# SUITE 606

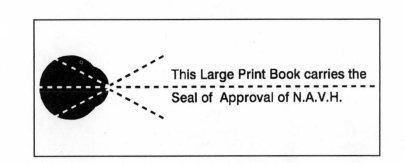
This Large Print Book carries the
Seal of Approval of N.A.V.H.

# SUITE 606

# J. D. ROBB
# MARY BLAYNEY
# RUTH RYAN LANGAN
# MARY KAY McCOMAS

**THORNDIKE PRESS**
*A part of Gale, Cengage Learning*

GALE
CENGAGE Learning™

Detroit • New York • San Francisco • New Haven, Conn • Waterville, Maine • London

# GALE
## CENGAGE Learning

**LIBRARY OF CONGRESS CATALOGING-IN-PUBLICATION DATA**

Suite 606 / by J.D. Robb ... [et al.].
   p. cm. — (Thorndike Press large print basic)
   ISBN-13: 978-1-4104-1103-7 (hardcover : alk. paper)
   ISBN-10: 1-4104-1103-6 (hardcover : alk. paper)
   1. Short stories, American. 2. American fiction—21st century.
3. Large type books. I. Robb, J.D., 1950– Ritual in death.
II. Blayney, Mary. Loves endures. III. Ryan, Ruth. Cold case.
IV. McComas, Mary Kay. Wayward wizard.
PS648.D4S835 2008
813'.010806—dc22                     2008039257

Published in 2008 in arrangement with The Berkley Publishing Group, a member of Penguin Group (USA) Inc.

Printed in the United States of America
1 2 3 4 5 6 7 12 11 10 09 08

# CONTENTS

■ ■ ■ ■

# RITUAL IN DEATH
# J. D. ROBB

■ ■ ■ ■

One owes respect to the living; to the dead one owes only the truth.

— VOLTAIRE

The belief in a supernatural source of evil is not necessary; men alone are quite capable of every wickedness.

— JOSEPH CONRAD

# ONE

Her feet were killing her. And made her imagine traveling back in time, hunting down whoever had invented stiletto heels, and beating the crap out of him.

What was the point of them other than throwing a woman off balance, making it next to impossible to run, and inducing foot cramps?

The question occupied Eve's mind as she tuned out the bulk of the party conversation buzzing around her like a hive of drunk hornets. What if one of the guests at this shindig went off and . . . stabbed somebody in the eye with a shrimp fork, for instance? How was she supposed to take him down dressed like this? And a foot pursuit in these stilts? Forget about it.

It was a hell of a getup for a cop, to her way of thinking. The flimsy excuse for a dress left most of her exposed. And she glittered. You couldn't have diamonds hanging all over you and blend.

Of course, you couldn't go to any sort of snazzy function with Roarke and blend.

The only advantage to the ridiculous damn shoes that she could see was the fact that they boosted her up so that she and Roarke were eye-to-eye.

They were stupendous eyes, bold and brilliantly blue. A look from them could give her a tingle in the belly — even after nearly two years of marriage. The rest of him didn't suck either, she reflected. The black silk fall of hair framed a billion-dollar jackpot of a face. Even now, as he glanced at her that sculpted, delicious mouth curved up in a slow, secret smile.

All she had to do, Eve reminded herself, was tolerate the goddamn shoes a couple more hours, then she'd have that mouth — and the rest of the package — to herself. Screaming arches were probably a small price to pay.

"Darling." Roarke took a glass of champagne from the waiter passing them, and handed it to her. Since the glass he'd traded it for had still been half full, she interpreted it as a signal to tune back in.

*Okay, okay,* she thought. She was here as Roarke's spouse. It wasn't as if he demanded she gear up like this and attend excruciatingly boring parties every day of the week. He was smooth about it — and as the man had more money than God and nearly as much power and position — the least she could do was play the part when they were doing the public couple thing.

Their hostess, one Maxia Carlyle, glided over in some kind of floaty number. The wealthy socialite was — by her own words — kicking into New York for a few days to catch up with friends. All of whom, Eve supposed, were wandering around Maxia's expansive tri-level hotel suite gorging on canapés and sloshing down champagne.

"I haven't had a minute to talk to you." Maxia put her hand on Roarke's arm, tipped her face to his.

They looked, Eve decided, like an ad for the rich and the gorgeous.

"And how've you been, Maxi?"

"Oh, you know how it goes." She laughed, shrugging one perfect bare shoulder. "It's been about four years, hasn't it, since we've seen each other. Never seem to land in the same place at the same time, so I'm especially glad you could make it tonight. And you," she added with a sparkling smile for Eve. "I was hoping I'd get the chance to meet you. Roarke's cop."

"Mostly the NYPSD considers me theirs."

"I can't even imagine it. What it must be like. Your work must be so fascinating and exciting. Investigating murders and murderers."

"It has its moments."

"More than moments, I'm sure. I've seen you on screen from time to time. The Icove case in particular."

And wasn't that one going to dog her forever? Eve mused.

"I have to say you don't look anything like a policewoman." Maxia's perfect eyebrows arched as she gave Eve's dress a quick scan. "Leonardo dresses you, doesn't he?"

"No, I usually do it myself."

Roarke gave her a little elbow poke. "Eve's oldest friend is married to Leonardo. Eve often wears him."

"Mavis Freestone is your oldest friend?" Now, in addition to interest and curiosity, considerable warmth infused Maxia's face. "I love her music, but my niece is a slathering fan. I took her to one of Mavis's concerts, in London, and arranged for a backstage pass. She was so sweet with my niece, and I've been the undisputed champion of aunts ever since."

She laughed, touched Eve's arm. "You *do* have a fascinating life. Married to Roarke, friends with Mavis and Leonardo, and chas-

14

ing killers. I suppose it's mostly head work, isn't it? Studying evidence, looking for clues. People like me glamorize it, think about policework the way it is on screen and at the vids. All danger and action, chasing madmen down dark alleys and firing off your weapon, when in reality it's brain and paperwork."

"Yeah." Eve controlled the urge to smirk. "That's about it."

"Being married to Roarke's action enough. Are you still dangerous?" Maxia asked him.

"Domesticated." He lifted Eve's hand, kissed it. "Entirely."

"I don't believe that for a minute. Oh, there's Anton. I need to snatch him away and bring him over to meet you."

Eve took a long, long drink of champagne.

"We'll meet this Anton, mingle another twenty," Roarke said, the faint hint of Ireland in his voice, "and slip out and away."

Eve felt a tingle of joy, right down to her numbed toes. "Seriously?"

"I never intended to stay above an hour or so. And certainly owe you for the points I'm making by bringing a Homicide cop to the party."

"It's all paperwork," Eve said dryly.

He skimmed a finger down her arm,

where a knife had slashed only days before. "Yes, your work is nothing but tedium. But I have to agree with Maxi. You don't look very coplike tonight."

"Good thing I don't have to chase down any psycho killers. I'd fall off these stupid shoes and embarrass myself." She curled her toes in them — or attempted to while she flicked a hand at the short, choppy crop of brown hair she'd recently taken the scissors to herself. Old priceless diamonds dripped from her ears. "I don't get parties like this. People standing around. Talk, talk, talk. Why do they have to get all dressed up to do that?"

"To show off."

She thought about that over another sip of wine. "I guess that's it. At least I don't have to gear up like this for the shower deal for Louise. Still, another party. More talk, talk, talk."

"It's a ritual, after all. When a friend's about to marry, her friends gather together, with gifts, and . . . well, I have no idea what happens then."

"If it's anything like mine, some of them drink till they puke, and others strip it off and dance."

"Sorry I'll miss it."

"Liar." But she grinned at him.

16

"Here we are!" Maxia came back, towing a portly, mustachioed man somewhere on the shady side of sixty. On his arm like a whippy vine twined a woman well shy of thirty with full, pouty lips, a bored expression, and a short red dress that covered very little of her expansive breasts.

"You simply must meet Anton and his lovely companion. It's Satin, isn't it?"

"Silk," the bored blonde corrected.

"Of course it is."

Eve caught the quick glint in Maxia's eyes and understood she'd *mistaken* the name deliberately. And liked her better for it.

"Actually we met a few years ago." Anton stuck out a wide, pudgy hand. "At Wimbledon."

"It's nice to see you again. My wife, Eve."

"Yes, the American cop. A pleasure, Detective."

"Lieutenant." Eve glanced down at Silk's sky-high heels. Just heels, she noted, with the feet arched into them bare on top. "I heard about those." She pointed. "People are actually wearing invisible shoes."

"They're not available to the public for another three weeks." Silk tossed her long mane of hair. "Sookie pulled some strings." She plastered herself against Anton/Sookie.

"Anton's produced several films about

17

crime and police and so on," Maxia commented. "So I thought he'd enjoy meeting one of New York's Finest."

"British-style procedurals." Anton patted Silk's hand as she tugged at him like a petulant child. "What we like to think of as crackling whodunits — with plenty of sex and violence," he added with a laugh. "And a slight connection with reality, as you'd know. I have been thinking about using an American setting, so I —"

"I don't see why a girl would want to be a cop." Silk frowned at Eve. "It's not very feminine."

"Really? It's funny because I don't see why a *girl* would want to be a bimb —"

"What is it you do?" Roarke cut Eve off, smoothly — giving her only the slightest pinch on the ass.

"I'm an actress. I just finished shooting a major role in Sookie's next vid."

"Victim, right?" Eve asked.

"I get to die dramatically. It's going to make me a star, isn't it, Sookie?"

"Absolutely, sweetheart."

"I want to go. There's nothing happening here. I want to go dancing, go some place with some *action*." She tugged hard enough to pull Anton back a few steps.

"He used to be such a sensible man,"

Maxia murmured.

"Guys of a certain age are especially vulnerable to bimboitis."

Maxia laughed. "I'm so glad I like you. I wish I wasn't due in Prague in a couple of days so I could get to know you better. I should mingle, make sure everyone isn't as bored as Linen over there."

"I think that's Polyester. Definitely man-made fibers."

Laughing again, Maxia shook her head. "Yes, I really like you. And you." She rose to her toes to kiss Roarke's cheek. "You look awfully happy."

"I am. And awfully glad to see you again, Maxi."

As Maxia started to turn, Silk's strident voice whined out. "But I want to go *now*. I want to have *fun.* This party is *dead.*"

Someone screamed. Something crashed. As people stumbled back, as some turned, shoving through small packs of others, Eve pushed forward.

The man staggered like a drunk, and wore nothing but spatters and smears of blood. The knife clutched in his hand gleamed with it.

A woman in his path fainted, and managed to take out a waiter holding a full tray of canapés with her. As shrimp balls and quail eggs rained, Silk shrieked, turned, and in a sprint for the terrace bowled over guests like pins in an alley.

Eve flipped open the next-to-useless bag she carried, tossed it to Roarke as she pulled out her weapon.

"Drop it. Drop it now." She sized him up quickly. About five feet, ten inches, roughly one-sixty-five. Caucasian, brown and brown. And the eyes were glazed and glassy. Shock or drugs — maybe both.

"Drop it," she repeated when he took another staggering step forward. "Or I drop you."

"What?" His gaze skidded around the room. "What? What is it?"

She considered and rejected just stunning him in a matter of seconds. Instead she moved to him, gripped the wrist of his knife hand, twisted. "Drop the goddamn knife."

His eyes stared into hers as his fingers went limp. She heard the knife hit the floor. "Nobody touch it. Stay back. I'm the police, do you get that? I'm a cop. What are you on?"

"I don't know. I don't know. The police? Can you help me? I think I killed someone. Can you help me?"

"Yeah. You bet. Roarke, I need a field kit ASAP, and for you to call this in. I need everyone else upstairs for now. I need you people to clear this room until the situation is contained. Move it!" she snapped when people stood, gaping. "And somebody check on that woman lying in the shrimp balls over there."

Roarke stepped up beside her. "I've sent one of the hotel staff down to the garage to get the field kit out of the boot of the car," he told her. "I've notified your Dispatch."

"Thanks." She stood where she was as the naked party crasher sat on the floor and began to shudder. "Just remember, you're the one who wanted to come tonight."

With a nod, Roarke planted a foot on the hilt of the knife to secure it. "No one to blame but myself."

"Can you get my recorder out of that stupid purse?"

"You brought a recorder?"

"If you need the weapon, you're going to need the recorder."

When he handed it to her, Eve pinned it to the frothy material over her breasts, engaged it. After reciting the basics, she crouched down. "Who do you think you killed?"

"I don't know."

"What's your name?"

"It's . . ." He lifted a blood-smeared hand,

rubbed it over his face. "I can't think. I can't remember. I can't think."

"Tell me what you took."

"Took?"

"Drugs. Illegals."

"I . . . I don't do illegals. Do I? There's so much blood." He lifted his hands, stared at them. "Do you see all this blood?"

"Yeah." She looked up at Roarke. "It's fresh. I'm going to need to do a room-to-room, starting with this floor. He couldn't have walked around for long like this. We start with this floor."

"I can arrange that. Do you want security to start on that, or sit on him while you do the room-to-room?"

"Sit on him. I don't want them to talk to him, touch him. What's that room over there?"

"It would be a maid's room."

"That'll do."

"Eve," Roarke said as she straightened. "I don't see any wounds on him. If that blood's someone else's — that much blood — they can't possibly still be alive."

"No, but we push the room-to-room first."

# Two

She needed to move fast. The amount of blood on her naked guy made it doubtful she'd find anyone alive — if she found anyone at all — so she couldn't putz around. While she didn't much like leaving her suspect with hotel security, even once she'd clapped on the restraints from her field kit, she couldn't afford to wait for her uniformed backup, or her partner.

For lack of better, she set her suspect on the floor of the maid's room, ran his prints.

"Jackson Pike." She crouched down on his level, looked into the glazed brown eyes. "Jack?"

"What?"

"What happened, Jack?"

"I don't . . ." He looked around the room, dazed and stoned. "I don't . . ." Then he moaned in pain and clutched his head.

"Uniformed officers are on their way," she said to the pair from security as she straightened. "I want him exactly where I've left him, and those people upstairs contained until I get back. Nobody comes in except NYPSD officials. Nobody goes out. Let's move," she said to Roarke.

"Guy's a doctor," she continued as they started out the door. "Thirty-three years old. Single."

"He didn't walk in off the street like that."

"No. Your hotel. Find out if a Jackson Pike, or anyone with a variation of that name's registered. How's this floor set up?"

Roarke pulled out his 'link as he gestured. "Four triplexes, one on each corner. One minute."

While he spoke to the hotel manager, Eve turned left. "Well, he left a trail. That's handy." Moving quickly, she followed bloody footprints over the lush carpet.

"No Jackson Pike, or any Pikes for that matter," Roarke told her. "There's a Jackson, Carl, on thirty-two. They're checking. On this floor Maxia has 600. Six-oh-two is occupied by Domingo Fellini — actor — I saw him at the party."

"Pike didn't come from there, trail's down this way." She picked up the pace as they started down the long corridor. "It's the sixtieth floor. Why isn't it 6002?"

"The sixth floor is the health club, the

pool, and so on. No guest rooms. The triplexes cater to those who can afford the freight, and we bill them as penthouses, or apartments. So it's Suite 600. Perception."

"Yeah, your perception's pretty screwed with all this blood on your carpet. Anyone in 604?"

"Not tonight."

"Empty suite's a nice spot for bloody murder, but the trail heads off." She kept moving, her weapon in her hand, her eyes scanning "Does every suite have the private elevator like Suite 600?"

"They do, yes. Those elevators in the center of the floor are also private, in that you need a key card or clearance for the trip up."

Emergency exits, all four corners, she noted, via stairs. But Jackson Pike hadn't used them. His trail led straight to the carved double doors of Suite 606.

Eve saw the faint smear of blood over the ornate zero.

Suite 666, she thought. Wasn't that just perfect?

She signaled for Roarke to stay back, then tried the knob.

"Locked. I don't have my master."

"Lucky for you, you have me." He drew a slim tool out of his pocket.

"Handy, but have you ever considered how a cop's supposed to explain — should it come up — why her husband's got burglary tools in his pockets?"

"For bloody emergencies?" He straightened. "Lock's off."

"I don't suppose you're carrying."

He flicked her a look, his eyes very cool. "While I didn't think it necessary to bring a weapon to a cocktail party, I got this from security." He drew out a stunner. "Civilian issue. Perfectly legal."

"Hmm. On three."

It wasn't their first time through a door. She went low, he went high into a large living area lit by hundreds of candles. In the flickering light blood gleamed as it pooled over the black pentagram drawn on the polished marble floor.

A body floated on that pool, the arms and legs spread to form an X at the center of the sign.

Gone, Eve thought, bled out. Throat slashed, multiple body wounds. She shook her head at Roarke, gestured to the left.

She moved right, in a suite the mirror image of Maxia's. Sweeping her weapon, she cleared a dining room, a short hallway, a kitchen, a powder room, making the circle that brought her back to Roarke.

"Bed and bath clear, this level," he told her. "Both were used. There's considerable blood — smears not spatters. Hers, I expect."

He wasn't a cop, she mused, but he could think like one. "We're going up." She did a chin point toward the elevator and tried to ignore the stench — not just death, but a kind of burning on the air. "Can you block that? Shut it down?"

Saying nothing, he walked to it, took out his tool again. While he worked, Eve circled the pentagram to clear the terrace.

"Done."

"What's the layout on the second floor?"

"Bed and bath, small sitting room to the left. Master suite — living area, powder room, dressing area, bed and bath to the right."

"I'll take the right."

The place felt empty, she thought. It felt dead. The metallic reek of the blood, the sickly sweet overlay of death mixed with candle wax smeared the air. And something more, that burning and a kind of . . . pulsing, she thought. Spent energy, the shadows of it still beating.

Together they cleared the second level, then the third.

She found evidence of sexual frenzy, of

food, of drink, of murder. "The sweepers are going to be hours in here, if not days."

Roarke studied the glasses, plates, half-eaten food. "What kind of people do murder, and leave so much of themselves behind?"

"The kind who think they're beyond or above the law. The worst kind. I need to seal this place off, all three levels, until crime scene gets here. Who was registered in this suite?"

"The Asant Group." On the steps, he stared down at the body posed on the pentagram. "Jumble the letters, and you've got —"

"Satan. God, I hate this kind of shit. People want to worship the devil, be my guest. Hell, they can have horns surgically implanted on their forehead. But then they've just got to slice somebody up for their human sacrifice and drag me into it."

"Damned cheeky of them."

"I'll say."

"Naked Jack didn't do this on his own."

"Nope. Let's go see if his memory's a little clearer."

The uniforms had taken over. Eve directed them to take names and contact info from the guests, then clear them out.

She sat on the floor with Jackson. "I need

a sample of the blood you're wearing, Jack."

"There's so much of it." His body jerked every few seconds, as if in surprise. "It's not mine."

"No." She took several samples — face, arms, chest, back, feet. "What were you doing in 606?"

"What?"

"Suite 606. You were in there."

"I don't know. Was I?"

"Who's the woman?"

"There were a lot of women, weren't there?" Again he shuddered in pain. "Were you there? Do you know what happened?"

"Look at me, goddamn it." Her voice was like a slap, shocked him back to her. "There's a woman in 606. Her throat's slashed."

"Did I do it? Did I hurt somebody?" He pressed his forehead to his knees. "My head. My head. Somebody's screaming in my head."

"Do you belong to the Asant Group?"

"I don't know. What is it? I don't know. Who are you? What's happening?"

With a shake of her head, Eve rose as the med-techs she'd ordered stepped in. "I want him examined. I want a blood sample. I need to know what he's on. When you're done, he'll be transported to Cop Central."

"Whose blood is it?"

"You're too late for her." She walked back into the living area to leave them to it just as her partner came in the main door.

Peabody's hair was pulled back in a stubby little tail that left her square face unframed and seemed to enlarge her brown eyes. She wore baggy dark pants and a white tee with a red jacket tossed over it. She carried a field kit.

"Who died?"

"An as yet unidentified female. Prime suspect is in there." Eve jerked her head. "Naked and covered with what is most likely her blood."

"Wow. Must've been a hell of a party."

"It happened on the other side. Let's go work the scene."

Outside the doors of 606 they coated hands and feet with Seal-It while Eve gave Peabody the rundown.

"He just walked into the cocktail party? And doesn't remember anything?"

"Yes, and so it seems. He doesn't come off as faking it. Both pupils are big as the moon. He's disoriented, motor skills are off, and he appears to have one major headache."

"Stoned?"

"Be my first guess, but we'll see what the

MTs have to say about it." Eve unsealed the door, and now used the key Roarke had acquired for her.

When she stepped in, the sturdy Peabody blanched. "Man. Oh crap." She bent over at the waist, pressed her hands to her thighs and took long, slow breaths.

"Don't you boot on my crime scene."

"Just need a minute. Okay." She kept breathing. "Okay. Black magic. Bad juju."

"Don't start that shit. We've got a bunch of assholes who had an orgy, topped it off with ritual murder using Satan as an excuse. Used the private elevator," Eve added, gesturing toward it, "most likely, coming and going. We'll want the security discs for that. Cleaned up after they did her. Evidence of that in the bathrooms, of which there are six in this place. Beds show signs of being used, and food and drink were consumed. Since I doubt the pentagram is part of the room's original decor, somebody drew it on the floor. A question might be 'Why?' Why use a fancy, high-dollar hotel suite for your annual satanic meeting?

"Let's get her prints, get an ID and a time of death." Since Peabody still looked pale, Eve opted to take the body herself. "Do a run on Pike, Jackson. His prints came up with age thirty-three, and an addy on West

Eighty-eighth. He's a doctor. See if he's got a sheet."

Eve stepped over to the body, doing what she could to avoid the blood. Not to preserve her shoes, but the scene. The air chilled, teased gooseflesh on her arms, and once more she felt, sensed, a pulsing.

She lifted the victim's hand to the Identipad, scanned the prints.

"Marsterson, Ava, age twenty-six, single. Mixed-race female with an address on Amsterdam. Employed as office manager at the West Side Health Clinic."

Eve tipped her head at the tattoo — a red and gold serpent swallowing its own tail — that circled the left hip. "She's got a tat on her hip, and it's not listed on her ID. Maybe a temp, or maybe fresh."

She took out her gauge. "TOD, twenty-two-ten. That's nearly an hour before Pike crashed the party down the hall." She replaced the gauge and studied the body. "The victim's throat is deeply slashed, in what appears to be a single blow with a sharp blade, right to left, slightly downward angle. A right-handed attacker, facing. He wanted to see your face when he sliced you open. Multiple wounds, slices, stab wounds, over shoulders, torso, abdomen, legs. Varying sizes and depths. Various blades held in various hands? Victim is posed, arms and legs spread, in the center of a black pentagram drawn directly onto the floor. Bruising on the thighs. Possible rape or consensual sex, ME to determine. No defensive wounds. None. Didn't put up a fight, Ava? Did they just take you down by slashing your throat, then have a party on you? Tox screen to determine presence of alcohol and/or drugs."

At the knock on the door, Eve called out for Peabody.

"I got it." Peabody hustled over, used the security peep. "It's Crime Scene."

In minutes the room filled with noise, movement, equipment, and the somehow cleaner smell of chemicals. When the crew from the morgue rolled in, Eve stepped away from the body.

"Marsterson, Ava. Bag and tag. Peabody, with me. Run this Asant Group," she ordered. "We're going in to shake what we can out of Pike."

"There had to be at least a dozen people in there, Dallas. Twelve, fifteen people by the number of trays and the glasses. Why come here to do this? You can't cover it up this way, and hey, party down the hall going on at the same time with a cop right there. By the way, you look totally mag. The shoes are up to wicked."

Eve frowned down at the shoes she'd forgotten she was wearing. "Shit, shit. I've got to go into Central in this getup." She'd also, she realized, forgotten Roarke.

He leaned against the wall outside Maxia's suite doing something that entertained or interested him on his PPC. And looked up as she approached.

"Sorry. I should've told you to go home."

"I assumed you'd want the code for the car since it's not one of yours. I had the garage bring it out front. Hello, Peabody."

"Hey. You guys look superior. It's really too bad the evening got screwed for you."

"It got screwed bigger for Ava Marsterson," Eve commented. "Maxia?"

"Took a soother and went to bed. I'll get myself home." He caught Eve's chin in his hand, skimmed his thumb down the dent, then kissed her. He handed her a mini memo cube. "Code's on it. Take care, Lieutenant. Good night, Peabody."

Peabody watched him walk away. "Boy, sometimes you just want to slurp him up without a straw." She wheeled her eyes to Eve. "Did I say that out loud?"

# Three

Grateful she kept some workout gear in her locker, Eve stripped off the party dress, pried her aching feet out of the hated shoes, then pulled on loose cotton pants and a faded gray tee. Since she couldn't walk around Central or successfully intimidate a suspect dripping in diamonds, she had no choice but to secure them in her locker.

Safe enough, she thought. If they'd been a candy bar, odds were lower that her property would be there when she opened the locker. But a small — probably not so small — fortune in diamonds, no problem.

After stepping into an ancient pair of skids, she met Peabody in the corridor.

"No criminal. Nothing, Dallas. He had a detained and released for disturbing the peace when he was twenty. Some college fraternity party. It wouldn't be on his record except the campus cops slapped the whole fraternity over it. He's from Pennsylvania, just moved here a couple of weeks ago. He's a doctor, pretty much brand-spanking-new, and just took a position on staff at —"

"The West Side Health Clinic."

"It's annoying to do the run if I don't get the payoff. Interview A. They got him cleaned up."

"The victim?" Eve asked as they walked.

"Clean to the squeaky level. Moved to New York about two years ago from Indiana. Both parents and younger brother still back there. We'll have to notify them."

"We'll take Pike first. They can wait a few hours to have their lives shattered." She pushed open the door to the interview room, nodded to the uniform.

The uniform stepped out, and Eve walked to the table where Jack sat in the orange pants and shirt of a con. "Record on. Dallas, Lieutenant Eve, and Peabody, Detective Delia, in interview with Pike, Jackson, regarding the investigation into the death of Marsterson, Ava."

"Ava?" Jack looked up, his face squeezed tight as if he struggled on the name. "Ava?"

"That's right, Ava. You've been read your rights, Mr. Pike, is that correct?"

"Ah, I don't know."

"Then we'll refresh you." Eve recited the Revised Miranda. "Do you understand your rights and obligations?"

"I think. Yes. Why? Why am I here?"

"You don't remember?"

"My head." He pressed both hands to his temples. "Was I in an accident? My head hurts."

"What do you remember about today?"

"I . . . I went to work. Didn't I? What day is it? Is it Tuesday?"

"It's Wednesday."

"But . . ." Jack stared up at her. "What happened to Tuesday?"

"What drugs did you take, Jack?"

"I don't, I don't take drugs. I don't do illegals. I'm a doctor. I'm on staff at . . ." He held his head again, and rocked. "Where? Where?"

"The West Side Health Clinic."

He looked at Eve, his eyes, his face slack with relief. "Yes. Yes. That's it. I just started. I went to work. I went to work, and then . . ." He moaned, shuddered. "Please, can I have a blocker? My head's pounding."

"You've got something in you, Jack. I can't give you a blocker until I know what it is. Did you go to the Palace Hotel with Ava? To Suite 606?"

"Ava . . . I can't . . . Ava works at the clinic." Sweat shone on his face from the effort. "Ava, manages . . . Ava. We . . ." Then

37

horror covered it. "No. No. No."

"What happened to Ava, Jack?"

"No. No."

"What happened in 606?"

"I don't know. I don't —"

"Stop!" She reached over, grabbed a fistful of his shirt. "You tell me what happened."

"It's not real. It didn't happen."

"What isn't real?"

"The people, the people." He surged to his feet, and Eve signaled Peabody to stay back. "The lights. The voices. Smoke and fire. And hell came." He lurched around the interview room, holding his head. Tears leaked out of his eyes. "Laughing. Screaming. I couldn't stop. Did I want to stop? We had sex. No. Yes. I don't know. Bodies and hands and mouths. They hurt her. Did I hurt her? But she was smiling, smiling at me. Then her blood."

His hands ran over his face as if wiping at it. "Her blood. All over me."

His eyes rolled up in his head. Peabody managed to break the worst of his fall by going down with him. "Jesus, Dallas, no way this guy's faking it."

"No. Let's get him into a cage. I want him on suicide watch. I want eyes on him." She stepped to the door at the knock.

38

"Screening on your suspect, Lieutenant. They said you wanted it ASAP."

"Thanks." She took the report from a tech, scanned it. "Jesus, what doesn't this guy have in him? Erotica, Rabbit, Zoner, Jive, Lucy."

"Sleepy, Dopey, and Doc," Peabody finished. Then shrugged at Eve's frown. "Bad joke. No wonder his head's screaming. Coming down off a cocktail like that's gotta rip it up."

"Get him into a cage, have a medic treat him. He's had enough for one night."

"He doesn't come across like somebody who could do what was done to that woman tonight."

"That much junk inside him, you don't know what he could do. But he's not a regular user. No way he could be a regular with that kind of habit and not have a single pop."

Eve started back to her office. A couple of uniforms led a weeping woman away in the opposite direction. Outside the bullpen a guy wearing a torn and bloody shirt sat laughing quietly to himself while he rattled the restraints that chained him to the seat.

She swung into the bullpen while he went back to giggling. In her office she hit the AutoChef for coffee first, then sat at her desk. She gulped caffeine while she booted up the security discs from the hotel.

She ran the VIP check-in first, the elaborate parlor reserved for guests in the tonier suites and the triplexes. She ordered the computer to coordinate with the time stamped on the Asant Group's check-in. And watched the parlor fuzz into white static. She ran it back, noted the glitch began thirty minutes before the log-in, and continued to twenty-three hundred.

The pattern repeated when she ran the security discs for the private elevator, and again when she ran the main lobby discs.

"Son of a bitch." She turned to her interoffice 'link. "Peabody, wake up your cohab. I need McNab in here to dig into the security discs. They're wiped."

If the boy genius from the Electronic Detectives Division couldn't dig out data, she had someone who could. She contacted Roarke.

"Why are you awake?" she demanded when her 'link screen showed him at his desk.

"Why are you?"

"Oh, just a little something about a ritual murder. I thought you'd want to know that all the security discs from your hotel are compromised. Nothing but static on all starting thirty minutes before the log-in for the Asant Group."

"Are you bringing them to me or am I coming to you?"

"I've got McNab coming in, but —"

"I'm on my way."

"Wait. Listen, grab me some work clothes, will you? And my weapon harness, and —"

"I know what you need."

Her screen went black. Pissed off, she thought, and couldn't blame him. She imagined a few heads would roll at Roarke's Palace, and in short order. But meanwhile, she had useless discs on her hands, a suspect with drug-induced memory blanks, and a mutilated body at the morgue.

And it was still shy of dawn.

She opened her murder book, set up her board. According to the hotel records, the Asant Group had booked the triplex two months prior, and secured it with a credit card under the name of Josef Bellor, who carried an address in Budapest.

She fed the data into her computer, ordered a standard run. Only to learn Josef Bellor of Budapest had died there five years before at the ripe age of one hundred and twenty-one.

"Gonna be hard-pressed to get him to pay the bill," she muttered.

One night's booking, she thought, going over the notes. All room service delivered through the suite's AutoChefs or pre-ordered and delivered prior to check-in. Five cases of wine, several pounds of various European cheeses, fancy breads, caviar, pâtés, cream cakes.

No point in ritual murder on an empty stomach.

So they ate, drank, orgied, she thought, pushing up to pace the small space of her office. Popped whatever illegals suited their fancy. Three floors of revelry, soundproofed high-collar digs with the privacy shades activated.

Would've saved the best for last, she decided. The sacrifice would've been the evening's crescendo.

Just how did a nice girl from Indiana end up the star of the show? How did a transplanted young doctor from Pennsylvania get invited and left behind?

"Lieutenant."

She turned to the sleepy-eyed McNab in her doorway. He wore pants of screaming yellow that matched the fist-sized dots shrieking over a shirt of eye-tearing green. His long blond hair was pulled back from his thin, pretty face into a tail. She wondered if the hank of it somehow balanced the weight of the tangle of silver loops in his ear.

"Doesn't it ever give you a headache?" she wondered. "Just looking in the mirror."

"Huh?"

"Never mind. Discs." She gathered them from her desk, pushed them at them. "Find something on them. Roarke's on his way."

"Okay. Why?"

"They're his discs. Palace Hotel security. I've already shot a report to your unit in EDD. Read it, work it. Get me something."

He stifled a yawn, then focused on her board. "Is that the vic?"

Eve only nodded, said nothing when he came in to study the board. He'd work better and harder, she knew, if he was invested. "That's fucked up," he said. "That's seriously fucked up. And that's gotta be more than one killer." He slipped the discs into one of the pockets of his pants. "If there's an image on these, we'll get it."

If there were no images, she thought when McNab left, it meant the security had been compromised on site. Knowing how tightly any ship in Roarke's expansive fleet ran, that would've taken some serious magic.

She turned toward her 'link with the idea of tagging Roarke on his way in. And he walked into her office.

"That was quick."

"I'm in a hurry." He set a bag on her visitor's chair. "Where are the discs?"

"I just passed them off to McNab. Wait." She shot out a hand as he turned. "If the security was breached on site, how could it be done?"

"I don't know until I see the discs, do I?"

"Be pissed off later. How could it be done?"

He made an obvious effort to settle himself, then walked to her AutoChef to program coffee for himself. "It would have to be through security or electronics, and one of the top levels. Most likely both, working in tandem. No one at that level would consider a bribe of any kind worth their position."

"Threat, blackmail?"

"Anything's possible, of course, but doubtful. It would be more to their advantage to come to me with the problem than to circumvent security."

"I'll need names anyway."

He set the coffee aside, took out his PPC. After a moment's work, he nodded toward her machine. "Now you have them. And if any of my people had a part in what happened to that girl, I want to know when you know."

He walked out, his barely restrained fury leaving a bolt of energy behind. Eve blew out a breath, and since he'd forgotten his coffee, picked it up and drank it herself.

# FOUR

Though she had no doubt Roarke's screening process was more stringent than the Pentagon's, she ran the names he'd given her. She got clean and clear on all. If, she decided, the word from EDD was an on site screwup, she'd run their spouses, when applicable, and family members.

But for now she couldn't put off informing next of kin.

It took, Eve thought when she'd finished, under thirty seconds to shatter the world of two ordinary people, with ordinary lives. More time, she reflected as she turned back to her board, than it had taken to slash Ava Marsterson's throat, for her brain to process the insult. But not much. Not much more.

She rubbed the heels of her hands over eyes gritty with fatigue, then checked the time. A couple of hours until she could bitch at the lab for any results, or go to the morgue for the same on the victim's autopsy.

Enough time for a shower to clear her head before nagging EDD. She picked up the bag Roarke had left her.

"Take two hours in the crib," she ordered Peabody when she stepped back into the bullpen. "I'm going to grab a shower."

"Okay. I ran the Asant Group from every possible angle. It doesn't exist."

"It's just a cover."

"Then I tried a search for any occult holidays, or dates of import that coordinate with today — or yesterday now. Nothing."

"Well, that was good thinking. Worth a shot. It was a damn party, that's for sure. Maybe they don't need an occasion. No, no," Eve corrected herself. "It was too elaborate, planned too far in advance to just be for the hell of it."

"For the hell of it. Ha-ha. God." Peabody rubbed her eyes. "I need those two hours down."

"Take them now. It's the last you'll be seeing of the back of your eyelids for a while."

She headed to the showers. In the locker room she checked the contents of the bag, noted that Roarke hadn't missed a trick. Underwear, boots, pants, shirt, jacket, weapon harness, her clutch piece, com-

47

municator, restraints, spare recorder, PPC, and cash. More than she normally carried on the job. She stuffed it all in her locker, grabbed a towel, then wrapped herself in it once she'd stripped off.

In the miserly shower cube she ordered the water on full at 101 degrees. It came out in a stingy lukewarm trickle, so she closed her eyes and pretended she was home, where the shower sported multiple and generous jets that pummeled the body with glorious heat. Then spun around, soaking wet, when her instincts tingled to see Roarke standing in the narrow opening, hands in pockets.

"If this is the best the NYPSD offers it's no wonder you're prone to hour-long showers at home."

"What's wrong with you? Close the door. Anybody could walk in here."

"I locked the door, which you neglected to do."

"Because cops aren't prone to sneaking peeks while another cop is in the damn shower. What are you doing?"

"Taking my clothes off so they don't get wet. That's the usual procedure."

"You can't come in here." She jabbed a finger at him when he draped his shirt over a bench. "Cut it out. There's barely room for me. Besides —"

"The security was breached on site. It's going to be a very long day. I want a shower, and since she's naked, wet, and here, I want my wife."

He stepped in, slid his arms around her. "Not only is this excuse for a shower stall the approximate size of a coffin, but it's bloody noisy for the amount of water dripping out."

"Who's the most likely to have compromised —"

"Later," he said, and drew her in. "Later," and covered her mouth with his.

She'd seen his eyes before their lips met; seen the worry and the fatigue in them. It was so rare for him to show either, even to her, that she instinctively wrapped around him. Need. She understood the need, not just for the physical, but for the unity.

Touch, taste, movement. Knowing who you were, each to the other, and what you became when that need brought you together.

"Anybody finds out about this," she murmured in his ear, "I'll get razzed for years." She bit lightly at his lobe. "So make it good."

Her heart slammed against her ribs when he drove into her. "Okay. That's a start."

49

He laughed, an unexpected and welcome zing of humor along with the pleasure. The old pipes clanged and rattled as he slowed his thrusts, smoothed the pace down from urgent to easy. He turned his head, found her mouth again, and drew them both down, deep, deep. Filled them both from the shimmering well of sensation and emotion.

He felt her rise up, the cry of her release tangled in the kiss. And let himself follow.

On a long, long breath, she dropped her head on his shoulder. "This is not authorized use of departmental facilities."

"We expert civilian consultants need our perks, too." He tipped her head up. "I adore you, Lieutenant."

"Yeah? Then shove it over some, pal. You're hogging what there is of the water."

When they stepped out and she began toweling off, he lifted a brow. "Towel over drying tube? Not your usual."

"I don't trust them in here." She gave the tube a suspicious glare. "You could get fried, or maybe worse, trapped. Anyway, I gave Peabody some crib time, but I'm going to cut it short, see if they've gotten to the vic at the morgue."

"I'll be going with you."

She didn't argue; it was a waste of time.

"You're not responsible for what happened to Ava Marsterson."

He watched her as he buttoned his shirt. "If you put one of your men in charge of an op, and there was a screwup, if a civilian lost her life, who does it fall on?"

She sat to pull on her boots, tried another way. "No security, not even yours, is completely infallible."

He sat beside her on the bench. "A group of people came into my place, breached the security from the inside, and ripped a woman to pieces. I need to know how, and I need to know why. If one of my people was part of it, I'm going to know who."

"Then I'd better roust Peabody. I hope you came down in my ride," she added. "That toy we drove last night won't hold the three of us."

"I drove something that will."

"This is so mag!" Peabody bounced on the backseat of the muscular and roomy all-terrain. "First we get to zip in that way-uptown Stinger, and now we're pumping the road in this."

"Glad you're enjoying yourself," Eve commented. "We wouldn't want murder to dampen your day."

"You've got to take your ups where you

51

get them. I've never even seen one of these before." Peabody petted the seat as she might a purring cat.

"It's a prototype," Roarke told her. "It won't go on line for a couple of months yet."

"Sweetness."

"Peabody, as soon as you finish enjoying yourself, run the heads of security and electronics in the file. Run their spouses, parents, siblings, cohabs, offspring, spouses and cohabs of offspring. I want to know if anyone has a sheet. I want to know if anyone's family pet has a sheet."

"They've been screened," Roarke told her. "Caro can forward you all the data."

Eve had no doubt his efficient admin could gather and transmit data in record time. "We need to confirm, and confirm through official channels."

When he said nothing, she took out her own PPC, copied all data to Dr. Mira's office unit. She wanted the department's top profiler and psychiatrist to review and analyze. Added to it, Eve thought, one of Mira's daughters was Wiccan. Maybe, just maybe, they'd tap that source.

The cold white tiles of the morgue echoed with their footsteps. Eve scented coffee — or what passed for it here — as they strode past Vending. She scented death long before they pushed through the double doors of the autopsy room.

Ava lay naked on a slab with Chief Medical Examiner Morris working on her. His delicate and precise Y-cut opened her, exposed her. Eve heard Peabody swallow hard behind her.

Morris straightened as they came in. The protective gown covered his silver-edged blue suit. He wore his dark hair pulled back in a long, sleek tail. "Company," he said, and the faintest of smiles moved across his exotically sexy face. "And so early in the morning. Roarke, this is unexpected." But his eyes tracked over to Peabody. "There's water in the friggie, Detective."

"Thanks." Her face glowed with sweat as she hurried over for a bottle.

"What can you tell me?" Eve asked him.

"We haven't gotten very far. You flagged her for me specifically, and I've only been in about an hour. And that's because the ME on duty was pissy that he couldn't get his hands in."

"I didn't want anyone but you on her. I'd rather wait. I have a pretty good idea how it went anyway. Can you tell me if she was raped?"

"I can tell you she had rough sex — very rough — multiple times. As to whether it was consensual or not? She can't tell us. But from the tearing, I'd say rape. Gang rape."

"Sperm?"

"They doused her — vaginally, anally, orally to remove. I've already sent samples to the lab, but I wouldn't hold my breath for DNA. I'd say multiple partners. She was brutally used, pre- and postmortem." He looked down at the body. "There are so many levels of cruelty, aren't there? And they all walk in our doors."

"What about the tat? It looked fresh and real."

"It's both. Inked within the last twelve to fifteen hours."

"They wanted her marked," Eve mused. "The throat wound came first. Death blow. Right-handed assailant, facing."

"If I were a teacher, you'd be my pet. There are sixty-eight other wounds, several of which would have been mortal on their own, some of which are relatively superficial. I want to run a closer analysis, but on a first pass, at least a dozen different blades were used on her. The bruising, from finger grips, hands, fists, feet. Some premortem. And yet —"

"Not one defensive wound," Eve finished. "No sign she was restrained. She took it. I need to know what she took or what they gave her."

"I've flagged the tox screen priority. I can tell you she wasn't a user, unless it was very rare, very casual. This was a very healthy woman, one who tended to her body, inside and out. There'll be a rape drug in her, something potent enough to cause her to tolerate this kind of abuse without a struggle."

"I've got somebody in the tank. He was loaded. I sent a sample to the lab. Her parents and her brother are coming in from Indiana."

"God pity them." Morris touched one sealed and bloodied hand to Ava's arm. "I'll see she's cleaned up before they view her." Morris glanced over at Roarke, with understanding in his dark eyes. "We'll take care of her," he said. "And them. You can be sure of it."

As they walked down the white-tiled tunnel, Roarke spoke for the first time. "It's a hard life you've chosen, Lieutenant. A brutal road that brings you to that so often."

"It chose me," she said, but was grateful to step outside, and into the cool air of the new spring morning.

# FIVE

Eve gave Roarke an Upper West Side address when they got back into the AT.

"Mika Nakamura's worked for me for nine years." He pulled out of the parking slot. "Four of those as head of security at the hotel."

"Then she must be good," Eve commented. "And should be able to explain what the hell went wrong last night. She was on the log from noon until just after twenty-three hundred. Do you usually work your people for an eleven-hour stretch?"

"No. She should have logged out at eight." His eyes stayed on the road, his voice remained cool and flat. "Paul Chambers came on at seven. I spoke with him last night, and again this morning. He took the main hotel as Mika told him she'd handle the VIP and Towers, as she had other work to catch up on. She also told him she'd be running some maintenance on the cams."

"Is that usual?"

"As head of security, Mika would have some autonomy. She's earned it."

*Touchy,* Eve thought. *Very touchy.* "Have you spoken with her?"

"I haven't been able to reach her. And, yes, I fully intended to see her in person before you contacted me about the discs." The tone, very cool, very level, spoke of ruthlessly restrained fury. "She wouldn't hold the position she does if she hadn't passed the initial screening, and the twice yearly screening thereafter."

In the backseat, Peabody cleared her throat. "She comes up clean. So does her husband of five years. One child, female, age three. Um, born in Tokyo, and relocated to New York at age ten when her parents — who also come clean — moved here for career purposes. Attended both Harvard and Columbia. Speaks three languages and holds degrees in Communications, Hotel Management, and Psychology."

"How did she end up yours?" Eve asked Roarke.

"I recruited her right out of college. I have scouts, you could call them, and they brought her to my attention. It's not in the realm of any reality that she had any part in what was done to that girl."

"She logged out about ten minutes before Pike walked into Maxia's party. And minutes before the security for the elevators and lobby cleared. We have to look at that. She could've been forced, threatened."

"There are fail-safes." He shook his head. "She's smart. She's too damn smart to get herself trapped that way."

Better to let it lie, Eve decided, until they spoke to the woman in question.

Security paid well enough, in Roarke's domain, to warrant a tidy duplex in a tony neighborhood. People clipped along the sidewalk wearing suits and style while they sipped what she assumed was fancy fake coffee out of go-cups. Pretty women with bouncy hair herded pretty children toward what, she assumed again, would be private schools. A couple of teenagers whizzed by on airboards while a third chased after them on street blades.

Eve climbed the short steps to the door. "You can take the lead with her," she told Roarke, "but when I step in, you have to step back."

Rather than respond, he rang the bell.

Privacy screens shielded the front windows, and the security lock held a steady red. As the seconds ticked away, Eve wondered how a woman might go into the wind with a husband and a kid. They had a weekend home in Connecticut, she mused, and relatives in Japan. If . . .

The security light blinked green.

Mika Nakamura was a stunner. Eve had seen that from the ID shot. But at the moment, she looked hard used. Sallow skin, dull, bloodshot eyes, the tangled mess of ebony hair all spoke of a hard night, or an illness.

"Sir?" the voice rasped. Mika cleared her throat, opened the door a bit wider. She wore a long scarlet robe messily tied at the waist.

"I need to speak with you, Mika."

"Of course. Yes. Is something wrong?"

She stepped back. Eve noted the house was dim, that the privacy screens had been boosted up to block the light. Even so, the interior was splashed with vibrant colors from rugs and art.

"Please come in. Won't you sit down? Can I get you some coffee? Tea?"

"Aren't you well, Mika?"

"I'm just a little off. I had my husband take Aiko out for breakfast because I can't seem to pull it together."

"Long night?" Eve asked, and Mika gave her a puzzled look.

"I . . . sorry?"

"My wife, Lieutenant Dallas, and her partner, Detective Peabody. I've been trying to reach you, Mika."

"You have?" She pushed her hands at her hair in an absent attempt to straighten it. "Nothing's come through. Did I . . ." She pressed her fingers to her temple. "Did I turn the 'links off? Why would I do that?"

"Sit down." Roarke took her arm, led her to a chair in as bold a red as her robe. He sat on the glossy black coffee table to face her. "There was an incident at the hotel last night."

"An incident." She repeated the words slowly, as if learning the language.

"You were on the com, Mika. You ordered Paul to cover the main hotel, though it was already covered. And you dismissed the tech from the screen room, telling them you'd be running some maintenance on the cameras."

"That doesn't sound right." She rubbed at her temple again. "It doesn't sound right."

Eve touched Roarke's shoulder, and though impatience flashed into his eyes, he rose. Eve took his place. "Just before sixteen hundred, you shut down the cameras in the VIP lobby and the private elevator for Suite 606. They remained off until approximately twenty-three hundred."

"Why would I do that?"

Not a denial, Eve noted. A sincere question. "A group checked into that suite. The Asant Group. Do you know them?"

"No."

"During the time the cameras were shut down, from your com, a woman was murdered in that suite."

Even the sickly color faded from Mika's cheeks. "Murdered? Oh, God. Sir —"

"Look at me, Mika," Eve demanded. "Who told you to turn off the cameras, to send your relief away, to dismiss the tech?"

"Nobody." Her breath went short as her pale face bunched with pain. "I didn't. I wouldn't. Murdered? Who? How?"

Eve narrowed her eyes. "Got a headache, Mika?"

"Yes. It's splitting. I took a blocker, but it hasn't touched it. I can't think. I don't understand any of this."

"Do you remember going to work yesterday?"

"Of course. Of course I do. I . . ." Her lips trembled; her eyes filled. "No. No. I don't remember. I don't remember anything, it's all blurred and blank. My head. God." She dropped it into her hands, rocked herself, much as Jackson Pike had. "When I try to

61

remember, it's worse. I can't stand the pain. Sir, something's wrong with me. Something's wrong."

"All right now, Mika." Roarke simply nudged Eve aside, crouched, and put his arms around the weeping woman. "We'll take care of it. We'll get you to a doctor."

"Peabody, help Ms. Nakamura get dressed. We'll have her taken down to Central."

"Damn it, Eve." Roarke shoved to his feet.

"Dr. Mira can examine her," Eve said evenly, "and determine if the cause is physical or psychological. Or both."

Roarke eased back, turned to help Mika to her feet. "Go with Detective Peabody. It's going to be all right."

"Someone's dead. Did I do something? If I did —"

"Look at me. It's going to be all right."

It seemed to calm her. But as she continued to tremble, Peabody put an arm around her to lead her from the room.

"Same symptoms as Jackson Pike," Eve commented. "Down the line."

"Eve —"

"I'm cutting you a break by not getting pissed off. Don't push it."

He merely nodded. "I'll stay until she's

ready to go. Then I've other things to see to."

"Good." She took out her communicator to arrange for Mika's transportation, then contacted Mira's office. She plowed through Mira's admin. "I'm pulling rank, are you hearing me? If necessary I'll go to the commander on this, and nobody'll be happy about that. I'm ordering a priority. Dr. Mira will clear her schedule as of now. Jackson Pike, currently in custody, will be brought down to her for examination. She has the file. If she has any questions, she can reach me. In an hour, she will examine Mika Nakamura, who will be brought to Central shortly. If you have a problem, you can take it up with me later, but you'll do exactly what I've told you, and you'll do it now."

Eve clicked off. "Ought to hook her up with Summerset." she muttered. "Couple of tight-asses." While Roarke watched thoughtfully, she contacted her own division and arranged for two uniforms to deliver Pike to Mira's office, ASAP. Satisfied, she shoved the communicator back in her pocket.

"Someone used her," Roarke began.

"Maybe."

"Used her," he repeated. "And a woman's dead because of it. Mika won't ever forget that."

"You can worry about that now. I can't."

"Understood. We're not on different sides, Eve. Just slightly different angles. She's in pain, and afraid, and confused. And she's mine. You understand that."

"Yeah." She understood that right down to the bone. "And Ava Marsterson's mine. Do I think your head of security suddenly thought it would be fun to help a bunch of lunatics carve someone up in the name of Satan? No. But there's a reason they used her, a reason they used your place, that room, that victim. There's a reason for Jackson Pike."

Eve stepped over as Peabody led Mika back into the room.

"Ms. Nakamura, do you use the West Side Health Clinic?"

"What? Yes. Aiko's pediatrician is there, and my doctor."

"Do you know Ava Marsterson?"

"I —" Mika staggered back, one hand pressed to her head. "Who? I can't think through the pain."

Eve glanced at Roarke. "I take that as a yes."

"She's straight, Dallas." Peabody brooded out the window of the AT. "She could barely stand for the pain, but she fought to push through it. Worried about her husband and kid, sick — seriously sick — at the idea someone died while she had the com." She glanced at Eve. "Just like Pike. So you have to think, given the circumstances . . . Ritual magic, on the black side, the gathering of, well, power. By all appearances and all evidence, the ability to cause two straight arrows to behave in a way opposed to their character. We could be dealing with a spell."

Eve's brown eyes narrowed. "I knew you were going to get around to that."

"It's not unprecedented," Peabody insisted. "There are sensitives, unscrupulous sensitives who've used their gifts for their own gain, their own purpose. Black magic's taking those gifts, that power, and distorting it."

"Jackson Pike was loaded with drugs."

"Add drugs to the mix, it's easier to bend the will. There was something in that suite, something left over." Peabody rubbed her arms as if suddenly chilled. "You felt it, too."

She didn't argue, because that much was true. "I'm not buying that some witch can . . ." Eve waved a hand in the air. "And get some normal guy to start hacking someone with a knife."

"I don't think he did. I think he was supposed to be another sacrifice — or maybe just the patsy." When Eve didn't respond, Peabody scowled. "You don't want to buy into the power deal, but going straight logic, why does this group plan all this and include some young doctor who's only been in New York a couple of weeks, and has no ties, *none* to anything off prior to that? You don't bring some newbie in on the big deal. You don't —"

"You're right."

"Listen, I'm just saying . . . I'm right?"

"About Pike, yeah, you're right. Maybe they were going to off him, too. Or maybe they pulled him in to take the rap. Drugged the shit out of him, left him behind. He's got no defense. Naked, full of illegals, covered with the vic's blood, and carrying around one of the knives used on her. Still, they'd have to figure we'd know he didn't do it alone, and once the drugs wear off, we examine him, work with him, he could start to remember some details."

Peabody pondered on it a moment. "Okay, look, you don't buy the magic, but you'll agree that people who get together to light candles, have orgies that end in human sacrifice probably do."

"I'll give you that."

"And can be persuasive — especially if they have a gift, are a sensitive, especially if the person they're persuading is doped up."

"Okay." Eve nodded.

"So, to *dissuade* we need someone with a gift, someone who believes, to break the spell."

"You want to bring in a witch? Christ."

"It's an option," Peabody pushed.

"Mira's going to examine them, and determine the root of the physical and/or psychological blocks. Let's stick with reality, for just a little while."

She shot up to a slot on a second-level street parking. "Trosky, Brian, on the desk at the time of the group check-in. Let's see what he remembers, or if he's got himself a really bad headache this morning."

Eve strode across the sidewalk and into the apartment building. As it didn't boast a doorman or clerk, she went straight to the intercoms, pressed the one labeled Trosky.

When no response came, Eve bypassed the elevator lock. "Third floor," she ordered.

The music blasted out the moment the doors opened on three. A woman stood beating on the door of 305, Trosky's apartment. "Brian, for chrissake, turn it *down*."

"Problem?" Eve asked at close to a shout.

"Yeah, unless you're frigging deaf. He's had that music blaring like that for over an hour. I work nights. I gotta get some sleep."

"He doesn't answer the door? Did you try his 'link?"

"Yeah. It's not like him, I gotta say. He's a nice guy. Good neighbor." She beat on the door again. "Brian, for chrissake!"

"Okay, move aside."

When Eve pulled out her master, the woman goggled. "Hold on, hold on a minute. You can't just go breaking into somebody's place. I'm calling the cops."

"We are the cops." Eve nodded at Peabody as she used the master, and Peabody pulled out her badge.

"Oh, wow, oh, shit. Is he in trouble? I don't wanna get him in trouble."

Eve pushed open the door, felt her eardrums vibrate at the force of the music. "Mr. Trosky, this is the police!" she shouted. "We're coming in. Music, off," she ordered, but the roar of it continued. "Peabody, find the source of that noise and kill it. Trosky! This is the NYPSD!"

She drew her weapon, but kept it down at her side as she scanned the living area — trashed — then the bump-out of the kitchen. She moved to the open bedroom door.

He lay across the bed, tangled in the bloody sheets. She swept the room and the adjoining bath, though instinct told her

Brian Trosky hadn't been attacked, that the hammer that had caved his skull — to stop the pain? — had been wielded by his own hand.

# Six

Same side, Roarke thought as he walked into Spirit Quest, different angles. Eve would always search for the logical, the rational. He was a bit more flexible. And so he'd come to talk to the witch.

The shop was pretty, even festive in its way with its crystals and stones, its bells and candles, its colorful bowls and thriving herbs. Its scent was spring meadow, he thought, with a hint of moonlight.

In the small space with the murmur of harps and flutes as background, people browsed. He watched a woman in a flowing white dress carry a ball of smoky crystal to the counter where the young, fresh-faced clerk instructed her solemnly on how to charge the ball by moonlight, how to cleanse it.

When the purchase had been made, wrapped and bagged, Roarke took a step toward the counter. He needn't have bothered, as she stepped out of the back room with an awareness in her dark eyes that told him she'd sensed him — or in the more pedestrian method, had seen him on a security screen.

"Welcome back."

"Isis." He took the hand she offered, held it — and yes, felt that frisson of something. Some connection.

"You're not here to shop," she said in her warm, throaty voice, "which is too bad considering the depths of your pockets. Come upstairs, we'll be comfortable and you can tell me what you need to know."

She led the way, through the back, up the stairs. She moved gracefully, athletically, an Amazon goddess of considerable height and generous curves. Her flaming hair fell in mad curls nearly to the waist of the snug white top she wore, just teasing the back of the first of the many layers of her skirt, a rainbow of hues. She turned at the door, smiled at him out of those onyx eyes. Her face was bold, broad featured with skin of a dull, dreamy gold.

"Once, in another life, we sought comfort together for more than talk." Her smile faded. "But now it's death, again it's death that brings you here. And weighs on you. I'm sorry."

She stepped into the living area of an apartment as exotic and appealing as her shop. "Your Eve is well?"

"Yes. Chas?"

She let out a laugh. "Snuck down to the deli for coffee," she said, referring to her lover. "We pretend he's having a walk. But you can't live with and love another and not know at least some of their secrets."

He stared into her dark eyes, so compelling — so eerily familiar. "Did I know yours, once upon a time?"

She gestured to a chair, took her own. "We knew each other, and loved very well. But I was not your love, your only. You found her then, as you've found her again. And always will. You knew when you first saw her. At the first scent, the first touch."

"I did. It was . . ." He smiled a little, remembering his first contact with Eve. "Annoying."

"Does she know you've come?"

"No. We don't always follow the same lines, even though we usually end in the same place. I don't know if you can help, or if I have a right to bring death to your door."

"Not ordinary death." Isis took a long, slow breath. "Has someone used the arts to cause harm?"

"I don't know. They have, at least, used

the illusion of them to kill an innocent woman. You haven't heard of this?"

"We've only just opened this morning, and I don't listen to the media reports." Rings glittered and gleamed on her fingers as she laid her hands on the arms of her chair, settled back. "What would I have heard?"

He told her then, watched her lovely skin pale, her eyes go darker yet. "Do you know of them? The Asant Group?"

"No, and I would have." Her fingers stroked the smooth blue stone of the pendant she wore, as if for comfort. "I hear both the dark and the light. Suite 606. Or 666 with such little change. You didn't know this girl?"

"No."

"You brought nothing of hers, nothing she owned, wore, touched?"

"I'm sorry, no."

Still pale, Isis nodded. "Then to help you, you need to take me there. To where they sacrificed her."

Eve shot over to the West Side Clinic. "They had to troll for the victim here. Scoop up the new doctor, connect with Mika. Somebody on staff, a patient, one of the goddamn cleaning crew."

"Do you really think Pike or Mika might try to kill themselves like Trosky?"

"Mira's notified. It won't happen. It's not even noon," Eve replied.

"Sure could use lunch though."

"Maybe he did slip out on them, or came to sooner than they figured. Walked into the party. Impromptu party, Maxia just planned it the day before. Couldn't know he'd walk right in to another penthouse. Couldn't know a cop and the owner of the hotel would be right there, that we'd find the body minutes later."

"Without the party he might've wandered around the floor for hours, or . . . gotten down to a lower floor, even the lobby," Peabody agreed. "Nobody would've zeroed right in on 606."

"What you'd get is a lot of civilian screaming, running, security taking him down. Cops get called in. At some point, they're going to check the discs, but they don't know the exact time frame, so it'd take a while, and a while longer to pinpoint 606 and find her. If three of the key players kill themselves before we interview them thoroughly, before they're examined by a professional, what've we got?"

"What looks like the new guy in town luring a pretty girl to her death, and being in league with the other two, being part of a cult."

"Yeah, you could waste some time on that. They may not be ready for us." Eve swung toward the curb, coldly double-parking. "Not quite ready." She flipped on her On Duty sign, stepped out, and walked to the clinic.

Babies cried. Why, she wondered, did they always sound like invading aliens? People sat with the dead-eyed stare of the ill or the terminally bored. Eve crossed over to the check-in desk where a brunette looked at her with tear-ravaged eyes.

"I'm sorry, we're not taking walk-ins today. I can refer you to —" She broke off when Eve laid her badge on the counter. "Oh. Oh. Ava." Tears popped out, fat and fast. "It's about Ava."

"Who's in charge here?"

"I — I — Ava really managed the clinic. She really handled everything. I don't understand how —"

"Sarah." Another woman in a smart suit stepped up, touched the receptionist's shoulder. "Go on into the breakroom for a little while. It's all right."

"I'm sorry, Leah. I just can't *stand* it." She rose, fled.

"I'm Leah Burke." The older brunette

held out a hand, gave Eve's a firm shake. "One of the nurse practitioners. We only heard about Ava a couple of hours ago. We're all just . . . Well, we're reeling. Please, come back. I need to find someone to cover the desk. We can use Dr. Slone's office, he's with a patient. Left, then right, then the third door on the right. I'll be right with you."

Eve tried to ignore the images of what might be going on behind the closed doors of examination rooms. She hated clinics, hospitals, doctors, MTs. If they were medicals, she wanted them to keep their damn distance.

Slone's office was polished and prim. Diplomas in black frames made the walls important, while a photo of a hot blonde on the desk added that personal touch. Sturdy, straight-back chairs ranged in back and in front of the wide desk.

"Run her," Eve told Peabody.

"Already am. Forty-eight years old, divorced. One child, female, deceased. Aw, jeez, hit while crossing the street. Drunk driver. Graduated Columbia Medical School. Put in ten years at the free clinic in Alphabet City, took five years as professional mother, did another two in Alphabet City, unemployed for a year after her kid

76

died, then came here. Six years in. No criminal. She —"

At Eve's signal, Peabody lowered her PPC. A moment later Leah hurried in. "I'm very sorry. We're all turned around and upset today. We're scrambling to reschedule appointments, and deal with patients when we can't. Do you want Ava's medical and employment records? Dr. Collins authorized us to turn them over to the police if you came for them."

"Yeah, we'll take them. And Dr. Pike's."

"Jack?" She seemed to sink. "We were afraid . . . We haven't been able to reach him, and he didn't come in for his shift. They were together last night. Their first date."

"Is that so?"

"Ava was so nervous, and Jack was so sweet. I can't believe they're dead."

"She is; he isn't. Where were they going?"

"What? He's all right?" Her eyes widened, went shiny with tears. "Jack's all right?"

"He'll do. Do you know where they were going?"

"Ah, just something casual. Dinner and vid, maybe a club. What happened? Can you tell us what happened? The reports don't make any sense, and when we call for information, we can't get any. We're all —"

She stepped aside as the door opened. He was an imposing man, maybe six-two, lean as a whip with a sharply chiseled face. His eyes were green with a touch of gold, his hair a deep bronze.

"Dr. Slone, this is . . . I'm sorry, I'm so turned around. I didn't get the names. The police."

"Lieutenant Dallas, Detective Peabody."

"Yes, of course. Leah, see to Sarah, will you? She should go home." He went to his desk, sat behind it. "What happened to Ava?"

"She was murdered."

"Mutilated, the reports say. The word was 'mutilated.' "

"That would be accurate."

He breathed slowly in, slowly out. "In a hotel room. I find it hard to believe Ava would go to a hotel room with Jack on a first date. With anyone for that matter."

"She was a young healthy woman. Young healthy women often go to hotel rooms on a date."

"She was shy, and what I'm sure you'd think of as old fashioned." The flare of anger brought out the gold in his eyes. "She must have been forced to go there, and Jack would never force her, or anyone. Where is Dr. Pike?"

"He's in custody."

Now Slone rose from his seat. "You've arrested him? For this?"

"I said he was in custody, not that he was under arrest."

Disdain tightened his face as he stared holes through Eve. "Does he have a lawyer?"

"He hasn't requested one."

"I won't have that boy accused of this. I brought him here. Do you understand? I brought him here."

"You recruited him," Eve said, thinking of Roarke's earlier statement.

"He's a fine doctor, a fine young man. A healer, not a killer. I'll personally arrange for his counsel."

"That's your choice. Where were you last night, Dr. Slone?"

"I beg your pardon?"

Eve often wondered why people used that phrase when they really meant "fuck you."

"It's routine. What time did you leave the clinic?"

"I left about four, and walked home. I believe I arrived close to five."

"Can anyone verify that? Your wife, your staff?"

"It was our housekeeper's day off," he said stiffly. "My wife was out. She got home shortly after seven. I resent the implications of this."

"I'm going to implicate the same to the rest of the staff and employees of the clinic. I can use your office, or conduct the implications downtown."

"We'll see what my lawyer has to say about that."

Before he could reach for his 'link, Eve snatched Peabody's bag, and pulled out the still of Ava at the crime scene.

"Take a look, take a good one." Eve slapped the photo on his desk. "Then curl your lip at my *implications* and call your damn lawyer."

He didn't pale; he didn't tremble. But he looked for a very long time. And when he raised his head his eyes were hard, and they were cold. "She was hardly more than a child. Use the office. I'll notify the others. They'll have to speak with you between patients."

He strode out, shut the door behind him.

"He's got a mean bedside manner," Eve commented.

"So do you, sir."

With a shrug, Eve dipped her hands into her pockets. "Run him. Run them all."

# SEVEN

While Isis gathered what she needed, Roarke took out his 'link to contact Eve. He struggled against the resentment that burned through him at the idea he felt obligated to get clearance from his wife to enter his own property. And, he realized, resented the struggle *against* the resentment.

Bloody cops, he thought, and their bloody procedure. And then, bloody hell when he was dumped straight to her voice mail.

"Well then, if you can't be bothered to answer your 'link, I'll tell you that I've my own expert. I want her to have a pass at the crime scene, so I'll be taking her there shortly. Any problem with that, well, you'll have to get back to me, won't you? And we'll see if I can be bothered answering my 'link."

When he clicked off he saw Isis watching him with amusement dancing in her eyes.

81

"Two strong-headed, strong-willed people, both not only used to giving orders but to having them obeyed. It must be an interesting and stimulating life you have together."

"There are times I wonder how we ever managed to get through two hours together much less two years. And other times I wonder how either of us survived before we found each other."

"She'll be angry with you for taking me to this place."

"No, what she'll be is right pissed. But they used my place, you see, and at least one of my people. So pissed she'll have to be. I'm grateful to you for doing this."

"Gifts aren't free. What I have, what I am makes its own demands. Will you take this?" She held out a small white silk bag tied with a silver cord.

"What is it?"

"A protection charm. I'd like you to carry it when we go in that room together."

"All right." He slipped it in his pocket, felt it bump lightly against the gray button he habitually carried there. Eve's button, he mused, and wasn't that a kind of charm? "I've been in before."

"Yes. And what did you feel?"

"Beyond the anger, the pity? I suppose if I were a fanciful man I'd say I caught the scent of hell. It's not sulphur and brimstone. It's the stench of cruelty."

Isis took a long breath. "Then we'll go. And we'll look."

In Slone's office, Eve glanced at the readout on her 'link, and let the transmission go to voice mail. Roarke would have to wait, she decided, and turned back to Sarah Meeks. The receptionist had a soother in her now, but tears still trembled.

"Where were Ava and Jack going?"

"They weren't sure. They both wanted to keep it light, you know? First date, and you work in the same place, so if it doesn't work out . . ."

"Did they leave together, from here?"

"No — I mean, I don't think so. She was — they were — still here when I left. But I know she planned to go home first. Even though it was casual, Ava wanted to fuss a little, so she was going home to change."

"What time did you leave?"

"About three. I came on at seven yesterday, and left around three."

"Who else was here when you left?"

"Oh, let's see. Dr. Slone, and Dr. Collins, and Dr. Pratt. Um, Leah, Kiki, Roger, one of our physician assistants, and . . ."

Eve took notes as Sarah listed names.

"Was Ava seeing anyone else?"

"No. I mean, she dated sometimes, but not a lot, and nothing serious. There was just this spark, you know, between her and Jack. We all thought they might . . ."

"Did she have any interest in the occult?"

"The what? You mean, like ghosts or something?"

"Or something."

"I don't think so. Ava was . . ." She trailed off again, as if trying to find the word. "Grounded. That's it. She was just really real. She loved her job here, and was so good at it. Good with the staff, the patients. She remembered people's names, and what they came in for, and what everybody liked in their coffee."

"Was there anyone who showed a particular interest in her — other than Jack?"

"Everyone did. She was like that. Everybody loved Ava."

Eve sent Sarah out, sniffling. "Anything pop on those runs?" she asked Peabody.

"Nothing that sings. You've got a lot of highly educated people on staff. Slone's married, two kids, no criminal. Wife's an interior designer. Homes in the city, in the Hamptons, and in Colorado. Collins, Dr. Lawrence, second marriage, two offspring from each, no criminal. Current wife is professional mother. Upper West Side digs here, and a home in Costa Rica. Pratt —"

"Copy the data to my pocket unit." Eve paced the office. "This is going to take a while. We need to split up. Go over and check Ava's apartment. Have EDD pick up her electronics. I'll meet you back at Central when we're done here."

"Okay. You know, Dallas, we're both going to need sleep at some point."

"We'll get to that. Tell them to get someone else in here."

At least one of the killers was here, Eve thought. She was sure of it. The vic hadn't been in the city two full years, and from what Eve had learned, most of her time and energy and interest funnelled into her work. These were her contacts, her people.

Pike, brand-spanking-new.

It was possible they'd run afoul of someone at Ava's apartment — and Peabody would ferret that out, if so. But logic said both Ava and Jack had known at least one of her killers well enough to trust.

And what easier place was there to drug someone than in a health center? The place was full of drugs — and people who, in Eve's opinion, just loved sticking them into other people. Subdue them here, she speculated, give them enough happy juice to make them compliant and transport them to the hotel, where one or more partners has already dealt with Mika and Trosky.

Get them upstairs, she imagined, and let the party begin. Had to be early. The whole thing had been done by twenty-three hundred, latest. It took time to eat, drink, orgy, and perform a human sacrifice.

She glanced up as the door opened. The man who hurried in was about five-ten and carrying a good five excess pounds in the belly. His round face held a pleasant if harried smile. Eyes of faded green radiated both fatigue and kindness. He scooped his hand through his short tangle of brown hair.

"I'm so sorry to keep you waiting. We're . . . well, we're short-staffed today, as you know. We didn't have enough time to notify all the staff, the patients, and close today." He sat, wearily. "I think we're all running on sheer nerves. Sorry, I'm Dr. Collins, Larry Collins."

"Lieutenant Dallas. I'm sorry for your loss."

"It's incomprehensible. At least a half dozen times today I've started to ask Ava for something. In the six months or so since she's been here, she's become the hub of the practice."

"You're aware she was planning to see Dr.

Pike last night, socially."

"Yes. We were all invested, a bunch of matchmakers." His lips compressed on the term. "And now . . . Jack couldn't have hurt her, Lieutenant. It's just not possible."

"What time did she leave yesterday?"

"Ah, let me think. I believe she was still here when I left, and that would have been close to five. Yes, yes, because I said good night to her and —" He broke off, looked away, struggled for composure. "— and good luck."

"Where did you go?"

"I went home, and had a drink." He smiled a little. "My last patient of the day was a very, let's say, active and opinionated five-year-old."

"You're a pediatrician?"

"That's right."

Eve nodded, watching him. "I have to ask, it's routine. Is there anyone who can verify your whereabouts from five p.m. to midnight?"

"My wife. She fixed me the drink, bless her. We had a quiet evening at home as the kids were spending the night with friends."

"All right. Who was here when you left, other than Ava?"

"I'm not entirely sure." He furrowed his brow in thought. "I think Rodney, one of our nurses, and Kiki, a lab tech. I know the waiting room was clear, because I commented on it to Ava. We try to close at five, but realistically it's nearer to six most days."

"Dr. Pike? Was he still here?"

"I didn't see him. Of course, he may have been with a patient."

"Thanks for your time. I may have some followups later, but for now, that's it. Would you send either Kiki or Rodney in?"

"I think Rodney's on his lunch break, but I'll see that Kiki's told you're waiting." He rose, walked to the desk where she sat, offered a hand. "Thank you, Lieutenant, for all you're doing."

She got to her feet first so their eyes would be level. She thought of when she might grab a meal, and took his hand. "It's my job."

"All the same." He held her hand, her eyes a moment longer, then released it. "Thank you."

She waited until he'd left the room before she spoke for her recorder. "Note, Dr. Lawrence Collins is a sensitive. And one who doesn't mind poking into another's mind without permission."

Hope he enjoyed her thoughts of pepperoni pizza, Eve mused. Then checking the time, pulled out her 'link to check her messages.

She was snarling and steaming before Roarke's message played out. "Son of a bitch!" She tagged him back. "You'd better answer, goddamn it, you'd just better — Stay out of my crime scene," she snapped out when his face came on screen.

"That crime scene is a suite in my hotel."

"Look, pal —"

"You look for a change. One of my people is in custody. Another, I've just been informed, is dead by his own hand. I won't sit and do nothing."

"I'm getting somewhere here, and I'll be in contact with Mira within the hour. She'll have finished the initial exams, and if she gets the results I think I may have enough for a search warrant."

"That's all very well, and good for you. Meanwhile, I've my own line to tug, and at the end of it, you may have enough for arrest warrants."

"You can't just walk into a crime scene and take someone with you. Who the hell is with you?"

"Isis."

There was a long, stunned silence. "You're taking a witch into my crime scene? What the hell's wrong with you? If the two of you compromise —"

"Your sweepers and techs have been through, the scene's been recorded and photographed, evidence removed and logged. You've been over that suite top to bottom yourself. Added to that, goddamn right back at you, I didn't come down in the last shower of rain. I know what's to be done to protect the bleeding scene."

"You both need a nap," Eve heard Isis say, very pleasantly.

"Listen. I'm on the Upper West Side, finishing up interviews with the staff at the health center. I'll be done in about thirty minutes, and can be at the hotel in forty. Wait. Just wait until I get there."

There was another silence, then she saw him nod. "Forty minutes," he said and clicked off.

Eve hissed out a breath, kicked Slone's desk. She might have kicked it a second time, but the door opened.

The woman who came in reeked of Neo-Goth. The black hair, red lips, and the silver hoop through her pierced left brow projected a kind of careless defiance that merged with the tattoo that peeked out from the slope of her breast.

Eve might have considered it all a matter of personal style, along with the snug black top and pants, the chunky black boots, but for the smug gleam in the black-lined eyes.

Weak link, Eve thought, and smiled. "Hello, Kiki."

"I'm swamped." She dumped herself in a chair. "So let's cut to it. I left about five — Ava, the pure and wholesome — was still here, all shiny-eyed about her date with Dr. Dull. I lit out, met up with some friends downtown. We hit some clubs, got trashed, hung out, and I got home about two. Is that it?"

"Not quite. I'll need the names and contact information for your friends."

Kiki shrugged, rattled off names and 'link numbers.

"You didn't like Ava?"

"Wasn't my type, that's all. Too bad she's dead and all that. Saint Jack probably freaked when she wouldn't put out, and did her." Now those eyes glittered. "But since I wasn't there, I don't know. Ava and I weren't buds, so I got no clue what she was into. You need more, you'll have to catch me later. I'm backed up."

"Thanks for your time."

"Whatev."

Eve waited a few seconds, then walked to the door, stepped out. She saw Kiki at the end of the corridor in an intense conversation with Leah Burke. The moment Leah spotted Eve coming toward them, she squeezed a hand on Kiki's arm to silence her, and started forward. "Lieutenant, can I help you?"

"I'd like to speak to Rodney."

"He's not back from his break." She checked her wrist unit. "He should be only a few more minutes. He's very prompt."

"Okay, I'll take Dr. Pratt."

"He's still with a patient. I can't —"

"I'll keep it short. I'm sure we'll all be happy when this is done. Before you interrupt him, what time did you leave last night?"

"Me? Ah, just after five."

"Was Ava still here?"

"No, she'd just left. I, ah, scooted her along, actually, so she could get ready for her date. I closed up last night."

"You were the last to leave?"

"That's right."

"And where did you go?"

"I went home. I, ah, walked home, changed, had some dinner."

"You didn't go out again?"

"No."

"Make or receive any calls, have any visitors?"

"No, it was a quiet night. Lieutenant, I

92

have patients myself."

"Okay. I've only got a couple more staff members, and I'll be out of your hair."

Eve stepped back into Slone's office. Collins, Burke, and Kiki, she thought, were top of her suspect list. She scanned Silas Pratt's data, but he didn't keep her waiting long.

He strode in, a sharply handsome man with an air of confidence. His eyes were a laser blast of blue, and she could admit they gave her a jolt. When he offered his hand she allowed herself to think just that: *Here's a great-looking man with killer eyes.*

He smiled at her. "Lieutenant, I'm Silas Pratt."

Her heart pumped a little harder as he squeezed her hand. She felt the probe of his gaze, and yes, of his power, like heat along her brain. "Have a seat, Dr. Pratt," she said and removed her hand from his.

"Can you tell me if you have any leads? Other than Jack. No one who knows him will believe Jack did this to our Ava."

"You've only known him a couple of weeks."

"That's true. Peter recruited him, but I like to think I'm a good judge of character. What they're saying was done to Ava, well, it's monstrous, isn't it? And to someone so young, so vibrant."

Now he did sit, and passed a hand over those potent eyes. "I thought of her almost as a daughter."

"You don't have children. According to your official data."

"No. But it was easy to feel a paternal kind of affection for Ava."

"I don't want to intrude any longer than necessary." And she wanted out, Eve admitted. There was a heat in the room now, a kind of singeing of the air. "When did you leave yesterday?"

"About quarter to five. Ava was getting ready to leave, I remember. Leah was shooing her out. She and Jack — well, you know about all that."

"Yes. Did you approve of that? One of your doctors dating your office manager."

He looked surprised by the question, even bemused. "They were both adults — and frankly, they seemed besotted with each other from the first minute."

"Where did you go when you left?"

"Home to change. My wife and I had a small dinner party last evening. A few friends."

"I apologize, but it's routine. I'll need the names and contact numbers."

"Of course." He smiled at her. "No apology necessary." And he gave her six names. She thanked him, dismissed him. Then added those names to her list of suspects.

# EIGHT

Roarke arranged lunch for himself and Isis
in the owner's suite of the hotel, and passed
the forty minutes eating food that didn't
interest him while making polite small talk
with a witch.

"When's the last time you slept?" Isis
asked him.

"I suppose it's been about thirty-two
hours now. She'll push herself until she
drops, you see. Eve."

"And you relax and recreate?"

"More often than she. But no, in this case,
in this particular case, I suppose we'll both
push. Her time's up, so if you've finished,
I'll take you to 606."

"First." She rose, stepped to him, and
placed her hand on his head. "No, relax,
just for a moment. Clear your mind. You
can trust me."

A warm flow, he thought. Not the quick
burst of energy that came from popping a

booster, but more of a slow, steady build of stamina.

"Better?"

"Thank you, yes."

"It won't last long, but between that and the little you ate, it should get you through. What you need is some rest." She picked up her bag. "I'm ready."

He led her to the elevator.

"You said there's a private elevator that opens into the suite, as well as the doors to the hallways."

"That's right."

"I want to see it from the outside first. I want to go through the door, not through a machine."

"All right. Sixtieth floor," he ordered. "Main bank."

"I'll ask you, whatever happens, not to leave me alone."

"I won't." When the elevator doors opened, Roarke took her hand.

The bloody footprints still walked the carpet. Blood smears marred the walls where Jack had laid his hand for balance. In Roarke's hand, Isis's fingers tensed.

"People think of it as a cliché." She stared at the door where the tail of blood made a six from the middle zero. "But it has power and meaning. It should be cleaned — all of this — with blessed water as soon as possible."

Roarke stepped forward, drew out his master. And Eve strode off the elevator like vengeance.

"Wait. Didn't I tell you to wait?"

"And so I did." Roarke turned to her, his gaze as icy as hers was hot. "You're late."

She put herself between him and the door. "I know who did this. At least I know some of them. I can close this without the mumbo."

"Nice to see you again, Eve."

Eve shifted her gaze to Isis. "No offense. I appreciate you being willing to help, and in fact, have some questions you may be able to answer. You don't have to see what's in there."

"I've already seen some of it, through him and now through you. Seen what's trapped in your minds. But I can't feel unless I go in. I can't feel or see what she saw and felt unless I go in. I might help, I might not, but he needs it."

Isis took Eve's arms so that for a moment, she stood as the link between Eve and Roarke. "You know that."

Eve yanked out her master and turned to the door. "When I say it's done, it's done," she stated.

Roarke slipped the protection charm into her pocket as she unsealed the door.

She stepped in first. "Lights on full." She turned quickly when she heard Isis let out a quick, shuddering breath. But Isis put out a hand, and took another step into the room.

"It reeks still, and will until it's cleansed. No one can stay here until a cleansing. You feel it, do you feel it? This is not the work of a dabbler, not the vile work of one who only seeks blood and death for their own sake. This is power and purpose, and it brought the dark."

"You're going to tell me they called up Satan?"

Isis turned her black eyes on Eve. "I imagine he has more important things to do than answer a summons. But evil can be called, and it can be fed. You can't do what you do and believe otherwise. Or see what you see."

She stared at the pentagram, and the pools and rivers of blood that washed over it. "She doesn't know me, neither in body nor spirit. I need some of her blood. Get that, while I prepare."

She knelt and began taking items from her bag.

Eve said, "Crap," but she stalked off to get swabs from the bathroom amenities.

"I'll need three. Head, heart, hand." Isis set out candles, crystals, herbs.

Though she rolled her eyes, Eve crossed to the pentagram. If she felt a pull when she stepped into it, she willfully pushed it away. She slapped a look toward Roarke as she coated the swabs. "If it ever gets out that I not only allowed but participated in some voodoo bullshit —"

He crouched beside her, took her free hand. "My lips are sealed as long as you want them to be. I owe you for this."

"Damn right you do."

"You're so tired, darling Eve." Before she could evade, he leaned to her, brushed her lips with his.

"There's power there, too," Isis murmured. "We'll need it. Light the candles, please, and stand with me. Together with me while I cast the circle. Hurry. I can't stay here long.

"The power of three in light," she said as Roarke lit the candles. "The power of three in flesh." She took a bag and walked a circle of salt around them. "Order the lights off," she commanded, and when only the candles lit the room, she began to chant in a language Eve didn't recognize.

With a curved knife she turned, like the hand of a compass. Her face glowed; her eyes burned. She placed crystals at the compass points of the circle, then sprinkled herbs into the water she'd poured into a small copper bowl.

Whether it was fatigue or the power of suggestion, Eve felt something cold, cold, brutally cold push against the air.

"It cannot enter what is light. It cannot enter what is bright. And we will not *open!*" Isis threw her hands high, and her biceps quivered with the strain. "I am daughter of the sun, sister of the moon. I am child and servant of the goddess. In this place, at this hour, I call upon her power. Into me, into mine, bring both light and sight divine. Set the murdered spirit free, send her essence into me.

"The power of three, by her blood."

Isis smeared Ava's blood on her forehead, on her breast, on her hand. And falling to her knees, she shook. Her eyes glazed like black glass while her face went white as wax. Horror etched into her features. Both Eve and Roarke dropped down beside her. Her hands grasped theirs, her fingers tightened like wires.

"She's in some sort of trance. We have to get her out."

"We gave our word," Roarke reminded her. "Christ, she's cold as ice."

Isis bowed back until her head nearly touched the floor. And screamed. For one mad moment, Eve imagined she saw a gash open and gush blood from her throat. And when the witch slumped, Eve wasn't certain if she was unconscious or dead.

"Fuck this, we're getting her out of here now."

"Don't leave the circle." Isis's voice was weak, but her eyes fluttered open. "Don't. The red bottle there. I need it, and a little help to sit up."

They eased her up, and taking the bottle, she sipped slowly from it. "It's not an illegal," she said, with both pain and humor in her eyes. "A potion. There's always a price for power."

"You're in pain," Eve said flatly. "We need to get you out of here."

"The circle needs to be closed as it was opened. Properly. Then, yes, we all need to get out of here."

When it was done, and her tools gathered again, Isis leaned on Roarke while Eve resealed the door.

"Can we go back to where we had lunch? I'll tell you what I can tell you, but I want to be away from here."

In the owner's suite, Roarke helped her to the couch, tucked pillows behind her head.

"What do you need?" he asked her.

"A really big glass of wine."

"I can get that for you. Lieutenant?"

"Coffee. I understand you're a sensitive," Eve began, "and you believe, strongly believe in your . . . faith."

"You sometimes hear the cries of the dead. Feel their pain, and know their need for you. We're not so far apart." Isis closed her eyes a moment, opening them when Roarke brought her wine. She drank slowly, as she had her potion. "She was a lovely child. I saw some of what they did to her. Not all, I think, not all, but enough. She was inside herself, screaming to get out, but trapped there. There are ways to trap a spirit, with drugs, and other methods. She drank what they gave her, ate, let them touch her. She had no choice. They marked her with a serpent."

Eve thought of the tattoo, said nothing.

"Sex for power. Well, for some of them, it was only sex — the greed for it, the meanness of it. No love, not even lust. Just greed and violence and power. The one they brought her first, not one of them. Trapped as she was. Something there."

Isis touched a hand to her forehead, sipped more wine. "Something light between them," she continued. "Light and

103

new, twisted now when they coupled on the sign. Snuffing out that fragile light with chants and drugs and power until it, too, turned mean. They raped her, took him away and raped her, again and again while she lay unable to fight, to resist. And her trapped spirit screaming, screaming."

"Easy now," Roarke murmured, and took Isis's hand. "Easy."

She nodded, gathered herself again. "They pulled her up, dragged her to the one who leads them. She looked at him. He said her name, and she looked in his eyes when he cut her throat.

"And they fell on her like beasts. I couldn't bear any more. I couldn't bear it."

Eve rose and walked away while Isis wept in absolute silence, while Roarke sat with her, held her hand. She walked to the wide glass doors, yanked them open, and stepped out into the spring air that buzzed like a mad hive from the city.

When Roarke came out, she continued to stare out at the snarls of traffic, the rush of people below. "What am I supposed to do with this?" she demanded. "Go to the PA and tell him I want to arrest these people because a witch communed with the tragic spirit of the victim?"

"Eve."

He laid a hand on her shoulder, but rather than turn to him, she curled her hands on the rail until they were fists. "I know she didn't bullshit that, okay? I may be cynical, but I'm not stupid. And I'm *sick* at the thought that she saw what she saw. Nobody should. Nobody should have to see that, feel that."

"No one but you?" he asked, and turned her to face him.

She shook her head. "I looked right in the faces of some of the people who did this to that girl. And I looked right in the eyes of one of them, the one I think cut her throat. And for a second — hell, longer — I was scared right down to my guts." She let out a breath. "Now, I'm just pissed off."

He pressed his lips to her forehead. "Then take them down, Lieutenant."

"I damn well will." She put her arms around him first, squeezed. "You pissed me off."

"Same goes. Now, it seems, I'm not. And I just love you."

"I'm still a little pissed." But she tipped her head back, looked into his eyes. "But I love you, too."

Stepping away, she went back to Isis. "Are you steady enough to look at some pictures?"

"Yes."

"Let's hope I don't need your statement, your ID, or . . . the rest of it to take these bastards down. But just in case." Eve pulled a stack of ID photos from her bag, spread them on the coffee table.

"Yes." Shifting to sit up, Isis took another sip of wine. Then, without hesitation, pointed out Ava's murderers.

# NINE

Eve rushed through Central, dodging other cops on the glides on her way to Homicide. The time with Isis had put her behind. She needed to meet with Mira, go over her notes, organize them. Then talk the PA into issuing more than a dozen arrest warrants.

And God, she needed coffee.

She veered toward her bullpen just as Peabody came out.

"I was about to tag you. Grabbing an energy bar first. You want?"

Eve started to decline, the things were disgusting. But they worked. "Yeah. I need to put a couple of things together, then meet with Mira."

At Vending, Peabody plugged in some credits. "You want the Razzmatazz or the Berry Burst?"

"What difference does it make? They're both revolting."

"I kinda like the Berry Burst." As Peabody

made the selections, the machine cheerfully congratulated her on her choices, then listed the ingredients and nutritional information. "I checked in with Mira since you were late getting back."

"Ran into stuff. Fill you in. Coffee."

Peabody hiked after Eve to Eve's office. "She said she needed another thirty minutes, that was about five minutes ago. Down-the-hall neighbor at the vic's apartment states the vic never came home after work yesterday. They were supposed to do the girl thing together for the date. Hair, outfit, like that. Ava never showed. Nothing in her apartment to indicate an interest or connection with the occult. EDD's got her electronics."

"She never went back to the apartment because they took her at the clinic." Eve took a bite of the energy bar, washed it down with coffee. She filled Peabody in, and as expected, her partner's eyes went big as planets.

"You — *you* did like a ritual?"

"You had to be there," Eve muttered.

"No, really happy to pass. Was it scary?"

"The point is, while I'm not sure how much weight the woo-woo might carry in court, Isis fingered every single one of the people on my list. Damn smug is what they

108

are, alibied up. Alibiing each other. Break one, break all. If Mira's got anything solid, we top it off. We've got enough to push for a search warrant on the clinic — and if we push right, on the residences of the staff. Contact the PA. Get them."

"Me? Me?" If she'd just been ordered to run naked through the bullpen, Peabody would've been less stunned. "But you should do it. They listen to you over there. What am I supposed to do?"

"Jesus, Peabody. Sing, dance, shed a goddamn tear. Put the package together and get it done. I've got Mira in fifteen. Go."

She all but shoved Peabody out the door, then closed it. Locked it. She two-pointed the rest of the energy bar into the trash. It wasn't doing the job. She needed five minutes down, she admitted. Just five. She set her wrist unit to alarm, sat at her desk, laid her head down on it, and shut her eyes.

She went straight under.

A sound woke her, a kind of humming. Voices, tinny with distance, tapped on her subconscious. One — young, male — spiked with excitement.

"Look! Flying cars. Look out the window! That is so *cool*."

Eve allowed herself a groan, started to slap

109

at her wrist unit. Opening bleary eyes, she stared groggily at the swirl of luminous blue light, and the man, woman, and child cloaked in its circle. Instinct had her reaching for her weapon even as she registered them — tall man, a lot of gold hair, slim brunette with startled green eyes, and a shaggy-haired boy.

She thought she heard the woman say, "Oops." Then they were gone, and her wrist unit was beeping.

"Okay, with a dream that weird, I need more than five minutes down." She turned off the alarm, scrubbed her hands over her face. After downing the rest of her now lukewarm coffee, she gathered what she needed for Mira.

As she left the office, she shot a frown over her shoulder. Weird, she thought again. The whole damn day was weird.

Mira's admin gave Eve a glare that turned the room into an arctic cave. Knowing the way to Mira lay at the dragon's feet, Eve cut through the bull. "I kicked you, and kicked you hard this morning." She pulled out one of the crime-scene photos. "She's why." And laid it on the desk.

The admin sucked in a breath, held it, let it out slowly. "I see. Yes. She's waiting for you, Lieutenant."

"Thanks." Eve picked up the photo and walked into Mira's office.

Mira wasn't at her desk but standing at the window, her back to the room. She looked smaller somehow, Eve thought. Almost delicate in her quiet lavender suit.

"Dr. Mira."

"Yes. Such a lovely day. Sometimes you need to remember the world is full of lovely days. You've had a very long one, haven't you?"

"It's got a ways to go yet."

Mira turned. Her sable hair curled around her pretty face, but her eyes looked tired and troubled. "Where do you want me to begin?"

"I know what happened, and I know who's responsible. At least the main players. I need to know what was done to Jackson Pike and Mika Nakamura, how it was done, and who did it. What was done to them was also done to the desk clerk at the hotel, and he bashed his own brains out with a hammer. So I need to know if it was done to anyone else."

Rather than sit in one of her cozy scoop chairs as was her habit, Mira continued to stand. "First, the toxicology screening showed a combination of drugs in their systems. I have that list for you. Both had a

111

hallucinogenic in their bloodstream and a drug we sometimes use to control patients with violent tendencies. As you know, both Pike and the victim were also given sexual drugs."

"Would that explain the headaches, the memory blanks?"

"The combination would likely result in a kind of chemical hangover, but no, not the violent pain. There may be blank spots as well, but again, no, that's not my conclusion."

She did sit now. "The drugs were used to begin a process, and to enhance it."

"They've been hypnotized."

"You're ahead of me."

"No, but I'm hoping we're on pace. At least two of the suspects are sensitives. They took a pass at me. Since I've dealt with a homicidal psychic before, I used the same method to block them, to steer them away. One of them, Silas Pratt, he's . . . Look, I know you've got a daughter who's Wiccan, and I get there are theories and faiths and even documentation, studies, blah, blah. I'm not big on that. But this guy?"

It went against the grain to admit it. "He's got a punch," Eve told her.

"You don't want to use the word 'power.' "

"It doesn't take power to load people up

with drugs, or to hypnotize them. It's a technique. You use it." She stuffed her hands in her pockets and began to pace. "One of these bastards is Mika's kid's doctor. She took the kid in for a standard checkup three weeks ago. So, we theorize Pratt hypnotizes her. Maybe they slip her something first to make her more susceptible, but he takes her under, and gives her the assignment. Post-hypnotic suggestion, right?"

"Yes."

"It needs a trigger — something she sees, hears. Easy enough to take care of that while she's on her way to work, maybe give her a booster shot. She goes in, shuts down the cameras. They had to get to the desk clerk. We'll find the intersect there, but they turned him on like a damn droid. They waltz Pike and the victim right in. They go along like puppies. They're loaded by then, and under . . ."

"A spell?"

"If that's the word. Pike's left as patsy, with that trigger still cocked in his head. The pain's impossible, and trying to remember takes it up to excruciating."

"I believe if you hadn't gotten them to me, into a controlled, medical environment when you did, they'd have ended it as the desk clerk did. I've had to use that pain to try to get to the trigger. It's . . . difficult."

Understanding, Eve moved to Mira's AutoChef. "What's that tea you're always drinking?"

Mira managed a smile. "It varies. I think jasmine would be nice. Thank you."

Eve programmed a cup, brought it to Mira, took a seat. "You're not hurting them. You know that. The one who cocked the trigger is."

"They, both of them, begged me to kill them." Mira sipped the tea, then eased wearily back in the chair. "It's taken hours for me to find the right method to dial the pain down. Not turn it off, not yet, but lower it from inhuman to hideous. Enough that Jack remembered a little. He remembered that Dr. Pratt called him into his office at the end of the day. He's not sure of the time, it's cloudy, but thinks it was after his last patient. Pratt gave him a cup of coffee, and after he drank it, it's more jumbled. He remembers being in a limo with Collins and Ava. He thinks there were more. I recorded everything, of course. He remembers having sex with Ava."

"Does he remember the murder?"

Her eyes troubled, Mira shook her head. "He's suppressing. Even without the trigger, his mind's not ready to go there. He next remembers waking in a bed, covered with blood, and a woman he called Leah sitting beside him, crying."

"Leah Burke. Good, that's good. I can break her, and she'll take them all down with her."

"It wasn't just a young woman killed in that suite, Eve. Parts of the two people I have sedated and restrained for their own safety were murdered in there. When I find the way to remove the trigger and they remember what was done, their part in it however unwilling, they'll never be the same."

"You'll help them deal with it, or find someone who'll help them deal with it. It's what you do."

"Take them down, Eve. Take them down hard. When I can tell Mika and Jack that's been done, we can start on the healing."

In all the time they'd worked together, Mira had never asked. Eve rose. "Like you said, it's a lovely day. Before it's over, they'll be down."

As she walked out, Eve whipped out her communicator to contact Peabody. "Search warrants?"

"It's looking good on the clinic. I just need to —"

"Put a hold on it. We've got a wit who puts

Leah Burke in Suite 606. We're bringing her in. Book an interview room."

"You want me to have her picked up?"

"Here's how it goes. Two uniforms at her door. If she's not home yet, I need to know ASAP. She's not under arrest, and she's not to be read her rights. Got that?"

"Got it."

"She's needed down here for further questioning. That's all they know. She's not to be permitted to contact anyone. She's not under arrest. I'll finish up with the search warrants."

Eve was still listing the names for the APA when she approached Homicide. What sounded like a small riot had her quickening her steps.

Then she smelled the pizza. "Yeah, I mean even the house in the Caribbean. I've got goddamn probable cause right down the line. I've got witness statements, and within two hours I'm going to hand you a confession on a goddamn platter that will take down every son of a bitch on the list I just gave you. They're going to have hoodoo voodoo crap tucked away," Eve said meeting Roarke's eyes as she stepped into the bullpen. "Because they believe it. A dozen blades were used on the vic. We're going to find some, most, or all of them."

She clicked off. "Figured you'd be back around after you got your witch home."

"You haven't eaten." He picked up a box of pizza while her men swarmed like ants over the five others he'd brought in. "Eat now."

She grabbed a slice, chomped a huge bite. "Oh. God. Good." She swallowed, took another. "I got them."

"I can see that. Can I watch?"

She took the tube of Pepsi he offered, guzzled. "It's a good bribe. Take Observation."

# TEN

Revived and revved, Eve stood with Roarke in Observation and watched Leah pace the interview room in her smart suit.

"She's already sweating. Ten minutes in, and she's already sweating. She's scared and guilty, and the doctors aren't here to tell her what to do, what to say."

"Why her? Out of all of them?"

"She cried." She glanced over as Mira came in.

"Word's out that you have one of them in," Mira said. "I wanted to see for myself."

"I haven't arrested her yet. Listen, I'm going to ask you not to turn on the audio until I give you the go. Actually, I'm not asking. I've got to get started."

"Will I be able to see Mika?" Roarke asked Mira after Eve stepped out.

"Not yet. She's comfortable for the moment. I've spoken with her husband."

"So have I. Is there anything I can do for her?"

"There will be." Mira laid a hand over Roarke's, and watched Eve enter Interview. "What she's going to say needs to be off the record. At least for my ears."

"Do you object?"

"No." Mira stared at Leah Burke through the glass. "No, I don't."

Inside, Leah spun toward Eve. "I demand to know why I was brought here, why I'm being treated this way. I have rights. I have —"

"Shut the fuck up. You've got nothing here until I give it to you. Sit down."

The words, the tone, had Leah's whole body recoiling. "I will not —"

"I'll put you down, bitch. Believe it."

The threat, so hot and hard in Eve's eyes, had Leah sitting at the small table. "You'll lose your badge." But her voice trembled, just a little. "Worse. There are laws."

Eve slammed both fists on the table, hard enough to have Leah covering her face in defense. "Laws? I bet you were thinking about *laws* when Ava Marsterson was being hacked to death. Jack remembers, Leah." She leaned close, snapped her fingers in front of Leah's face. "Boom. Spell broken. You've got one shot. One, then I move on to the next. But I'll hurt you first."

"You can't touch me. You can't put your hands on me. I want —"

"I know how to hurt you so it won't show." Eve let the heat burn in her eyes as she circled the table. "Your word against mine. Decorated cop against murder suspect. Guess who they'll believe? I haven't put this on record. I haven't read you your rights. And we're all alone here, Leah. One shot once I turn on the record. You don't take it, I move to Kiki or Rodney, to Larry's wife, and down the line — and you go back to a cage blubbering with the pain.

"Everybody gets one shot. Take it, I deal down to Murder Two. You'll do life, but you'll do it on planet. Pass? And you'll find out what hell really is because you'll be in some concrete cage in an off-planet penal colony where I will personally see that word gets out you fucked with tiny little children. Do you know what cons like to do to people who fuck with tiny little children?"

"I've never touched a child —"

"I'll lie." Eve grinned. "And I'll love it. One shot, and if you so much as *think* lawyer, it's done. You only get the chance because Jack's soft-hearted enough to think you feel real bad about what happened. Me? I'm hoping you pass so I can look forward to getting the reports on how many inventive ways the other cons and the guards rape you over the next, oh, fifty years."

She came around the table, whispered in Leah's ear. "They find ways to get sharp, ugly tools into those cages, Leah. They'll slice and dice you, let them stitch you up again just so they can slice and dice some more. The more you beg, the more they'll enjoy it."

She watched tears plop on Leah's trembling hands, on the rough surface of the table. And thinking of Ava, felt no pity. "She trusted you, you bitch."

"Please. Oh, please."

"Screw you." Eve walked to the door, stepped out. She took a deep breath, signaled Peabody. "Let's do it." Walking back in, she nodded toward the observation glass. "Record on. Dallas, Lieutenant Eve —"

"Please, please. I'll tell you everything."

"Hey, great." Eve slid into her chair, composed and easy. "Let's just get everything on record first, and read you your rights."

When she'd finished, she nodded to Leah. "What do you want to tell us, Ms. Burke?"

"I didn't know it would be like that. I swear, I swear I didn't know."

"Like what?"

"So much blood. I never thought they would really kill her."

"Be more specific."

"I thought it would be a symbolic death."

"Bullshit." Eve leaned back in her chair with the warning in her eyes clear. *Lie, and your one shot dies.* "You knew exactly what was going to happen, and when it did, you couldn't handle it. If you want me to go to the PA and say you came in, you confessed, you gave the details and feel remorse, don't bullshit me. Did you participate in the ritual murder of Ava Marsterson?"

"Yes. I didn't understand. Believe me, I didn't understand. I thought I did, but . . . She didn't accept, and neither did Jack. Not like Silas said they would."

"Silas Pratt participated in the murder of Ava Marsterson?"

"He cut her throat. She just stood there, and he cut her throat, and the blood gushed out of her. She didn't accept. She didn't know what was happening, so how could she accept?"

"Accept what?"

"Her sacrifice. That she would be the gift."

"Whose gift?"

"The gift from us to the prince. To Lucifer."

"How long have you been a satanist?"

"I am *not* a satanist. I am a disciple of the One."

Eve gave it a moment, unsure if she was amused or irritated by the obvious insult in Leah's voice. "Okay. And does the One demand the murder of innocents?"

"Your God murdered my child." Leah's hands balled into fists, beat lightly on the table. "He took her, and what had she ever done? She was just a baby. I found my way back. I found my strength and my purpose."

"Silas Pratt showed you the way back."

"He's a great man. You'll never understand. A man of power. You'll never hold him with your pitiful laws and your bars."

"But he lied to you, this great man, this man of power," Peabody put in. "He lied to you about Ava and Jack."

"No, I think . . . No, he wouldn't lie. I think he miscalculated, that's all. She just wasn't ready. Wasn't as strong as Silas thought. Or maybe it's me. Maybe I'm weak. I couldn't stand what they did to her."

"Tell me who they are. Every name of everyone who was in Suite 606."

"Silas and his wife, Ola. Larry — Dr. Collins, and his wife, Bria." In a dull, empty voice, she gave Eve a dozen names in addition to her own. "And Ava and Jack."

"Dr. Slone?"

"No. Peter and the others from the clinic who weren't there aren't disciples or priests. It's important, Silas thinks, that there are those who aren't part of us — and to know who is open to our faith, and who would be closed. Everyone who is of our group attended. It was an important ritual, a celebration."

"A celebration?"

"Yes. It was Silas's birthday."

"I've seen his records. It wasn't his birthday."

"His date of rebirth in the One."

"Right." Eve sat back again. "Why Ava and Jack?"

"Ava was the gift. Silas recognized her as such the day she came in to interview for the position. And Jack . . . the sexual energy between them would be a vital element to the ritual."

"Why that room?"

"We'd considered other venues, but . . . A palace, it seemed right. And Larry's connection to the head of security gave us the way in. I'm only a disciple. I don't plan." She folded her hands now, bowed her head. "I follow."

"You followed them into that suite. But first you helped drug Ava and Jack at the clinic."

"We gave them what would open them to the coming ritual, what would help them accept, and embrace Silas's power."

"He used hypnosis, Leah, on top of hallucinogens."

Tears continued to gather and spill. "You don't understand. You're closed."

"Fine. You used chemicals to open Ava and Jack, without their knowledge or permission."

"Yes, but —"

"And once they were under that influence, you took them to the hotel. Correct?"

"Yes."

"There, Mika Nakamura and Brian Trosky had also been drugged, and *embraced* by Silas's power. That power caused them to shut down the security cameras to the lobby, and to the elevators for the sixtieth floor. It also, as had been done to Jack, caused them to forget what had been done, or suffer pain."

"The pain is only if they refuse to accept, only to help them —"

"Inside the room, you ate and you drank, you engaged in sexual activity."

Color flushed into her cheeks. It was amazing, Eve mused, what embarrassed murderers.

"Sex is an offering."

"Ava didn't offer, did she? After you'd feasted and stoked up, painted your pentagram, lit your candles, said whatever it is you people say, you stretched out a drugged, helpless, naked woman on the floor, and told a drugged, helpless man to have at her. He cared for her. They cared for each other, isn't that true?"

"Yes, yes, but —"

"And when he finished what he'd have never done of his own will, the rest of you raped her."

"Yes." Tears rolled down her cheeks. "Everyone was required to take from the gift, and to give of ourselves. But I felt . . ."

"What?"

"Cold. So cold. Not the heat, not the fire, but ice. I heard her screaming in my head. I swear I *heard* her." She covered her face with her hands. "But no one would listen. They pulled her to her feet. Kiki and Rodney. Silas stepped into the circle, and the cold, the cold was terrible. Her screaming was like spikes in my head. But no one heard her. He slashed her throat, and her blood sprayed all over him. Everyone rushed forward when she fell to take more blood, to make more blood. Jack passed out, so they coated him with her blood. They took him upstairs, left him in bed while they finished with her. Larry told me to go up, to take one of the knives and put it in Jack's hand, and to give him another round of drugs so he'd overdose."

"The plan was to kill Jack, leave him behind, so it looked as if he'd killed Ava."

"Yes. Yes. But I couldn't. I couldn't give him more. Her blood was on my hands, and I could hear her screaming." She laid down her head and wept.

"Give her five minutes to pull it together," Eve told Peabody. "The charge is Murder in the Second, two counts," she added, thinking of Trosky. "Additional charges are kidnapping, two counts, rape, inducing chemicals without consent or knowledge, including illegals. Have her booked and bolted. I'm going to go get us a shitload of warrants."

Lack of sleep didn't put a hitch in Eve's stride as she walked to Silas Pratt's front door. Big, fancy house, she noted. Well, he'd seen the last of that. The droid that answered looked down its nose. "Dr. and Mrs. Pratt are unavailable at this time. Please leave your name and state your business, and —"

He didn't get any further as Eve shoved him aside. "Shut that thing down," she ordered the uniforms that trailed after her and Peabody. She walked into the spacious living area where the doctor and his wife were sipping martinis.

"Exactly what is the meaning of this?" Silas demanded as he surged to his feet.

"Deal with the woman, Peabody. He's mine. Silas Pratt, you're under arrest. The charges are Murder in the First Degree in the death of Ava Marsterson, a human being. Murder in the First Degree in the death of —"

"This is absurd. You're absurd."

Eve felt that *punch* of his, accepted the ice that coated her belly. Even welcomed it. "Don't interrupt. Resist, by all means, because I'd love to spend the next several minutes kicking your ass. Jesus, Peabody, can't you shut her up?"

"She's a screamer," Peabody said cheerfully as she passed the hysterical Ola to waiting uniforms.

"Now where was I? Oh yeah, the death of Brian Trosky, another human being. We've got kidnapping charges, illegals, fraud, medical abuse, and just for fun, destruction of property. You guys seriously trashed that suite. You have the right to remain silent," she began.

"You can go to hell."

"Thanks, but New York's close enough for me." She grabbed one of his arms to pull it behind his back as she read him the rest of the Revised Miranda. When he tried to shake her off, she gave herself the pleasure of slamming the heel of her boot into his instep. He cursed at her, snarled at her as she clapped the restraints to his wrist. "What is that, Latin? Greek? Or is just all made up?"

He struggled as she frog-marched him across the room, which, she thought, it could be argued was the reason his head smacked into the doorjamb. "Gee, I bet you're going to have a headache now. Cut it out, before you hurt yourself."

"I'll drink your blood from a silver cup."

"That's just disgusting." She moved her mouth close to his ear. "You don't have any power here, asshole. Getting arrested, dragged out of your fancy house in front of your fancy neighbors, and hey, look, it's Channel 75." She beamed, pleased her heads-up to her contact there had brought the media. "Nothing like humiliation to water down power. I bet even the devil himself's embarrassed."

She muscled him into the back of the police car. She fixed dark glasses over his head, over his eyes. "Remember he's a sensitive," she told the cops she'd put in charge. "He goes straight into isolation."

She slammed the door, put her hands on her hips. "Go home, Peabody," she said when her partner stepped beside her and yawned until her jaw cracked. "Get some sleep."

"I am so on that. Some day, huh?"

"Yeah, some day." Eve stood where she was, watched Roarke come to her. Gosh, she thought, pretty. And realized sleep deprivation had gooed up her brain.

"I imagine this arrest will be playing on screen for some time."

"That's entertainment." Eve gave him a quick smile.

"Please tell me you're not going to make all the other arrests personally, then deal with the ensuing paperwork tonight."

"Nah, I just wanted this one, 'specially. I delegated, and the paperwork'll wait till morning. I'm pretty close to falling on my face."

He put his arms around her, amused that she was tired enough not to resist even though some of the media remained. "I want to go home, sleep with my wife. For days."

"Settle for eight straight hours?"

"Deal."

With their arms around each other's waist they walked to the car. Roarke got behind the wheel; Eve slid into the passenger's seat. And, he noted, got started on that eight hours immediately.

# EPILOGUE

Jack sat up in bed when Eve entered his treatment room. He was pale, and bruises of fatigue dogged his eyes. No doubt she'd had a more restful night than he had. "Doctor?" he began.

"Lieutenant. Lieutenant Dallas. Do you remember me?"

He stared through her for a moment. "Yes. I remember." He held up a hand, a signal to wait. And shutting his eyes, breathed. "I remember. You were at the hotel, but not, not in that room. And you were talking to me in another room. The police station. Am I under arrest?"

"No, Jack. I know you're working with Dr. Mira. She says you're better than you were, and you'll be better yet."

"The drugs are out of my system. It helps. The headaches . . . it's not as bad. Ava's dead. I was there." The words trembled out. Once more he closed his eyes, breathed. "I was there. I raped her."

"No, you didn't. They used you both. You're a doctor, Jack. I know Mira told you what they'd put in you, and you know what those chemicals can do. You were drugged, put under hypnosis. Kidnapped. Nothing that happened was your fault or responsibility. You were a victim."

"I'm alive. She's not."

"I know. That's hard. You're afraid to remember, afraid to ask if you used the knife you had in your hand."

His eyes welled, and tears leaked out. "How can I live with that? Whatever they put in me, whatever they did, how can I live with that?"

"You don't have to. You didn't use the knife. I have a number of statements from people who were there, who were involved. Every one of them says you passed out. They put the knife in your hand when you were upstairs, unconscious."

"The blood. Her blood."

"They put it on you. You were supposed to die, holding the knife, covered in her blood. There would have been questions, sure, a lot of questions. Who else was with you. They had two other people they believed would be dead who'd be tied in. One of them is dead, Jack — he didn't do anything, and he's dead. Another is across the hall in a room like this, struggling to deal with what happened. They drugged her, used her. Do you blame her for Ava?"

"No. God."

"Why blame yourself?"

"I couldn't get out. I couldn't get *out* of . . . myself, and help her. Even when I heard her screaming. In my head."

"Thirteen people killed Ava. You weren't one of them. Because you lived, we found them. Every one of them is locked up. Every one of them is going to pay. You lived, and you found me, Jack. I was in suite 606. I saw what was done to her. I had her blood on my hands. She was in my head, too, Jack. I'm telling you, she doesn't blame you. She doesn't want you to carry this."

He put out a hand, took hers. "They're going to pay?"

"Every goddamn one."

"Thank you."

She stepped out, and watched through the observation window as Roarke leaned over and kissed Mika on the brow.

"How is she?" she asked when he came out.

"Better. Better than I'd hoped, really. Mira said she has a strong mind. How about your Jack?"

"He'll get there."

Roarke took her hand. "Another long day, Lieutenant, with all your interrogations and reports and media conferences."

"You had one, too, I imagine, making up for the time lost yesterday. Buying up wide chunks of the universe takes it out of a guy."

"Yet I feel surprisingly . . . fresh."

"Good, because I want to go home and sleep with my husband — in a much more active sense than last night." She let him keep her hand as they walked away from the treatment rooms. "You know, I found this little bag full of stones and flowery things in the pocket of the jacket I had on yesterday. How do you suppose that got there?"

"Hmm. Magic?"

She gave him a shoulder bump and let it go. As far as she was concerned, the only magic she'd ever need was the good strong grip of his hand in hers.

■ ■ ■ ■

# LOVE ENDURES
# MARY BLAYNEY

■ ■ ■ ■

Maristeve and Curt Bradley
Suzy and Ronnie Kerns
Kit and Cliff Needham
Betsy and John Saunders

With thanks to Riggs National Bank for
bringing us together

# ONE

*London 1814*

"Mama! Mama! Wake up. Someone is knocking at the door."

Summer Cassidy bolted upright in the chair, moving from sleep to wakefulness before her daughter finished the sentence. "What, Kitty? Someone is at the door? At this time of night?" The first flush of fear gave way to relief. "I am sure it is only your father. Without his key. Again." Standing, she stretched the crick from her neck and drew a deep breath as though she could draw in vigor from the air around her.

"Shall I go and let him in, Mama?"

"No, darling, that is not a chore for a four-year-old." She tucked the covers around her sweet baby. "Go back to sleep."

"Have him come tell me a story," Kitty murmured as her eyes closed. Summer watched her daughter for a moment, kissed her temple, praying she would have only the sweetest dreams.

The pounding echoed through the house again. *Damnation.* She glanced back at Kitty, who stirred but did not open her eyes.

Summer's maid stuck her head out of the dressing room as Summer passed by. "Do you think it could be robbers?"

"No, Carroll, I do not." *Was this girl stupid or merely overly dramatic?* "First, there is nothing here worth stealing. Second, I do not think robbers would knock first."

Carroll nodded slowly as though she were trying to think of another, even more ghastly explanation for a late-night caller.

"Should I go wake Mrs. Rawley?"

"No, by the time you wake her, Reggie's knocking will rouse the whole neighborhood. I will go down."

"In your nightclothes?" Carroll's shock was sincere enough to make Summer wish she could do without a maid completely.

"I am wearing a robe and slippers. The neighbors are either out or asleep so they will not be shocked, will they?"

The maid's nod was not enthusiastic. As Summer hurried down the stairs she heard the clock chime. Only midnight? Reggie's day had barely begun. He would not be home this early if he had won. *Damnation.* She winced. Add cursing to her growing list

142

of bad habits. Soon she would be right at home on the streets.

The knocker thumped loudly again. She pulled the door open even as it registered that this did not sound like Reggie's knock. His was impatient though rarely demanding. This authoritative, arrogant rap was completely different.

The sound matched the man standing in the doorway.

Lord Stephen Bradley. *Damnation* did not do her feelings justice. He looked not a day older than the last time she had seen him five years ago.

Tall, handsome with the exotic coloring of his Spanish mother and those dark blue eyes. The fact he was the third son of a duke had nothing to do with his appeal. He exuded a charisma she had not been the first nor last to find so compelling.

How was it that the mind could think a dozen thoughts — present, past, even future — all in an instant? What did he want? Did he see how quickly she had aged? Did those shared weeks at Linton House five years ago haunt his dreams, too?

She pushed the door closed, doing her best to banish the unwanted memories. Lord Stephen spoke before she could shut him out. "Wait, Summer. Reggie has been hurt. You must let me in."

She did not have to do anything *he* told her. One man as her lord and master was quite enough. But his words "Reggie has been hurt" conquered her pride. Summer pulled the door to her, looking around the edge of the frame, trying to hide her dishabille.

"Hurt? How badly?" A bump on the head, a broken arm? Let him be abed for the rest of the Season. She could hope.

"Badly, Summer." He stepped into the house, filling the small entry hall. He took up too much space.

His blue, blue eyes were still commanding. Before, she had completely misunderstood what he wanted from her. She'd thought it was *Love. Passion. Forever.*

All he had really wanted was her surrender.

Now he was demanding cooperation. He closed the door and moved to the salon that Reggie used as his private sanctuary. He took over as though this were his home, not hers.

"I need more details." Summer folded her arms across her thin robe. This was her house even if it was only rented.

"He was set upon by thieves." He rubbed the back of his neck as he spoke. "He had just left . . ."

Lord Stephen paused. Was he searching for words or just reluctant to continue?

"He was coming from a brothel or a gaming hell." She finished his sentence. "Please do not try to spare my feelings."

He rubbed the back of his neck again. Had he taken some injury, too?

"Reggie was alone and drunk." Stephen did not hesitate at that, drink being her husband's most faithful companion.

"He was set upon by thieves. Reggie decided to fight them and lost." The last word came with the smallest shrug, disbelief in his voice. "I think his neck is broken."

Summer Cassidy stood quite still, remembering Reggie that evening, twirling Kitty in the air, insisting it would bring him "the best luck."

"Reggie cannot die." She met Lord Stephen's worried eyes, then squeezed hers shut to stop the spinning. "Even he cannot be that selfish."

"Summer?" Stephen took her by the shoulders, his fingers strong, his touch a bruising caress. "For God's sake. Do not faint." He grabbed her chin. "Open your eyes."

She did and saw his demanding strength, resolution.

*All those virtues have been used up,* she thought. *I am so tired. I cannot do this.*

He nodded. Surely she had not spoken aloud.

"Put some clothes on. The others will be here with Reggie in five minutes. Where is your footman?"

"Off for the night." They had not been able to afford a night footman for more than a year.

"Then Reggie's valet."

"Fired last week and not yet replaced." Reggie had never realized that you have to pay a valet to keep one.

"Your housekeeper. Where is she?"

"Mrs. Rawley is a fine housekeeper with only one drawback. She is as deaf as a post. She will sleep through the whole." Summer moved to the stairs. "I will manage. My maid will help me." Tears filled her eyes, causing her to miss the first step.

Stephen came up behind her and steadied her once again. "Do you want me to help you up the stairs?"

It was his brusqueness that made her stiffen. Did she want him to come with her? Not in a hundred years. Not when his touch was beyond bearing. Turning back toward him she gave him her coldest expression. "No, my lord. I do not need your help."

She shrugged off his arm and began to climb the stairs as quickly as her nerveless legs would allow.

"Summer, ask your maid to open the door to his room so they know where to take him."

"It's at the front of the house," she said and kept on climbing. Pushing open the door to Reggie's room, she walked through it. Without a valet the room was untidy, clothes everywhere, shoes and bits of paper scattered about. A mess was Reggie's idea of comfort. She picked up some of the clothes and dropped them on the chair, kicked the shoes under it and then went to his bed, turning the covers back.

The sheets were as white as London wash water would permit even if they were mended in several places. Summer remembered when they were new, when their marriage was new. She had worked so hard to make life with Reggie what she wanted it to be. When had she given up? Tears filled her, but she did not weep.

There was fuel for a fire and she lit it. Once the fire caught and a weak heat warmed her chilled hands, she stood and went through the connecting door into her own chamber.

Carroll already had clothes out for her. A

black dress. She did not even know she owned one.

"I am so sorry, ma'am."

"Not a black dress," Summer said, looking away from the maid's tear-filled eyes.

"But you are a widow now . . ."

"Not a black dress. Not yet." She put her hand on Carroll's arm in apology for her curtness. "We only have Lord Stephen's word that my husband's neck is broken."

Carroll nodded and went back into the dressing room.

What would they do with no money and an endless mountain of debt? *Please, let Stephen be wrong,* she prayed.

The blue dress Carroll brought was a much better choice. Summer stripped off her nightclothes and picked up her shift. She turned so that Carroll could lace her stays. The familiar routine woke her from her half-dream shock.

Should she offer the men a drink? Some wine or would they prefer brandy? The doctor. Surely they could find a physician willing to attend Reggie.

She wound her braid into a coil and let Carroll fix it with two pins.

One of the men who brought him home would go for the physician. Or the surgeon that had tended Kitty's last cough. Stephen could be wrong. Reggie could recover. Even if it took weeks. Yes, that sounded so much better than planning a funeral.

Carroll handed her a pair of slippers and Summer put them on, not bothering with stockings.

She would feed him soup and Kitty would make him smile. A four-year-old was very good at that. He would not be winning money to feed them. He would not be losing any either.

They would manage. *She* would manage.

At least last night he had come home with his purse full. He had poured the coins into her hand, demanding a kiss. Reggie in a good humor was hard to deny.

Even as she dressed and her brain rattled through a dozen considerations, she could hear the men arrive, come up the steps, and turn down the hall. They were gone too quickly. Her heart ached, this time with fear. She went out into the hall as Lord Stephen came to the top step.

"Have the men gone?"

He nodded.

"Why did you not offer them something?"

"They expected nothing, Summer."

*Ah, they did not want to see me.*

"Lockwood offered to go for my physician and a surgeon." He paused a moment and then shook his head. "The physician will come. But, Summer, it is too late."

Stephen Bradley watched as his words destroyed her life.

"What? What do you mean it's too late?" She ran into the bed chamber.

Stephen followed her. No one should have to face this moment alone. She was beside her husband, holding his hand. "It's all right, Reggie," she whispered.

Stephen stood by the door and watched.

Summer kissed her husband's forehead and stared at his face as though willing him to open his eyes.

Her devotion amazed him. Love was incredibly powerful if it could so dim all a man's shortcomings.

"He's not dead. His hand is warm. He's not dead," she insisted with a mix of belligerence and desperation, her eyes gray-green pools of misery.

"Reggie's not breathing, Summer." He clenched his fists. His eyes watered at the sight of her pain.

"He's still here. Can you not feel him in this room?" As she spoke she watched Reggie and shook her head.

Stephen looked around the room, at the dresser with Reggie's shaving mirror, the chair full of clothes, an empty bottle on the table. "This is his bedroom. Of course you will feel him here."

She put Reggie's hand down gently, still watching his face. He understood her confusion. Reggie did look as though he was no more than asleep and would open his eyes and make some joke.

"How could you let this happen, Stephen?" She spoke softly at first, accusing him with her eyes as well as her words. "How could you let him go off on his own, in the middle of the night? You know how dangerous the streets are."

"I am not his nursemaid." It came out more harshly than he intended.

"You are the clever one," she said, ignoring his excuse, no longer whispering. "You are the one who thinks before he acts. You are his best friend. He would do anything you asked. If he is dead it is your fault."

"Summer, you must listen to me." *Best friend?* He had barely seen Reggie these last five years.

"*Must?* I must listen to you?" Her voice vibrated with anger. She took a step away from her husband's body, then stopped. "Go away. We will be infinitely better off without you."

"As you wish, madam." He bowed curtly.

151

Stephen's anger took him only as far as the front room where he would wait for the physician. He headed straight for the brandy, poured generously and drank.

Summer had changed. It was not only the circles under her eyes, the lines around her mouth. The shy sweetness he had so loved was gone. Erased well before tonight's loss most likely.

"It *is* my fault." He spoke to the brandy glass and took another long drink. Reggie had won a hefty purse from him. Enough to win him entrance into the latest high-stakes hell. He was in such a hurry, not willing to wait for any of his friends. No, he had to go to Maude's immediately. Reggie was so sure that he would miss the best play of the evening if he arrived after midnight.

Stephen's eyes stung. He rubbed them and looked around the room, desperate for a diversion from his guilty thoughts.

It was furnished with large pieces that took up too much space: a desk littered with papers, a sideboard with bottles and glasses, dirty and clean. Reggie called this his library, even though there was not a book in sight. The rug was threadbare in one long path down the center. All those elements registered along with something else.

The hall door was open so he would not

miss the physician and he could hear Summer crying. It was more than crying. Great choking sobs of rage and loss. And pain that transcended words. Grief twisted through him until he thought his heart would fail.

Stephen knew he should pray for Reggie. What he wanted to do was damn his soul to hell. Once Reggie had been his best friend, but five years ago, Reggie's lie had put an end to it.

That sunny sweet afternoon he had offered Summer a love that grew from passion. She had felt the same for him, he was sure. Reggie had lied to them both. Told her — no, convinced her, with contrived evidence and skilled playacting — that Stephen's love was false, his actions those of a cad. On top of that, he'd lied to Stephen about Summer's change of heart. But then, her feelings weren't a lie, were they? They were the product of Reggie's falsehoods. Reggie had won Summer by cheating, by treating her as a prize and using their hearts as pawns.

No matter what Summer believed, Stephen had loved her then and he loved her still. He took some more brandy, knowing that the only way he could comfort her now was to leave her alone with her grief.

# TWO

Reggie did not like being a ghost. He considered the empty brandy bottle on the table near the fireplace. Frustration edged into anger at his inability to touch it or drink it. At this point, he would settle for inhaling the fumes. He had been without its comfort for so long that one deep breath of the smoky liquid would be as good as a taste.

Nothing was going as he'd hoped. He floated back to the chair near the window and tried to bend his form to fit into it. The room was the one he had called his own for the last five years. It suited him well enough though he did miss the house on the square. Challoner Street was quiet, if that was possible in London, and had made a good day's sleep possible. Even though it was a nice room, he had no desire to spend eternity here.

Was he truly a spectral being? That was *their* term. *Ghost* was the word he used. Was there a difference between the two? He had not thought to ask.

Where were the powers he could use to terrify people? Those would have given him a true advantage. No shopkeeper would insist on payment after a visit from his spirit self.

He seemed to have no ability other than floating and he had grown bored with that after the first day. It had been four months and not a single person had seen him. Not that there had been anyone except Mrs. Rawley.

At first she had spent days in the room, cleaning ruthlessly. He had told her to leave everything as it was, but she had ignored him. While she had not thrown a thing away, she had found a cabinet or armoire for every single item. She did not understand that he would not be able to find anything if he could not see it. After that bout of industry the housekeeper came in only to dust and mop.

There was no sign at all of his wife and daughter. Now he understood why ghosts stayed around so long. Nobody ever came to call.

As he had the thought, Reggie heard a familiar voice in the hall. Lord Stephen Bradley. Perfect. Stephen was the fellow he most wanted to see.

"I thank you very much, Mrs. Rawley."

Even with the door closed he could hear the words. Stephen was shouting so that the deaf beldame could hear him. "I assure you, once again, that I have Mrs. Cassidy's permission."

That was ridiculous, Reggie thought. Summer would no more allow him here than she would go to a gaming hell.

Mrs. Rawley opened the door and closed it after Stephen had crossed the threshold. He stood there, scanning the room, as if trying to decide where to start.

"Hi-ho," Reggie called out in his most jovial voice. Stephen ignored him, heading instead for the shaving stand. He proceeded to open the drawers and look through the contents.

"Stephen, damn it, look at me." Reggie jumped up from the chair he had posed himself in and stomped, more like sailed, over to the dresser. "I am right here. Behind you. Right here!" The last was a shout and still there was no response.

"To hell and back," Reggie swore with vehemence. Then it occurred to him that was a phrase he'd best avoid using. It was too close to what might happen. He looked up at the ceiling. "How am I supposed to do this if no one can hear me?"

There was no answer, at least not in a voice loud enough to hear. The thought did echo in his head that Stephen had seen enough of him for one lifetime.

"They must be here somewhere, Reggie. Unless they were thrown away in the cleanup. God knows you did not pay off your gambling debts."

Aha, Reggie thought. "Thinking aloud, eh, Stephen? Damn, ahem, darn annoying habit that finally has some use." He floated over to the clothespress. "In here. Inside those shoes that I never wore. Too tight."

Stephen went to the wardrobe, still not acknowledging him. As Reggie watched Stephen search every coat pocket it occurred to him to wonder why Stephen wanted them. "You planning to pay 'em for me?" He started to laugh at the thought, but the laugh sounded more wicked than amused and he pressed his lips together.

"In the shoe," Reggie shouted as Stephen closed the door, completely ignoring the pile of boots on the floor of the armoire. "This is not fair," Reggie shouted to the ceiling. "I cannot right wrongs or whatever it is that I am supposed to do if no one can hear me!"

Stephen moved on to the jars on the

mantel, pausing with a piece of Greek statuary in his hand.

Reggie floated back to the chair and curved his form into it again. Then he noticed what Stephen was holding. "Aha, the statue. Do you remember how we bargained the shop owner down on that piece? Still don't know if it's real or a fake, but it reminds me of our adventure. We shared so much before that June ruined our camaraderie. Do you remember?"

Lord Stephen Bradley abandoned his search and sat in Reggie's chair. Stephen shivered as Reggie pushed through him. "No need to sit right on me, Stephen."

Reggie floated over to the fireplace.

"We were all of twenty, so sure the Grand Tour had made us men of the world." Stephen leaned his head back on the edge of the high wingbacked chair as he spoke.

"We were men of the world, eh, my lord." Reggie sighed. "We met women who showed us what it meant to have a lover, be a lover." Stephen still did not hear him. Reggie chattered on nonetheless. "We learned more about art and antiquity than I ever wanted and gambled in three different languages."

"Paris was my favorite," Stephen announced to the room. "After Paris, Kent seemed so provincial. I never guessed that when I went to see the property there, it would change my life. I met Summer. Hazel eyes, hair like ripening wheat and lips just as sweet as she was."

"Need I remind you that she was *my* fiancée?" Reggie sailed to the ceiling.

"She was so shy at first." Stephen's smile was one of those mawkish sentimental ones. "But once I knew her, she seemed all wrong for you, and you for her."

"Nonsense. We had practically grown up together. Everyone expected us to marry. I thought she would do what was expected and not question me overmuch."

Stephen sat with his eyes closed and Reggie waited to see what confession would come next. Maybe this was his punishment. To hear what his friend really thought of his wife when he, as her husband, was dead and could not call him out.

"Why did I open the note?" Stephen shook his head and then smiled. "I would do it again, bad manners or no."

"Tell me which note. We sent messages back and forth constantly."

"You were trysting with the milkmaid. What a fool you were Reggie." He opened his eyes now but still seemed far, far away. "It really was all your fault. You had the golden one and preferred the dross."

"Oh, that note." Reggie frowned. The last thing he needed was to be reminded that Stephen had never abandoned his love for Summer. He knew it, but it was still biting to hear.

"Five years and this is the first time I have admitted it aloud." Stephen shook his head.

"What happened in the maze?" Reggie had always wondered.

"I was only going to tell Summer that you were nowhere to be found."

Reggie waited, but Stephen had lapsed into a gloomy silence that was no help at all. Unless he could read minds. Reggie floated closer and set his hand on Stephen's head. Nothing.

Stephen shivered and stood up abruptly. Instead of leaving he walked straight to the door that connected to Summer's bedroom. He pushed the panel open and just stood there. "Jasmine and vanilla. Sweet secrets and practicality."

Reggie shook his head. What nonsense. It wasn't like Summer used perfume. It had been years since she had tried to tempt him.

"Now it's over. All over," Stephen announced as he headed for the door.

"Not quite, old chap," Reggie shouted to the empty room.

Summer had no sooner stepped into the front hall than the oppression settled on her. The scent of dust and old flowers would forever remind her of this house. She had hoped it would feel differently now that Reggie was gone. Four months. They had been in the country for four months and nothing had changed. It was as though time stood still and she was back to the night of his death, even though it had been six months ago to the day.

She squeezed her daughter's hand. "You see, Kitty, no one is here except Mrs. Rawley."

"Papa is here. It is why I wanted to come. Why I had to come." Kitty's voice was a high-pitched whine. Her insistence had been heartbreaking at first. Now the petulance was unbearable.

"Kitty, Papa is dead," Summer insisted with more annoyance than understanding. "He was here. Now he is in heaven."

"No, Mama." She stamped her foot, on the verge of a tantrum. "I will show you."

Twisting from her grip, Kitty ran up the stairs and into her father's bedroom.

Summer turned to Carroll, who was

directing the placement of their baggage inside the door. "Everyone was so sure that the trip would help her."

"Children sometimes see things that we do not. Could be she has a bit of the fairy in her." Carroll made the prospect sound like something to be greatly desired.

"Well, there is no fairy blood on my side of the family," Summer said in a voice laced with sarcasm. "Carroll, please go find Mrs. Rawley and let her know we are here. Some tea and biscuits would be nice." That should keep her maid's mind off fairies and ghosts for a few minutes.

With a perfunctory, "Yes ma'am," Carroll headed toward the kitchen.

Summer moved to the stairs and then stopped, as she saw Stephen Bradley coming down them. All her effort at composure was replaced by a stream of thoughts: *It must be my imagination. He looks so sad. I am wearing the most hideous bonnet.* "What are you doing here, my lord?"

"I called earlier this week and Mrs. Rawley told me that you would be back on Monday. Yesterday."

"We were late starting so we made the trip in two days instead of one. Not that I owe you any explanation."

"I only came today to be sure all is well

with you." He didn't react to her anger, merely nodded in understanding.

She wished she had told him she was in the midst of a torrid affair and was loathe to leave her lover behind. Or some other outlandish tale that would make it clear that her life was none of his business.

"Kitty has not lost any of her energy." Stephen waved at the stairs. "She rushed past me with barely a greeting."

"What were you doing abovestairs?"

"When you were not here I decided to pay a last visit to Reggie."

"You visited him?" Panic gripped her. Please, not another person seeing ghosts.

"Well, I visited his room," he said as though he agreed but he made no move to go. "You were right when you said you could still feel him there. It's as though . . ."

He stopped speaking mid-sentence.

Did he see the tears fill her eyes? Summer lowered her head. There was no ghost, but spirit or no, he was still here in so many ways. They would move. Soon. Very soon.

The silence grew uncomfortable. Finally, she looked up so he could see that the tears were gone. He smiled at her. That sweet, loving smile that she had not seen for lo these many years.

"How are you, dearest?"

She lost herself in his eyes. Their warmth heated her and she almost told him. That she was afraid, so alone, just as she had been for too many months to count. But the endearment brought a memory, the way he had held her, kissed her as though he could not have enough. The recollection was as good as a slap.

"I am not your 'dearest' anything, Lord Stephen. I never was and I never will be. Leave my house."

His smile changed to an arrogant twist, as though he knew she was trying to wrest control from him.

He still did not leave.

"Do you ever wonder, Summer, how many other lives were changed at the heart of the maze at Linton House?"

"My life was not changed, despite your best efforts at seduction. Efforts that failed, I might add."

"Is that how you remember it?"

"I do not remember it at all."

"Yes, you do, Summer." He came down the final two steps and still towered over her. "You remember. I know I do."

"Do not use my name. I am still Mrs. Cassidy to you." She stared at the wall, not at him, so that she could not see him laughing at her. She still felt like a green girl of eighteen. He had seen the world while she had spent her life in a tower or, yes, at the heart of the maze, waiting for rescue.

"Go away, Stephen. You have done a fine job of ruining us. You took Reggie to every new hell, urged him to gamble. Would not leave him alone." Anger took the place of tears and she whirled back to let him see her resolve.

"Summer, that is not true. If Reggie told you that, it was a lie."

"What a convenient accusation that is, when he can no longer defend himself. It does not matter how often you were together. You were with him that night."

"Yes, that's true, but you are wrong about so many other things. When you are ready, come to me and I will explain."

"Absolutely not," she said with renewed determination. "I hope I never see you again."

As soon as she spoke she wished she could stuff the words back into her mouth. It was exactly what she had said to him then, after Reggie had told her that Stephen's kiss was nothing more than a bet between them.

"Does that mean you want to take up where we left off?"

"God forbid."

He had no answer for that, at least not

with words. His eyes demanded something she could not interpret.

"What is it that you want, my lord?"

"Exactly what I wanted then, Summer. You. Only you. I thought I would have to wait days and I have waited five years."

"You thought you could seduce me. You were wrong. That has not changed. I am the one thing you cannot have."

He picked up his hat and gloves before he spoke. "That, my dear, will be your choice."

Without giving her a chance to sputter her revulsion, he left. She closed the door firmly and locked it, relieved that she would never have to see him again.

She did not want to go upstairs. Did not want to go near Reggie's bedroom. She went into his library instead and wondered why his presence was not as strong here as it was upstairs.

Taking off her hat and cloak, she sat in the chair nearest the cold fireplace. She would think about the future and ignore the past Stephen had brought to mind.

She was going to move as soon as she could. She would be as properly independent as London would allow, raise her daughter, and introduce her to society when the time came.

She was looking forward to that. Her own

mama's death had cut her Season short. Then Reggie had proposed and a second Season was not necessary. It *was* so sensible until that afternoon in the maze when Stephen had come instead of her fiancé.

# THREE

That June day five years ago had been nearly perfect. Fine days were not that rare in Kent but still worth honoring. Summer asked Stephen to deliver a note to Reggie asking him to come to her at the heart of the maze at Linton House. She could have asked a servant, but Stephen was more likely to know where he was.

Summer had not heard him approach, totally engrossed in the poems she had brought, still trying to decide which of Shakespeare's love sonnets to read aloud. When she saw that it was Stephen, she blushed and snapped the book shut.

Lord Stephen Bradley appeared slightly discomfited himself. "I'm so sorry, Summer. I found Reggie. But he is caught up in some business and cannot come." He handed the note back to her.

"Some impromptu horse race? Or has he a wager on which ant will reach the anthill first?" She laughed and hoped it covered her hurt. "I should have known he would not abandon his entertainments for anything as cryptic as my invitation." It was the way Reggie was, she understood that.

Stephen smiled, but did not even nod at her conjecture.

"Your loyalty is admirable, my lord. I hope it can be an inspiration to Reggie." She stared at her hands in her lap, embarrassed that she could not even give him the simplest of compliments without her cheeks turning red. Summer made herself look up into his face as she continued, "I am sorry if I sound like a shrew."

"Never," Stephen said, his eyes as intense as his voice. With a sudden jerk of his head he looked away from her, taking in the bower she had created. A moment ago it had seemed the most romantic spot, now it was no more than a childish indulgence. He probably thought it was stupid.

The grape arbor was entwined with old lace she had taken from the attic, the spring green grass a carpet beneath a small table and two chairs. She'd found a lovely floral fabric to cover the table set with champagne and savories awaiting Reggie's arrival.

"This is quite lovely, Summer. Like a forest glade from *A Midsummer Night's Dream* with you as Titania."

"You are exactly right," she laughed, brightening. "Reggie would never have figured it out."

"Only because he has never read Shakespeare. He would know this for a small bit of paradise even if he could not place it."

That was the moment she knew.

The sun still shone with springtime warmth. The birds trilled nearby. This part of the earth was as it had always been, yet something profound had changed.

Summer realized she was about to marry the wrong person.

How could she consider spending her life with someone who thought love poems were foolish, who did not know Shakespeare from Molière and was happiest playing whist for a penny a point?

Her father would be disappointed. Reggie's parents crushed. Summer lost track of time, not at all sure how long she sat there, her head buzzing with what it would mean to change her mind this close to the wedding.

Without asking permission, Stephen took the book from her hands, looked at the title, and began to speak without opening it.

"Shall I compare thee to your namesake,

a summer day?
Thou are lovely and more temperate;
Rough winds do shake the darling buds of
May,
And summer's lease has all too short a
date.
Thy eternal summer shall not fade,
Nor lose possession of that fair thou ow'st,
Nor shall death brag thou wander'st in his
shade,
When in eternal lines to time thou grow'st.
So long as man can breathe, or eyes
can see,
So long gives this and this gives life to
thee."

A breeze ruffled the lace and the table covering, nature's accompaniment to the sonnet. It filled the silence between them.

"You left out the middle" was all she could think to say.

"But not the most important part." He took her hand and drew her to her feet. "Let me replace the lost words with this."

He bent to kiss her, waiting that fraction of a second, his eyes asking, *"Yes or no?"* She answered by leaning closer. *"Hurry, yes, please, now."* The touch of his lips was as magical as the poem, as the setting, as the heart of the maze.

Summer pressed herself to him, her mouth to his and wanted more. Her whole body felt the kiss, the deepest part of her longed to feel him fill her. It was more than wanting that made her open her mouth to his, that welcomed his hand on her breast, that sighed as she fit perfectly to him. This was belonging, a home of the heart, where she, where *they* were meant to be. Together. She had never felt like this with anyone else.

The crushed note cut into her finger and it reminded her of Reggie. The man she was supposed to marry.

Stephen would not let her pull away from him but held her against him, her head pressed to his heart.

"You are marrying the wrong man, dearest. He is my best friend and your fiancé, but that makes it even more imperative that we tell him. Admit what you know. I beg you."

She nodded and then said, "Yes."

He took the note from her, kissed the tiny bloody spot on her finger, and kissed her again, this one meant to comfort. She wanted more and he obliged until they were both breathless.

Without words they sat together on the stone bench, across from the cushioned chairs. The table and its treats were the least of the temptations they felt.

Stephen held her hand with both of his. "I love you, Summer. I love you enough to risk my friendship by going to Reggie and asking him to let you end the engagement. Only if you feel the same, though. Only if you are willing."

"Yes," she said. She laid her head against his shoulder. "Yes, Stephen, but it makes me feel like the worst traitor in the world. Fickle is the kindest word I can think of."

"We have fought this long enough. From the first moment I saw you, months ago, I knew you were meant for me."

"Really? I did not know until you took my hand when we were introduced. Even then I decided it was nothing more than the attraction a woman might feel for a handsome man."

"Was that inexperience or self-deception, Summer?"

"Inexperience. Every time we were together, playing badminton, watching you play cricket, all the dinners we had together. It was you who made me laugh, or blush at a compliment. Reggie was attentive, when he was not distracted by his games, but you were far more thoughtful. I thought it was your way of taunting Reggie and no more."

"You cannot know how lovely you are,

Summer. By candlelight, in the sun, you outshine them both. You are an amazing mix of practical and secretive. I cannot count the times I wondered what you were smiling at, or why you were frowning."

"See now I am blushing at the thought of you watching me. What I feel is so very uncomfortable. How can it be love?" She did not wait for an answer but went on. "When I gave you the note to take to Reggie, I thought it was one way to tell you that I did not notice your interest. That I wanted only Reggie." She turned to face him with a sad smile. "That was self-deception."

He kissed her again and she was afraid that the kiss would not be enough, she wanted him so totally. Summer had never realized that there was such wantonness in her. It frightened her enough that she stood up to put a little distance between them.

Stephen followed her and put his arms around her, under her breasts. She leaned back against his chest.

"Life takes such odd turns, does it not, Stephen? It was what one would expect, that your uncle would introduce you to Reggie when you were first at school. Mr. Bradley knew you would be neighbors some day."

"You think that set it all in motion?" Stephen kissed the top of her head. "But would my uncle have introduced me to Reggie if I were not to inherit his estate? I imagine we could trace this moment all the way back to at least the Tudors. That is how our family came to own the property. I do believe that our love was meant to be."

The memory of that day was so clearly etched in her mind that Summer could still recall the certainty that overshadowed her distress. As she fully returned to the present moment, in Reggie's library, still dressed for traveling, she realized that it was the last time she had looked at Stephen Bradley with anything more than disgust.

Summer made her way up the stairs, exhausted by more than two days of travel. Following the sound of Kitty's chatter, she wound up at Reggie's bedroom door.

"There were kittens and puppies in the country. Aunt Beckett said we could have one of each, but Mama said they would not do well in town. You would have loved them. They would keep you company when I am not here."

Summer paused. Who was Kitty talking to? Mrs. Rawley?

"Be a dear, my itty-bitty Kitty, and find your mama and bring her here."

Not the housekeeper, Summer thought,

her heart pounding, her stomach in a knot. Reggie was the only one who had ever called their daughter "itty-bitty Kitty."

More than that, it sounded exactly like him. With a nauseating mix of panic and fear, Summer pushed the door open and hurried into the room.

The bed was empty without a wrinkle in the tightly drawn coverlet. Relief began to overtake anxiety until she turned toward the fireplace and found Reggie in his wing-backed chair with Kitty sitting restlessly at his feet.

Dear God in heaven. What was he doing here? *No. No. No.* She thought the words, tried to speak them, but she could not quite catch her breath. Her protests came out as barely audible cries.

"I told you, Mama. I told you. He might be dead, but he is still here. I told you. He is a ghost." Kitty bounced up and down from her kneeling position.

If Kitty had not been between them, the screams building inside Summer's head would have come out of her mouth as shrieks that would have pleased her maid no end.

"Isn't it wonderful, Mama?"

Her maid's imagination and her little girl's happiness made her control the terror that

176

distorted rational thought. She pressed a hand to her chest. She would not faint.

"Hello, Summer." Her husband smiled, that winning grin to which she had never quite grown immune, the one that made overwhelming debt seem a mere detail. Living without it had made life so much less complicated. She closed her eyes, refusing to allow her sensibilities to take over. This is what happened when one was exhausted. She opened her eyes.

"Still here." He grinned even more broadly.

"Yes, Mama, and he is never leaving, are you, Papa?"

"Sit still, you jack-in-the-box," her father said and, as always, Kitty obeyed him immediately. "I must talk to your mama. Go up to the nursery and find your favorite book and when we are done I will read to you."

Kitty's petulance came back instantly.

"Do it right now, Kitty, or I will disappear."

With that threat, the child jumped to her feet and ran from the room.

"Can you disappear?" Summer asked, walking closer. It was hard to move forward when all she wanted to do was turn and run.

Her heart was still slamming against her

ribs but her brain appeared to be functioning in spite of the fear. He looked real enough but there was a dark shimmer around him that was not natural.

"Can I disappear? I have no idea but I do know that I cannot leave this room. Mrs. Rawley has not seen me and I have been haunting this room for near on four months. Stephen could not see me either. He left just before my Kitty came in."

"You are not a ghost. You cannot be. The next thing you will tell me is that there is such a thing as time travel and that Suite 606 really exists."

"Summer, yes, time travel does exist. It is its own magic and very few can do it. As for Suite 606, there are such places all over the world, some are rooms, some are caves, some are sheltered places in nature. Once you enter the realm, if your dreams are a fantasy then you can live them out there. If you want to know the truth then you can find that there."

"Reggie, that sounds like a fairy tale." Summer regretted her cynicism, but Reggie must think that she would believe anything. Of course she had heard of Suite 606, even though she had not had a traditional Season. She had laughed at it when she first came to London as a bride. Years later she decided it was a man's way of describing a high-priced whorehouse so as not to offend a woman's sensibilities.

"It is more than a fairy tale. It is as real as ghosts are. In fact, I know many of nature's secrets now. It is quite gratifying."

"Why not describe a few. Then Kitty will not have to bring you a storybook."

"Your cynicism is not an attractive quality. I am a ghost. Admit that makes other fantastic things, including Suite 606, possible. You were never one to deny the truth."

"You mean I didn't make an art of the lie as you did."

"Oh, that wounds me. Come closer. See if you can touch me."

Summer shook her head, walking around the chair, studying the situation, trying to be practical. As she looked more closely, she realized that he was not sitting in the chair so much as occupying the space, his form bent at the angle to sit but not really resting on the cushion or the back of the chair.

"This is not possible." Could it be done with candles and some theatrical effect? Was someone trying to prove her insane?

"You have not gone mad, Summer. Stop wasting time on disbelief. Do you remember when we saw the woman reading in the summer house at Linton? And when we reached there she was gone? And the time we were in the graveyard and the summer air was suddenly chill?"

"Yes."

"Ghosts." He spoke the word with authority and a firm nod.

"Nonsense."

"Then what about that time we were playing hide-and-seek in the attics? You saw a baby in a cradle. It disappeared when you reached for it."

"I never told anyone about that. Not even you." Summer shivered. She had never gone up to the attic again.

"It was the ghost of a babe who died in the plague."

"Certainly infants would go straight to heaven."

"Not that one." He shrugged as though he did not care to waste any more time on that lost soul. "I am still here because I have work to do before I go on."

"Go on to where?" she asked cautiously. If she persisted in carrying on this conversation, Carroll would be more than justified in calling someone from Bedlam to take her away.

"I hope I will go on to heaven."

"You do not know? Tell me why someone

as selfish as you would end up in heaven? The entrance test must be very simple."

"Well, I am not quite sure," he spoke slowly, "but I think *this* is the test."

"So like you to rush back to earth without all the details."

He grew sulky at the insult, just as he had when alive.

"But you did not rush back, did you, Reggie? You have been dead for six months and here for only four."

His sheepish grimace told her without words.

"You made a bet and lost?" Oh, this most certainly was Reggie. No one but him would take that kind of chance.

He nodded.

"You tried to gamble with God?" she asked incredulously.

"No, not God. Some sort of demon angel or devil, definitely not God because she was a woman."

"And it did not occur to you that she was one last temptation?"

"You were always smarter than I was, Summer. One of the most annoying things about you." He made the observation with casual offense, as though it were as much a compliment as a criticism. "Yes, I lost the bet. This is my last chance."

"Tell me what it is you have to do."

"You will help me?" he said with undisguised relief.

"Tell me what you must do and then I will decide. As much as I want you to disappear, I will not compromise my future and what little money we have in order to satisfy some demon you are trying to please."

# FOUR

"It is simple." Reggie shrugged. "In order to leave earth completely I must undo, or at least admit, some wrongs."

"You shrug as if admitting those wrongs is going to be easy for you."

"It is now. The stakes are pretty high, you know."

"Well, go ahead. This will be interesting." She could feel herself being drawn into his web. It would not be as simple as he insisted. It never was.

"Right-o, Summer, but you see, I am not sure what the wrongs are and what I can do to make them right."

"Oh yes, I do see that could be a problem. If you tried to right all of them Kitty would be ready for her come-out before you were done."

"Precisely," he said as though proud of it.

"I think you can forget the little ones."

"Like telling you I was going to White's

when I was really headed to a hell."

"Or the clothes that you were able to buy 'for a song.' "

"Or when I told Kitty that all the ices had melted at Gunter's."

"That was not true? Oh, Reggie."

"I had to be at the fight to make my wager. If I had taken her out for a treat I would have been too late."

Even as he listed the wrongs, most of them lies he'd told, she noted that the aura around him began to lighten a little. Not much, not nearly enough to make him look angelic.

"Reggie, I think it must be the big wrongs that are the key to your spot in heaven."

"I expect so. She did not give me a lot of direction."

"Was she too busy laughing at how easy you were to trick?"

"Hmmm" was his only answer.

Silence fell. Summer shook her head. Here she was talking to her ghost-husband as though he were real and still a part of her life. To think she had believed that Reggie could not dictate to her from his grave. Apparently, she was wrong. "You know, Reggie, I could leave the house. Leave you here for eternity."

"Yes, you could, but what would God say

about that?"

"That it is what you deserve?"

"Yes, yes, Summer, I see that I treated you shabbily, but you do not have to be such a shrew about it. Your bad temper is enough to handle."

"My bad temper!" she began and then stopped. If she lost her composure now, it would only prove his point.

"Summer, I think I must ask you to help me pay some of my gambling debts."

"Of course. I will be delighted to do that. Your debts are so much more important than food for your daughter." Sarcasm was such a weak weapon, but nothing impressed him. Rage was not worth the effort.

"There will be food. We both know that. You would never let the house accounts fall behind. Please, Summer. I am sure this is one of the things that must be set right."

The anger drained from her, replaced by a fatigue that left her weak. The web was tightening and she did not have the energy to fight it. "Tell me where they are."

"Capital, Summer. Look in the clothes-press. In the shoe on the far right."

The handful of papers she pulled out was not a complete surprise. She took a few moments to look them over. Halfway through she gave her husband her full attention.

"This money could have kept us comfortable for a year, two even."

"You don't have to pay them all. Just a few."

"Can I not just pass them on to your executor?"

"My brother? No, that won't work." Reggie flowed up from the chair. "Let me see the list."

Summer gasped and stepped back from his floating form.

"That hurts, wife. There's nothing to be afraid of. Look, I cannot even touch you." He reached out to her and she shivered.

"But I can feel you. Cold and empty." Rather like his life.

"All right, I'll stay here by the chair. Read me the names. I will tell you who needs the money now. Then go to Matthew, my man of business. He will tell you how to proceed with the rest."

"I still think I should go to your brother. Tell him how much it would have meant to you to have these debts paid."

"No, he would not be at all receptive if you are the one who asks for money."

"Why not?"

"Well, you see" — he hesitated, scowling as though in pain — "when I would go to them for money, for a loan, I mean, I told them that you had learned to love gambling as much as I do. It was your lack of restraint that had the creditors at the door."

"That explains why his answers to my letters have been so curt. He actually believed you?"

"I convinced him that I won most of the time and if you had been more responsible we would have managed well enough."

"That sounds like a pretty big wrong to me." Summer pressed her lips together. "Do you feel any better?"

"Not really. In point of fact, a headache is starting."

"How can ghosts have headaches?"

Reggie thought about it for a second and then shrugged.

The last item refueled her anger. This packet was bigger than the rest. She opened it and her fatigue disappeared, anger overwhelming her so completely that she crushed the note in her hand. "You owe Lord Stephen Bradley one hundred and fifty pounds?"

Reggie snapped his fingers or tried to. "That must be what he was looking for when I found him prowling around up here. Not to worry, dear girl. One hundred fifty pounds is hardly anything between us. Over the last year I've won ten times that from him. That one is old. Meaningless. Tear it up."

"I will not. If you owe Lord Stephen one hundred fifty pounds then it will be paid."

"With what, Summer? You hardly have that kind of money in your reticule. There are debts that are far more pressing."

"A debt is a debt, Reggie. A simple concept you never seemed to understand. They must all be paid once I am sure that Kitty and I will have shelter and food and a little to live on. I can start with the money you hid under your mattress."

"You found that, did you? What about the money in the hatbox on the top shelf?"

"How many hiding places do you have?" she asked in a voice that was louder than she intended.

"Never found that spot, did you?"

"Tell me the other hiding places," she said, more quietly this time, controlling her temper with effort. "I know you kept money from us. We were reduced to porridge and milk for dinner, but you always had money for the hells."

He was about to speak but she stamped her foot and raised her voice. "What a disgrace of a husband." Rage pounded through her. "You were nothing more than a faithless, feckless gamester. I've spent the last five years struggling with the details you thought unimportant."

"I loved you."

"Please God I will never know that kind of love again."

"Then you had best avoid Stephen Bradley."

"No need to remind me of that. You know I hate him."

"You just said that you are going to pay him one hundred and fifty pounds. I tell you that debt does not matter. It is an old, sentimental debt that he has long forgotten."

"You are not being honest, Reggie."

"Why do you say that?"

"Your aura is darkening again. Before, when you told the truth, it would lighten. Tell the truth, or I will know you lie."

"It goes back to the incident in the maze. The one just before our wedding."

Summer looked at the packet again. Now her heart did miss a beat. It was the paper she had used to write Reggie the note that day and on it was scribbled "£150." "I never knew how much money was involved. So, to tempt me beyond bearing was worth one hundred fifty pounds?"

"I am long over the insult of that indiscretion, Summer." Reggie waved it away. "But

I remember quite well how hurt you were. If you must pay Stephen, send someone with the money. He is as devilish now as he was then and everyone knows how susceptible widows can be to such temptations." He floated back to his favorite chair. "Have one of the servants take the money to him."

"You and Stephen took my innocence with that bet, Reggie. It is one of the most awful things that ever happened to me."

"Worse than my death?"

"Nightmares. They are both nightmares." In fact, they marked the beginning and end of a living nightmare. That it should go on beyond his death was intolerable. She dropped all the slips but the one.

"Where are you going, Summer?"

"Do not say another word. I am going to my room, to think about whether I am willing to help you or will let you haunt yourself for all eternity. If I do decide to help, the money you owe Lord Stephen Bradley will be at the top of the list."

Reggie hated being alone. Where was Kitty with that book he was going to read to her? How much time had passed? That was another problem with this ghost life. Time was hard to pin down. He could have spent five minutes or five days talking to Summer.

He had no idea how long it would take for Summer to decide whether to help him or not. He would not have thought her vindictive, but when it came to that incident with Stephen her passions were involved and her passions had always been intense.

He posed in his chair, trying to recall what had actually happened and what he had contrived to his advantage.

Stephen had come to him to tell him that he and Summer were in love and she wanted to be released from her engagement. It had come as a blow, a fearsome one. Reggie had been counting on that marriage and had made a few wagers, expecting money to be in his hands within the month.

He did not have to pretend shock. It was so unlike his loyal friend and innocent fiancée to present him with such a disaster. Thank God for his quick thinking.

"I vow this is a shock." Now there was the truth. "But I am forever impressed with your loyalty, Stephen. That you would come to me with this and not cuckold me. So much easier to flirt with a man's wife than to be leg-shackled yourself."

"I would not subject my best friend and the love of my life to such dishonor, Reggie. Summer has not been as much in society as we have. You know she would not live such a lie."

"You sound like a buffoon, Stephen. But that is what love does to a man. For my part, I like Summer and thought we would deal well together, but I cannot stand in the way of true love."

He laughed. It was amusing now but at that moment his brainbox had been too busy concocting a plan to see the humor. He knew he could make Summer happy. The passion Stephen offered would burn itself out and leave them with nothing in common.

"I say, this can be a good turn for both of us. How about if you forgive the one hundred fifty pounds I owe you from our last trip to town and I will be happy to hand over one virgin bride. She is still a virgin, isn't she?"

"You will sell her to me? Is that what you are suggesting?"

"If you want to be crude about it. I prefer to think of it as a way for both of us to finish as winners." He pulled the much abused note from his pocket and found something to write with.

He wrote the sum carefully on the outside of the folded paper, followed by the words "Won and owed by RRB."

He handed the note and pen to Stephen. "Sign across it and I will go to Summer and tell her that she is free."

Stephen did not take the pen but stared at the paper.

Reggie had counted on that and he tucked the note into his pocket. "All right. I can see your feelings are too pure for such a commercial exchange. I will go to Summer and be sure that this is what she truly wants."

"That is asking too much, Reggie." Stephen rubbed the back of his neck. "I will tell her."

"Do you not see, Stephen —" Reggie stayed this best of friends with a shake of his head and a touch to his arm. "— I must do what is honorable and be sure this is what she wants. That you are not pressuring her or even making this story up completely."

Stephen believed him. The man who had laughed, gamed, and traveled with him for the last five years actually believed him. Seeing through a lie was one skill Stephen had never perfected.

# FIVE

"I am going to sleep near Kitty tonight, Carroll."

"Because of the ghost?"

"Because Kitty thinks there is a ghost and I want to be close in case she has bad dreams." There was no way in heaven that she was going to admit to Carroll that there *was* a ghost.

"May I sleep up there as well, ma'am?" Carroll raised one hand to her face as though she was afraid of the answer to come.

"Yes, you may."

"Oh, thank you, Mrs. Cassidy. There are the strangest noises coming from the master's room."

"Yes, I expect that we should have the man who traps rodents come." How she wished it was that easy to rid herself of the pest that was actually in residence.

Summer and Carroll made their way

upstairs to the nursery floor. Summer settled into the bed across from Kitty and let Carroll have the room that was for the governess they would never be able to afford.

It took Summer a little longer than usual to settle her daughter, who wanted to sleep downstairs in her mama's bed, but then decided, "I will sleep near you, Mama, so you can call me if *you* have a nightmare."

The child's hug brought tears to Summer's eyes and laughter as well, since it *was* far more likely that Mama would need comfort than Kitty.

By the time her daughter was asleep, the clock was striking nine. Summer was still wide awake and almost shaking from the effort to control hysterics. Her husband was a ghost. Unless he could find a way to clean his slate, it was possible Reggie would haunt her forever.

As if his debts were not enough to upset her life. What would she do when the estate was settled and she found out how much or how little money they had? Please, please, God, she prayed, spare me the need to marry again.

It seemed the wisest thing to do was to keep the appointment she had made with Reggie's man of business. Mr. Matthew would know the amount of debt to be dealt with by the executors and how much would be left for them.

She would explain that she did not want his advice, only information. She prayed that the man would cooperate and wondered where this new religious devotion had come from.

Summer had not prayed in years, having found God remarkably unresponsive to her prayers. Reggie's death might be construed as an answer to her most desperate of pleas, but the bills and the uncertainty of her future made her doubt it.

If God would not listen then she would take care of herself and her daughter first. She would not pay Reggie's gambling debts if it meant that her daughter would be left wanting for food and shelter. They had been close to that too often. Now it was in her power to end it. She would use the money Reggie had hidden to support her family long before she would pay off his debts.

Except for the one hundred fifty pounds Reggie had owed Lord Stephen for these five years. Even then Reggie's first thought had been for money. She remembered the details quite clearly.

"You cost me a tidy sum, my dear," were the first words he said to her the next morning. Her father had allowed them to make a circuit of the garden as long as they did not go into the maze. Reggie walked with her until they were out of sight of the house, over a hill, and down toward the folly. He kept silent until they reached the gazebo and the bench that overlooked the river.

"You lost a bet because of me?" She laughed, not sure whether to be flattered or not.

"I did and while I hope we can laugh together about it someday, right now it is no source of amusement for me." He took her hand, which made his words less hurtful, but his solemn face added fear to the hurt.

"Sit down, sweetheart. This is so much more awkward than I thought it would be."

"Is it about me and Stephen?" It took all the courage she had to ask, but waiting for Reggie to speak the words was more than she could bear.

"Yes. Your dalliance with him has cost me dearly."

"Dalliance?" Even as she asked the word, tears filled her eyes. "It was more than a dalliance."

"You had sex with him? Oh, Summer, I assure you that was not part of the wager."

"No, never! It was nothing more than a

kiss." It was so much more than a kiss but not as tawdry as Reggie implied. Then the last part of his sentence registered. "It was a bet?"

"I am so sorry. It was a foolish suggestion. We were on our fifth bottle and I was out of money. So Stephen suggested that I win it back by betting that he could not seduce you."

"Seduce me? Do you mean that he kissed me, he said all those things as part of a bet?"

"Shh, I do not want to know what happened." Reggie raised a finger to her lips. "I only want you to forgive me."

"Forgive you?" She felt like a puppet and no wonder. "I am little more than a toy to both of you."

"No, no, no. We are the fools. Not you. Never. I was so sure that you would not succumb to him and he was his usual arrogant self. I thought I would use the money to buy you a pretty trinket."

"How could you? How could he?"

"How could you, Summer? You and I are engaged. I thought at the very least I could count on you to be loyal. I am the only one who should have your kisses."

Remorse overtook her anger. If they had been cruel, she had been foolish. "Do you want to end our engagement?" She was so afraid of his answer.

"No, never, Summer. We are human, after all. I gamble more than I should, you know. Lucky that we have such a respectable fortune between us and marriage will surely distract me."

He did not kiss her, even though she leaned close to him. She wondered now if Reggie had turned away because he did not want to give her a basis for comparison. Then, she recalled, she had felt like a slut for inviting it.

"I will spend my life making it up to you, Reggie. I am so sorry." He ran a hand over her hair and when he let it rest on her shoulder she could not resist the comfort he offered. "I thought he loved me."

"The bastard. I shall call him out. I will kill him for the lie."

"No, oh no. Please do not fight." She raised her face to him. He looked angry. Reggie never looked angry. "Please, just make him go away. Forever."

"I can if that is what you want." He rocked her in his arms. "He is only jealous of what we have. A lifetime of love, shared friendship, families that know and respect each other. We are comfortable together, Summer. That is something he will never understand."

It went on and on, the assurances beginning to outweigh his shock at her behavior. Then he began a round of apologies for his part in accepting the wager. Summer knew now that it was the technique Reggie used when he knew he was guilty and did not want to have to actually do anything about it.

Stephen Bradley had earned that one hundred fifty pounds and humiliated her in the process. Now she would humiliate him. He would have his winnings. She would eat dinners of milk and porridge for a month if she had to. It was her way of winning.

She willed herself to sleep, and sleep came, dreamless, though when she woke she felt dampness from tears on her pillow.

Carroll brought her some warm water colored with some very old tea leaves. Even though it was less than weak, the warmth of the liquid was welcome.

She sipped her drink while Carroll laid out her clothes. An appointment with Mr. Matthew was the wisest first step, but she was not close to a decision as to whether she should help Reggie or not. If only her father had not been so distraught when the settlements were set up, still mourning her mother. He surely would have insisted on more in case of Reggie's death. As it was, there was only that useless piece of land in Northumberland.

The moment Carroll left with the tea tray, Kitty came into the room and climbed up on the bed. Summer could feel her excitement and had a good idea where the girl had been.

"Papa cannot wait to see you. He says that when he goes to heaven he will ask God to send me something very special."

"He did not say that!" Summer leaned back, then wondered why she was surprised at this callous use of his child. As he said, the stakes were higher now.

"Yes, he did, Mama. He promised that if he has to leave to go to heaven he will make it worth my while. Doesn't that mean that he will bring me a present?"

"He is trying to trick you into nagging me to help him."

"Why would you not, Mama?"

"Because he . . ." She stopped, unwilling to put into words how his demands might leave them penniless, as close to the poorhouse as they had ever been.

She could see herself spending the rest of her life righting his misdeeds, which was all wrong when she was the one who had endured the worst of them. That sounded awful, but in the last few years Reggie had brought out the worst in her.

"Of course I will help him, once I am sure what is the best course of action."

"I will go tell him." Kitty popped out of bed.

"No, I will, but first I must dress for an appointment. Mrs. Rawley said she would take you to the park. The weather is too fine to spend all our time indoors."

Kitty considered her mother's word as if she had a choice, and then bounded off, calling out to her papa that she was "going to play with her friends, but I will visit you when I come back."

Summer was almost asleep when Carroll came back. "I had to iron the creases out of this dress, Mrs. Cassidy. I was talking to Mrs. Rawley. Bloomsbury is a proper enough neighborhood, but is it wise to visit your husband's man of business at his home? Who knows what could happen?"

"Carroll, he is recovering from a broken leg and his wife will be with him. They have servants. I am welcome to bring my own. You sound more and more like a worrisome grandmother."

"Yes, but promise me you will not tell him about Kitty's ghost."

"No, I will not."

For all of Carroll's fretting, it felt like nothing more than a perfectly respectable morning call. The butler met her at the door and invited her in. There was fresh tea in the salon and Mrs. Matthew stood to greet her, as did Mr. Matthew's assistant, while Mr. Matthew was forced to keep his seat.

"It was so kind of you to come to us, Mrs. Cassidy."

It was obvious that Alan Matthew was mortified — by his inability to rise, by the white bandage covering his leg, by the two sticks that sat nearby.

"Think nothing of it, Mr. Matthew. But do tell me how it happened."

"How did I break my leg?"

Summer nodded as she sat in the chair Mrs. Matthew offered. It was a selfish comfort to find that she was not the only one struggling with misfortune.

"I was given a coin. The one that is sitting in the dish beside you. I was told to wish for something. At first I said that I had all a man could want, but then realized that I would like to have more time with my family. Not five minutes later I stepped into the street, stumbled, fell, and broke my leg. I have been home and abed for weeks."

"I suppose the lesson is to be careful what you wish for." Summer smiled at his fanciful tale. The coin was a strange one, but did not seem anything more than that. The true story was more likely an embarrassment.

"Indeed," Mrs. Matthew agreed. "Or perhaps not to trust in magic coins."

"That may be true, my dear," her husband teased, "but magic or not, coins do help to solve any number of worldly problems."

"Which very neatly brings you two to the business at hand." Mrs. Matthew smiled at her husband, curtsied to Summer, and excused herself from the room. As she closed the door, Mr. Matthew cleared his throat and picked up a ledger on his desk. Summer closed her eyes. It was now her turn to be discomfited.

"I will be frank with you, Mrs. Cassidy. Your husband owed a great deal of money." He looked over his spectacles. "He even managed to convince the flower sellers to accept a promise of payment. I hope you enjoyed the nosegays," he said with a smile.

Summer nodded, lowering her gaze to the list he was showing her. She had never seen one of those blooms and did not want to know who had.

"It is the role of his executor to settle

204

those bills. There will be enough to clear these . . ." His voice trailed off.

"But you do not know how we will manage on what is left?"

"Mrs. Cassidy, I am sorry to be so blunt, but there will be very little for you and your daughter except for the property in Northumberland that your father asked to be sold to provide for you and any children should Reggie predecease you."

"Reggie never sold the land, did he?"

"No, I'm afraid not. I reminded him of it every year when we would meet but he was sure he would be able to provide enough for your support. I'm sorry."

"Because you could not foresee his death at such a young age? None of us could, Mr. Matthew." She swirled the last bit of tea in her cup and then set it on the table. "If there is anything, I will be grateful. I can manage. If there is one thing I know, sir, it is how to make a guinea stretch. Hardly something I learned in the schoolroom, but then my governess actually believed that a husband would be the solution to all problems."

She was being too frank. That is what came from sitting in a salon at his home instead of at his place of business. The truth was that if Reggie had not shocked him, then she would not.

"There will be something and surely Mr. Cassidy's brother can be won over."

Summer bit her lip. So he knew they were not on good terms. "Mr. Matthew, whether he can be won over or not, I value my independence and would prefer to do everything in my power not to have to ask anyone for help. If there is as little as one hundred pounds a year, I can manage."

"There will surely be more than that. I know that you will put your daughter's needs before your own, and trust that she will be the measure by which you decide what is best for both of you."

"Thank you for that confidence and I promise you that is what I will do. Kitty will be well cared for no matter what it costs my pride."

"I hope it will not come to that." He handed the boxed papers to his assistant. "What I would like to do is give you these bills to examine. As I said, the financial matters will be handled by the executor, his brother, but I think it only fair that you have some sense of what is involved since the settlement of the estate will affect you and your daughter directly."

"Thank you, Mr. Matthew. Though I do feel as though it will be like opening Pandora's box."

"Not at all. These are only paper and have no inherent evil power. Allow my assistant to take you to the library, where you can have some privacy to examine them. When you are ready, we can discuss the situation and I can answer any questions."

His secretary was efficient, offering her more tea as he escorted her to the room nearby. It was a true library and Summer marveled at the collection even as she pulled off her gloves and settled down to work.

Forty minutes later she knew the worst.

Reggie owed money to everyone in London. His bills were years old in some cases. He owed money to every tailor he had ever visited, and he had spread his business around, most likely going to a new tailor when he had run up too many bills with another. Bills for books she had never seen, jewelry she never wanted to see, flowers dead longer than Kitty had been alive.

She had been so sure that she would feel better once she knew the extent of his debt. And she did. Still her hands were shaking. Standing up, she drew a deep breath and started to examine the books that lined the shelves. The words would not register. So she began to count them in an effort to distract herself from the anxiety that hovered like a dark angel.

She knew the worst, she reminded herself, and if there was more bad news to come, she would find a way to handle it. There had been hard times before: her mother's death, her discovery that Reggie was not faithful. The last time she had spoken to Stephen Bradley as a single woman.

# Six

Summer remembered that evening more vividly than her wedding the next day. They gathered for dinner at home, her father insisting that formal mourning for her mother was over and he would welcome the dinner at Linton with Summer as his hostess, "practice for your fancy London life."

It was a glorious June evening. The windows were open to let the cooling breeze entertain them. The scent of roses filled the house, a poignant reminder of her mother's absence.

They had been a year now without her mother and there was no longer any reason to delay the wedding. All the proper steps had been taken: notice of their engagement, the banns announced at church. Tomorrow they would marry.

Summer so longed to talk to her mother: Surely she could have helped Summer understand the chaos of sensibilities that left her restless in a way that had nothing to do with fatigue.

Her maid helped her dress in her favorite stays, stockings picked with a delicate rose at the ankle with garters to match, and the shell-pink gown she had been saving for a special occasion. She did her best to think about Reggie and the guests who were coming.

There would be twenty-four, which made it easy to avoid Lord Stephen. He should not have been there at all. How had she let Reggie convince her that it would have caused gossip if he suddenly disappeared? They could have easily explained that he was called away.

Seated halfway down the table, Stephen was as far from her as it was possible to be. He might be the son of a duke, but the rest of the party were older, dearer friends of some rank themselves.

After dinner, the ladies retired to the music room. Mrs. Ladlaw entertained them at the pianoforte with some lovely pieces by Mozart. She was an accomplished musician and none of them had to pretend their applause. With her guests entertained, Summer left the room to check on the tea tray.

She had suggested that they leave the dining room doors ajar to allow the small breeze to cool the gentlemen. As she went downstairs, she could hear their boisterous laughter and smell the tobacco her father was so fond of sharing.

Halfway down the hall to the kitchen stairs, someone called to her.

"Summer, I have to talk to you."

Without waiting for her permission, Stephen took her by the arm and led her to one of the alcoves that lined the hall. It gave them a sense of privacy but any of the servants coming from the kitchen would pass this way and see them.

"Summer, what happened? Reggie said that you were determined to go on as planned."

"Yes, I am. We are." She pushed back from him until she felt the wall at her back. "In the maze, that was a moment of insanity on our part. I set the stage for seduction too well."

"That was not seduction. It was" — he paused a moment — "it *is* the undeniable attraction two people feel for each other."

She looked him in the eye. "I know about the bet, Stephen."

"The bet?" He rubbed the back of his neck. "That is beside the point. What is between us is not about money. You know that."

"Do not toy with me this way." Anger roiled through her. "It is an insult, the worst insult."

"Never an insult. Admit it, Summer."

She tried to push past him. He pulled her into his arms. "I can prove it." He raised his hands to frame her face and lowered his mouth to hers. This time he gave her no chance to pull away. For a moment the erotic thrill held her still, then she melted against him, the promise of pleasure so complete that she could feel it echo through from every part of her body.

He stopped only a moment before she surrendered completely. "Let us find some privacy." He kissed her neck as he whispered the words. "There is so much I have to say to you."

"No," she spoke near a shout, pushing herself out of his arms, her sensibilities aroused beyond bearing. "You are trying to complete your seduction to win that unholy bet. Reggie told me," she insisted. "He and I are friends and we share the truth. I will share the truth with you, too. He wanted to call you out and I told him not to. Now I wish I could run you through myself. I never want to see you again."

She pushed him away and ran upstairs, rejoining the ladies, explaining away her tears by telling them that it was at times like these that she missed her mother the most. They were all quite comforting, two shedding tears of their own. It was impossible to escape, no matter that all she wanted was to plead a headache and avoid the gentlemen, and Lord Stephen.

By the time the men came to their ladies, they were in need of something more than tea to restore their spirits, and Summer did have a headache. It helped when Reggie told her that Lord Stephen had left to attend to some emergency at his uncle's estate. At the same moment, Mrs. Ladlaw began a reel. Soon they were all dancing informally, Summer and Reggie allowed to partner each other as many times as they wished. After all, the next day they were to be married.

Married-to-mother-to-widow in five years. Naïve girl to disillusioned woman in less than that. If it were not for Kitty, she would be lost in bitterness, but her daughter had come from her misguided marriage and she could already see that Kitty had the best of both of them — Reggie's winsomeness and her mama's practical nature, her father's smile and her eyes. Summer hoped she lived long enough to see her darling girl settled happily. For now it was all she had to hold on to.

■ ■ ■ ■

By the time Mr. Matthew's assistant came for her, she had recovered her equanimity and could draw a breath without the threat of tears.

"Does your study of your husband's papers answer your questions?" Mr. Matthew asked as his secretary poured more tea.

"Yes, sir. I was not at all surprised by the bills that have accumulated."

Mr. Matthew looked vastly relieved.

"Mr. Matthew, I am sorry for the position you are in as the bearer of difficult news when you are not well yourself, but anyone who knew my husband would know exactly what to expect at his death. A mess left to someone else. Yes, I do resent what he has done to his daughter's future, but we will manage."

"Thank you. You are all that is generous."

"I wish these bills could be the end of it, Mr. Matthew, but there are other debts."

"I wondered. Do you have some unpaid bills you would like to add? From the green grocer, the butcher?"

"Oh no. I have been responsible for those. There are some that are outstanding, but none in arrears, thank God." She drew a breath. "No, sir, I am referring to Mr. Cassidy's gambling debts. There are some that must be paid. Must." Or else Reggie would haunt her forever.

"But, Mrs. Cassidy, I would expect that most would be forgiven. Have been forgiven on his death. It is the custom, you know, and it has been several months. Has anyone pressed you for payment?"

"One or two have come to call, but no one has asked outright. And yes, two have written to assure me that the debts are cancelled."

"Are there money lenders involved?" He hated asking that question. She could tell by the way he winced.

"No." There was no point in being offended at the question. This debacle was not her fault. "I have no doubt that would have come in time, but he was winning more in this last year."

"To be honest" — much more honest than she wanted to be — "while he might not have dealt with money lenders, few of my husband's associates were members of acceptable society. Most of them live by their gambling. They need the money."

"Yes, I see that you would be sympathetic to their situation."

"Then you will also see why I will not hand these gambling debts to his executor who, I am sure, would ignore them unaware that there are some, like me, who need this money to put food on the table." She was being too frank again. "Besides, it is what Mr. Cassidy wants." She corrected herself quickly. "It is what he *would* have wanted."

Mr. Matthew accepted her change of wording with a nod. Of course, it could be that he would believe in ghosts, especially if he believed in magic coins.

"Thank you so much, Mr. Matthew." She stood up.

"Mrs. Cassidy —" Mr. Matthew began.

"I know what you are going to say, sir. I promise I will give careful thought to the debts I pay and I assure you I will feed my family and staff first."

He seemed only a little pleased by her attempt at moderation. She picked the coin out of the dish and forestalled any more advice.

"I will wish on the coin, if that will make you feel better. I wish for a solution to all my problems." She dropped the coin back in the bowl and put on her gloves.

"I think you will find your way in this without a magic coin. Do take it with you, Mrs. Cassidy. Pass it on to someone who you think might believe in such enchantments."

"Lord Stephen was not 'at home' the first two times I went. The third time he said that he did not want the money."

Carroll's eyes were wide. Summer considered that her maid's thoughts were exactly what she herself was imagining. Stephen was looking for a way to blackmail her into a personal visit.

"Do you think he wants you to bring the money so he can seduce you? Could it be that with him you could find what you both truly want? That you will find Suite 606 and all your dreams will come true?"

"No, Carroll." Summer laughed, truly amused by her maid's fascination with all things dramatic. "Suite 606 does not exist any more than your idea that he wants to seduce me."

"Then why would he refuse me and Mrs. Rawley?"

"Because he wants to humiliate me."

"But why?"

"I have no idea, Carroll." Let the girl's imagination run wild. She was not going to encourage it.

"Perhaps if Miss Kitty went with me?"

Carroll began.

"No. I am not going to involve my daughter in this."

"We could hire some stranger, some man, to take the money to him."

"Carroll, what exactly would stop the messenger from keeping the money for himself?"

"Oh, yes, there be so many looking for work these days."

"Thank you, Carroll. Stop worrying. I will find a way to give him the money that will not compromise my reputation. Would you go find out from Mrs. Rawley what time dinner will be ready?"

"Yes, ma'am." Carroll bobbed a curtsy and left her alone.

Finally.

"Summer? Summer, are you in there? Come talk to me. It is amazingly boring in here. I will die if I have to be by myself much longer."

She bit her lip to keep from stating the obvious.

"Oh, yes, I'm already dead. It could be you are right and this is hell, total and complete torture to have only myself for company."

Moving as quietly as she could, Summer opened the dressing room door, found her hat and the pelisse that matched her gown, and then tiptoed out into the hall. She would take Kitty to Gunter's and use the time to try to come up with a plan for giving Stephen the money without having to see him.

Kitty was playing with a family of dolls covered with handkerchiefs. "A ghost family," she explained. "If you will not let me visit Papa, I will pretend that he is here with me."

She pointed to a chair covered with a holland cloth and with a head made out of a pillowcase stuffed with something. On it Kitty had drawn eyes, nose, mouth, and the heavy eyebrows that were her father's most distinctive feature. It actually did look a little like her papa.

Kitty was frantic with excitement at the unexpected treat. They were both out of breath at the pace she set to reach Gunter's. It was as crowded as one would expect on the first sunny day after a week of rain. The diversity of the groupings always amazed Summer. There were couples flirting, older couples enjoying the younger ones, governesses with their charges, and even two women sitting together but otherwise unescorted. On seeing them, Summer immediately felt better about going to such a frivolous place when she was still in mourning.

She nodded at one or two acquaintances and found a table in a corner with her back to the room. That, and her black gown, should make it clear that she was only entertaining her daughter. Kitty ate her ice, a pineapple-flavored concoction that Summer thought sounded dreadful. A minute later, Kitty asked if she could sit with the girl beside her. Summer nodded her thanks to the other girl's nurse.

"I am happy to see that you are going out these days."

She did not have to see who was speaking to know it was Lord Stephen Bradley. It was more than the scent he favored, a sharp, spicy blend, more than the color of the greatcoat she recognized. There was physical awareness, her body responding to his. Her body wanted one thing. Her mind insisted not.

She stood up so as to feel more his equal, stepped back to put some little distance between them, and said exactly what was on her mind. "How is it, my lord, that we have not seen each other in five years and now we are running into each other all the time?"

"Mrs. Cassidy." His hat was already in his

hand and he pressed it to his chest as he bowed to her.

"How did you know I was here?" she persisted.

"I called at your home and Mrs. Rawley told me."

"Go away. People are watching."

Stephen turned away, but did not leave. Instead he bowed to the obviously interested onlookers.

"Stephen," Summer whispered, much as she would to a badly behaved child.

"There is nothing amiss here. I am a friend of the family. Besides you are a free woman now."

Summer was not going to ask him what he meant by that comment. There was a devil-may-care air about him that made her feel cautious enough for the two of them.

"I left a note with Mrs. Rawley, but since you are before me now, let me take this opportunity to tell you that it is pointless to send your maid, your housekeeper, or even the adorable Kitty to my door."

She raised her chin, wishing she could leave, well aware that every eye in the place was on them.

"Listen to me, Summer." Stephen closed the distance between them and put his hat down on the table. "I do not want the money." He spoke with a firm emphasis on the sentence, as though she had not understood it the other times he had said it.

"I respond with equal insistence that I will find a way to pay what Reggie owes you." She began to pull on her gloves, determined to leave without any more discussion.

"What Reggie owes me?" Stephen moved a little, effectively blocking her way. He waited until she stopped fumbling with her gloves and looked him in the eye. She saw longing, confusion, even anger. "You are what Reggie owes me. If you want to get rid of the money, then you can. Bring it to me yourself."

Summer stared into his mesmerizing blue eyes, demand and desire holding her as surely as his hand could.

"Come tomorrow, or even later today, Summer. Tomorrow evening I am expected at the Bennetts' party, but I will send a regret if you will come."

"I will not." There was an urgency in his voice that made her wonder what he was planning.

"Please, Summer."

He moved a little closer even as she moved a step back.

"As soon as you can manage the time away from home. I will send my carriage for you. We can talk in private."

"No. I will not visit you alone at night. You are absurd." Summer brushed past him. The contact cost her. From shoulder to hand where their clothes brushed she felt him, his strength, his tenacity. He had not changed. Nor had her reaction to him. He was an overwhelming presence that could make her forget everything but the longing to take what he offered, even if it meant losing everything else.

"I do not want the money, Summer." He stopped her by taking hold of her arm. "There is only one thing that Reggie ever took from me that I want."

"Me? You wanted me?" Summer faced him again, feeling as though they were creating steps to some intricate dance that was entertaining everyone in the room. "Leave me alone." It sounded like begging. She straightened her spine. "You only want me in bed." She scanned the room, hoping no one had heard.

"This is about more than sex." He leaned closer, testing or tempting her, she could not tell which. "But, my darling girl, it would be more than one night and not necessarily in bed."

"You disgust me." She whirled away from him so he would not see how shocked she was. Men and women coupled in places other than beds? Where, she wondered. On the floor? On the desk? She remembered their kiss. She would have given herself to him right then in the maze on the grass.

Oblivious to the tension between them, Kitty came up to her mama to ask if she could go home with "my new friend, Veronica." It took Summer all of ten minutes to explain why that was not possible today and to suggest that the governess bring Veronica to the park near their home tomorrow.

By the time she was finished, Lord Stephen had invited himself to join the two ladies who were sitting alone. The three were laughing, the new center of attention.

Kitty was as slow walking home as she was fast before, singing a song to herself, kicking whatever pebbles she could find. Summer considered Stephen's demand. He wanted her to hand him the money. Was he so sure that she could not resist him? She smiled and encouraged Kitty to move a little faster.

What if she made an appearance at the Bennetts' party and gave him the money there? It would be scandalous to appear uninvited and in mourning, but scandal was expected there and just as quickly forgotten. If she went, it would end this once and for all.

# SEVEN

"Papa says I can go with you to Lord Stephen's house, Mama. Papa says Lord Stephen will have a sweet for me."

Summer hoped that Reggie understood the look she gave him. Keeping her voice level, she smiled at her daughter.

"How generous of you, Kitty. Perhaps later. Carroll is waiting to take you to see Veronica. Her governess is working with globes today and she thought that you might enjoy sharing the lesson. Please go on, we do not want to keep them waiting."

"Oh, yes," Kitty popped up from the cushion at her father's feet. "I want to see how fast the globes can spin." She raced from the room.

"Quite a little student, our Kitty."

"Reggie, if you ever use our child like that again, I will leave you here and let you find your own way to heaven."

"Yes, your eyes told me that quite effectively. If I was not dead already your expression would have stopped my heart."

He laughed, a breathy sound that was not attractive.

"Listen to me, Summer! You cannot go there." Reggie put a hand to his heart and appeared shocked at the suggestion. "My wife at the Bennetts' party? It does my memory no honor. You are still in mourning."

"I told you before I took Kitty to Gunter's that I will help you, but we are doing it on my terms."

"My dear wife," Reggie began.

His tone was so condescending that Summer decided that even if he gave her good advice she was going to ignore it. She tapped her foot and waited for him to go on.

"The whole purpose of the Bennetts' party is to give men and women a chance to make connections of an intimate nature."

As if she did not already know that.

"That sort of connection would not interest you at all, Summer."

Which showed exactly how intimate she and her husband had been. When she thought of the way Stephen made her feel, just the sight of him or the thrill that she felt when he stood next to her, she understood that she and Reggie had done no more than procreate. Making love was an experience she would never know.

"Summer, pay attention to me. If this is your way of helping me right wrongs then you must rethink your plan."

When he would have gone on, Summer held up her hand in protest. "You have no say in this. I have finally realized that you may be here but I am the one in charge. It is an exhilarating sensibility after five years of marriage."

"By all that is holy, this is a maddening experience." Reggie sailed across the room with more speed than usual. "I have lost all my authority. I can talk and explain what is the best course of action, but you persist in doing whatever you want."

"That describes my life for all of our marriage." Summer hated the bitterness in her laughter. "You will find no sympathy from me, Reggie."

"Is that the reason you are specifically going against my wishes and taking this money to Stephen?"

"No, I am doing it because I want to use this new power to put an end to one of the worst episodes of my life. I will embarrass Stephen as much as he embarrassed me."

"There will be gossip." Reggie ran a hand

through his hair, something he only did when he was wildly frustrated.

"No, there will not. What happens at the Bennetts' house is never bandied about. Why do you care so much?"

"I am thinking of Kitty."

The aura around him darkened a little as he spoke.

"You're lying. Is it because you do not want me to spend any time with Stephen? On that we completely agree. This is a way to do what he wants, but on my terms."

"I *was* thinking of Kitty. You should, too."

"Think of Kitty! Did you just say that I should think of Kitty?" She picked up a pillow and threw it at him. It passed through his leg. "If you had thought of anyone but yourself once in the last five years, Kitty and I would not be in this situation. Think on that awhile, Reggie Cassidy."

She went into her bedroom and slammed the door. With tears threatening, she went on into her dressing room and closed that door firmly. If she was going to cry she would do it in private.

Summer sank onto the slipper chair next to the clothespress as the tears began, uncontrollable and overwhelming. "I'm sorry, I'm sorry." She sobbed, using a chemise to blot her eyes.

The truth was that she had been nothing but a witch since Reggie had died. No, since he had come back to haunt her. How was it that she had managed with a smile before and now it was all she could do not to shriek her rage?

There was more than one reason for that: Reggie in the other room was one. Righting his wrongs was another. It seemed like an endless process that did nothing but stir up painful memories. It was as though a wall collapsed and she was living those days five years ago even as she remembered them. As if memories were not enough, Stephen Bradley had come back into her life, too.

Hiccoughing back the last of the tears, Summer did not even try to pick which reason caused such upset. Instead she opened the clothespress and considered what dress to wear.

When she had spent five minutes finding fault with every one she realized that she was as good at telling a lie as Reggie was. If she had to think this long about what to wear, when she had only four gowns, then she was not being honest with herself.

She spread two dresses on the chair and went to help Mrs. Rawley with the dusting. It would give her time to think, to be honest with herself, if no one else.

By the time every piece of furniture was dusted, the stairs and railings as well, she was sure she was going to the party for all the wrong reasons. She wanted Stephen to know that if he had not treated her love as no more than a wager to be won, they could have had a wonderful life together.

If he had loved her. If. She was going to show him what he had missed. Something worth so much more than one hundred fifty pounds.

She would wear the black wool. It was theatrical in its severity. Dramatic in cut and lack of color. The wool was so dark that it reflected no light, focusing all the attention on her face. It was something an actress might wear when she wanted to assume a bold façade. It was exactly what she needed.

Riley Bennett finished his story and everyone around him laughed. Stephen had not heard a word of it, but he smiled and nodded with the others. Even as Bennett raised a glass to toast this "escape from the ordinary," Stephen realized that this party was no longer such a risqué gathering.

Since Bennett's obviously satisfactory marriage to Eleanor Wilstrom, the annual gathering was much less shocking. Not that Eleanor had put a leash on her husband any more than he had on her. By her own admission, marriage had been "a steadying influence on two wild hearts."

The music began again and Stephen wandered into the game room, just the place to be when he would rather think than dance.

The gaming was anything but conventional. It should have been entertaining, but when one woman tossed her wedding ring out as a bet, it reminded him of Summer and Reggie's wedding day. He let his memory take him there for the first time in years.

Stephen had gone to the ceremony. He had been invited and he was determined to make an appearance. Sitting to the side, among the locals he counted the guests who had come from as far away as Sussex. Summer's father was well liked for his calm, good nature. His wife had been the opposite and had been vastly entertaining. Uncle Bradley had a dozen stories of her dramatic sensibilities, rather like a bonfire that would flame quickly and fade as fast.

From a distance of five years and a well-lived life, he realized that Summer's inclination to temper came directly from her mother, balanced by some of her father's restraint. Living with her would have made life very interesting indeed.

On Reggie's wedding day Stephen was confused. How had Reggie convinced Summer that she was better off marrying a childhood friend? Each word of the ceremony was like a step toward a disaster he could not prevent. When Summer repeated the vows he felt as though he had been kicked in the gut. How could this have happened? Where had he gone wrong?

The newly married couple turned to leave and sign the registry. They passed right by him. Stephen ignored Reggie and did no more than whisper Summer's name. When she turned toward him, he dropped all pretense and let her see his heartache.

Stephen was not sure what she saw in his expression, but hers went from confusion to dismay. It lasted a long moment, nothing more. As she turned away at Reggie's urging, a voice echoed in Stephen's head. "Reggie lied to her so he could win."

He knew not where the voice came from, but he knew it was the answer. He turned, walked out of the church, said good-bye to his uncle, and traveled back to London, determined never to see his supposed best friend again. It had been the end of a dream and the beginning of a life whose total focus was forgetting.

Stephen walked back into the Bennetts' ballroom as one of the more sensual waltzes ended. Just then the butler announced another guest, "Mrs. Reginald Cassidy."

Summer? Summer was here? Stephen turned toward the door, along with a few of the guests close enough to hear her name called. She paused in the entrance as she searched the room. The effect was dramatic. Her black gown called attention to her as surely as the butler's announcement.

Was he the only one who thought that the years had made her more beautiful? He'd thought her sweetness gone but he had glimpsed it once or twice in their few meetings. It had mixed with hardship, creating a woman whose beauty radiated strength.

She came to him, directly across the floor, her magnificent eyes flashing anger and determination. Even though he knew her anger was aimed at him as surely as if she held a gun, he did nothing to stop her. He wanted her as much that moment as he ever had, though surely she was as far from wanting him as it was possible to be. In the eternity of time that it took for her to come up to him, he wondered how long it would be before he could court her.

Stephen knew the other guests were anticipating a scene. The chattering had stopped.

He bowed to her. She did not curtsy. "Summer, can we go somewhere more private to talk?"

"That may be what you want, my lord, privacy with me, but all you said was that I had to give you the money in person." Despite her quiet tone of voice, he was sure that her words carried, or were repeated, to every corner of the room. "I choose this place to repay my husband's debt to you."

"I do not want the money." He raised his hand to the back of his neck. An ache settled there, one that had nothing to do with his height compared to hers.

"All you can have is the money, Lord Stephen. I am not for sale. Once I would have been yours for no more than the promise of love. But you were too much of a cad to say it and mean it."

"Please stop. Do not do this." It was the wrong thing to say. Her eyes lit with fire and she slapped him. The crack echoed through the room and one or two of the ladies gasped.

Summer took a step back and raised her voice. "My virtue is worth far more to me than this paltry one hundred and fifty pounds." She pushed a heavily weighted bag at him. He raised his hands to refuse it, just as she let go. The suede bag fell to the floor, breaking open, the coins scattering underfoot, rolling to the corners. One even made it all the way to the entrance hall.

"It was never the money I wanted from you," he whispered. "All I wanted was your love."

Summer shook her head and with an air of panic turned and ran from the room. A buzz of interest followed her. Some guests began to collect the coins.

Stephen hurried after her, determined that Summer would not leave without him. He did not care who claimed the money.

His progress was slowed by several idiots who stopped him to ask for the story. Ellie Bennett interrupted the curious by clapping her hands.

"If you cannot see that this is a romance gone awry then you are sillier than Lord Vilforth's pet monkey. This story is not over yet. Let him leave so we can learn the ending."

He bowed to his hostess who mouthed, "Good luck."

As he was going through the door Stephen scooped up the one errant coin that was trying to escape as surely as Summer. He put it in his pocket, as a memento, though he knew he would never need a reminder of this evening.

# Eight

"I beg your pardon, ma'am." The groom touched his head in a gesture of respect. "Few hackneys come to this neighborhood."

Yes, everyone here had their own coaches.

"I should not leave the horses." His expression showed honest concern and decision in the next second. "The coachmen are throwing dice in the mews. I can go find you a hackney on Park Lane if you will call one of them should a need arise."

When she nodded, he headed down the street at something less than a run but more than a walk.

"Hurry, please," she called out and then glanced over her shoulder and whispered, "I need to leave now."

Summer wished she felt better. She was so sure that once she had given the money to Stephen, she would feel a great release. Instead, she heard from his lips what she had seen in his eyes five years ago on her wedding day. "All I wanted was your love."

If that was true, why did he make that bet with Reggie?

"Summer, thank God you are still here."

No, no, she was not going to talk to him now, not when she was confused and heartsick. Summer lifted her skirts and began to run down Upper Grosvenor Street.

It did not take long for Lord Stephen to catch up to her. Her shoes were not made for dramatic escapes. He took her arm. "What are you doing? Where do you think you are going? Calm down, Summer. It's not safe to be on the street at night."

"Let go of my arm." She swatted at him with her other hand. "I want to go home."

"Then I will take you up in my coach." His voice had a coaxing quality as though she was completely insane. "It is right at the front door." He took her arm in his and walked her back.

"Oh, stop being solicitous. I am upset not crazed." Summer tried to pull her arm free. He did not release her. "You have your money. I even gave you Mr. Matthew's magic coin. There is nothing left to discuss."

"I need to talk to you about the past, Summer." His urgency equaled hers. "You have to listen. Then if you still hate me, I will leave you alone, never bother you again."

"The past is just that. It is over." She could hear the metal clang of horseshoes on the quiet street and hoped it was her hackney. "Why do you need to talk about it now?" The carriage passed them without slowing. She wanted to scream with frustration. Why would he not leave her alone?

"Because of this." The urgency was gone from his voice. Even as he spoke, he pulled her close and kissed her. The touch of his mouth, of his lips, the feel of his body pressed to hers — it was memory and moment at once, filling her with pleasure and the longing for more.

He ended the kiss and stepped away, far enough so that no part of their bodies touched. "Only an expert at self-deception could ignore that. It has been five years and I do not even have to kiss you to know how truly we belong together. I have only to touch your arm." He did so and she knew exactly what he meant, had known that day at Gunter's, perhaps even the night six months ago when she had seen him again.

"Reggie lied to us, Summer. He lied to both of us."

"What are you talking about?"

"I will tell you. I have to tell you. Not here

though. Come with me. I will take you wherever you wish to go, but I will not leave you until you let me explain."

"I do not wish to go anywhere."

The porter was running back, his expression regretful. "I'm sorry, ma'am, but I cannot go any farther from my post."

"Thank you for trying."

Stephen took the coin from his pocket to hand to the porter. The servant did not see the gesture. He was running to the door where the Bennetts were saying good-bye to a guest.

Stephen turned back to Summer. "I wish there was a place where you would feel safe enough to listen to me, just listen."

"Lord Stephen." Ellie Bennett came down the steps; her husband followed. "I think we can help you." She turned to her husband.

"Suite 606?" Bennett asked with a roguish smile.

"Yes, I think so."

Stephen bowed to her, still holding onto Summer's arm. "Does it really exist?"

"They are teasing, Stephen. There is no such place."

"Oh, it does exist, truly, Mrs. Cassidy. How do you think Bennett and I resolved that awful muddle we were in?"

"You, yourself, were in the suite?" Summer tried to phrase the question to be sure she had the truth.

"Yes. We found the answers we needed. It took two days and two blissful nights." Riley Bennett's smile was charming, and wicked.

"I am not looking for a love nest, Mr. Bennett."

Stephen tried not to smile. Summer sounded so prim.

"Suite 606 is what you want, Mrs. Cassidy." Bennett spoke with rare earnestness. "There you will find whatever it is you need. You will be safe. You will have complete control."

Summer's disbelief must have been obvious.

"Yes, it's quite simple," Ellie Bennett added. "If your dreams are a fantasy then you can live it out there. If you want to know the truth, as we did, then you will find that there."

"Where is it?" Summer knew those words were a weakness.

"My coachman will explain to yours. It's not far, but it's not easy to find."

"Are you willing to try, Summer?"

Stephen was allowing her to decide? Easy enough to do for a place that might not exist. But not long ago she would have thought that ghosts were absurd as well.

"Yes, we can go. The truth is worth the risk of the Bennetts' game with us."

They rode in silence. Summer might have agreed to listen, but the set of her shoulders, her stiffness, made it clear to Stephen that she was not going to listen with an open mind.

The creaking of the coach and the strike of the horses' hooves were the only night sounds. Fog had settled around the coach. His world was beside him, nothing else mattered.

Stephen watched her grow more reluctant, the way she pressed her lips together, drew a deep, uncertain breath. Would taking her hand help or hinder?

Before he could act, the coach stopped. Stephen opened the door and jumped out before the coachman could come off his perch. The fog was roof-high here and he could see the houses were close together and unremarkable except for one in the middle of the block, twice as big as the others and bright with lamplight.

The windows were lit as well though there were no sounds from the house, as though the owners were away for the evening.

Stephen went up the flight of steps and knocked. A porter opened the door, a jolly-faced man in bottle-green livery.

"Good evening, my lord. Are you here for Suite 606?"

"Yes." Stephen felt as cautious as he was curious, not in danger but not in control either. Before he could tell her to wait, he heard Summer coming up the steps behind him. He went down a step to stop her, not sure they should go on.

"I know it seems odd, my lord," the porter said, nodding, "and rest assured it is. But it is not anything you need fear. Unless you fear the truth."

"The truth is precisely what we are looking for."

"If you and Mrs. Cassidy will come with me, please, I will take you to the place where you can find it."

The porter stepped back into the house, leaving the door open. From where he stood, the cavernous entry hall managed to have a welcoming air. The golden pillars that rose to the ceiling and the gold-threaded marble glowed with a warmth that was an invitation in itself.

"It looks rather grand, but not off-putting." Summer whispered, tucking her hand in his arm. "How did he know my name?"

It felt so right to have her hand on his

arm, her whisper for his ears only. Of course she might not feel that way at all. Fear made for unwelcome allies.

"He knew me as well. I have no idea how, dearest, but it is in keeping with the 'oddness' he mentioned. Do you wish to leave?"

"No." Her one word was firm. "Even if it is a trick, no more than a way to embarrass us, we will have a place to talk, to end this farce."

"I would prefer you were less practical and more optimistic, but must admit the same had occurred to me." Was it a good sign that they were taking this step in agreement?

The night porter smiled when they finally entered. He closed the door behind them and ushered them to the staircase. The grand sweep of steps led them to another, smaller hall. They were led down it, the length of the house. Despite the well-lit hallway, they were alone, passing neither owners nor servants. He felt as though they were being drawn deeper and deeper into a mystery. They had slowed considerably.

The porter reached the set of double doors at the end of the hall well before they did.

"It feels as though we are leaving the world behind." Summer spoke quietly but her words echoed in the silence.

"Yes, yes it does. The halls are well-lit, the path back to the front door easily found. We can leave if you wish."

"No, but I do not care for surprises. If I was alone, I would be running back to the door right now."

"But you are not alone. We are together." He stopped as the power of those three words sunk in.

She met his eyes and watched him steadily as she considered his words. "Yes, we are. Do you think that is the key to learning the truth?"

"I hope so." He urged her forward again. "I think we are about to find out." He nodded to the porter who opened the double doors and bowed them into a small anteroom facing another set of doors.

A brass plate labeled the room Suite 606.

"Inside you will remember a place where you last knew the truth. If you cannot resolve your differences there, then they cannot be settled, which may be for the best or may be the biggest mistake you will ever make." The porter paused in the act of closing the door. "You are free to leave, alone or together, any time you wish."

Stephen nodded. He believed the man, he had no idea why, except that it was unlikely that the home of truth would allow a minion to lie. Without delay, Stephen opened the suite even as the porter closed the outer door.

The two of them stepped into sunlight, into the heart of the maze at Summer's home at Linton. It was just as he recalled, the arbor trimmed with lace, the table set, and the book of poetry on the seat where he had found her that day.

"Oh, it cannot be." Summer spoke in a choked whisper. Stephen looked back. The door to the suite was still there.

"It is magic," she said in a more normal voice, but he could hear her amazement, a shade detached from fear. "If it is not magic, we have very, very good imaginations."

"He said we would recall a place we shared." Stephen came to stand at her back. Jasmine and vanilla surrounded him.

"How can it be?" She laughed. "Never mind. I never believed in any number of things before. Now I realize that there is more to this world than we can imagine. Perhaps there is even magic in coins."

Stephen fingered the coin in his pocket. He had wished for a place where Summer would feel safe enough to listen to him and none could be better than this. They would have to talk about that later.

"Now we are in the place where it all began. Where we admitted our love, where we both told the truth."

"Is that how you think of it?" Her words were coated with a distaste bordering on belligerence. "For me, this is the scene of the worst trickery I have ever been subjected to."

"Yes, it happened at Linton, but not here. I spoke from my heart here. The trick was not mine." When she did not move to sit, Stephen went to her and took her by the shoulders. "Will you listen?"

"I will, because I said I would."

He had never thought of her as stubborn, but he could feel her resistance.

"It does not matter anymore, Stephen." She shrugged out of his grasp.

He saw in her eyes resignation, if not defeat. He heard it in her voice and it made him angry.

"This place is only a memory. Life has drained the optimism you're looking for."

"That's nonsense, Summer."

"Do not tell me that what I think is nonsense." She crossed her arms and prepared for battle.

"I do not want to argue. Surely there is another way to find the truth."

"Not if you belittle my sensibilities and tell me I am nonsensical." She held her ground. When she glanced at the door, he was sure she was ready to walk out.

"Yes, well." Stephen prayed that what he was going to say was not more truth than she could bear. "Tell me something. If what happened here no longer matters to you, then why did you insist on paying the bet, giving me the one hundred fifty pounds?"

She dropped her arms and found something of great interest on the grass at her feet. After the longest minute of his life, she nodded, not to him but to some debate in her head. With a deep breath she nodded again and took off her cloak, bonnet, and gloves and dropped them on the bench.

He tossed his own hat and greatcoat on the stone bench and waited.

"I suppose, the truth is, that we sometimes lie even to ourselves." Her words were spoken in a slow cadence as though it was painful to speak them. "Of course it still matters. It was so important to me that I made a spectacle of myself and then agreed to go to a place I did not believe existed to listen to you."

She had not looked at him since her outburst. She walked to the chair that she had been sitting in that day.

He came closer and stood over her. When she still did not look up, he stooped down so he could look up and see her face.

Her eyes were closed, her lips curved in a small smile and he wondered where she had gone in her memory. When she began to talk, she opened her eyes and he could see a sheen of tears that made her smile a sad one, painful to witness.

"You told me once that the bet with Reggie was unimportant," she began. "I thought you meant to flatter me, to say that seducing me was a pleasure whether you won or not."

"Yes, I can see how you would interpret it that way." He stood up and moved the chair from the other side of the table so he could sit next to her. "It was not until the next day at your wedding that I understood what had happened."

She closed her eyes again and he took her hand. They might be talking of the past but he wanted her with him in this present, as odd as it was.

"Reggie told you we had a bet, didn't he, Summer? He showed you the note on which he had written the amount and then added his initials."

"Exactly." She tried to pull her hand from his and he let her.

"He tricked me. He tricked us both."

She stood up and went to the stone bench, her back to him again.

"Summer, I have never lied to you and will not start now."

She came back to him and sat down again. "No, the lie was Reggie's specialty. Tell me the truth, Stephen."

Summer listened as he explained. When he reached the part about her wedding day, her only reaction was to lean closer and closer to him as the story unfolded.

"When I saw your expression, Summer, I knew that he had lied. To both of us. And it was too late to do anything."

"If I forget everything else about this life I will never forget your face that day." She put her hand on his arm, her brow furrowed with confusion. "How could you remain friends with Reggie after that?"

"I didn't." He took her hand and kissed it. "I went back to London the moment I left the church. When Reggie called on me after your wedding trip I told him that he had played me for a fool and that our friendship was over."

"He told me that you did everything together," she began and then stopped. "Was that a lie, too?" She shook her head, dismay replacing disbelief. "Does he know how to live any other way?"

"I think lies became truth for him. In time he could not tell the two apart."

"Yes, he is the most disingenuous man I have ever known. Stephen, I thought you were just like him."

Her detachment was a puzzle until Stephen realized she had lived with it every day and night for five years. If it were not for fate and a group of thugs it could have been so much longer. Anger at Reggie pounded through him. Summer must have felt it, she moved her hand from his arm.

"I suppose I should feel guilty for being so angry with a man who is dead."

"I remember how angry my brother was when our mother died just after he left for school. My father never once reproved him. Now I understand why.

"The truth is" — Summer closed her eyes and bent her head — "I have not loved Reggie for years."

Stephen knew that *he* should feel guilty for the dart of joy that came with that confession.

"Not because I was attracted to anyone else," she added quickly as if he needed that reassurance.

"Oh, Summer, you do not have to explain to me. Our Reggie loved himself enough for the two of us."

She laughed at that and he felt as though an ice dam was melting. Her laughter was the first giant crack.

He listened to her. Stephen did not brush off her thoughts or ignore them. He listened. No man had ever done that before. She sat straighter. "How is that you were with him the night he died?"

He took her hand and this time she curled her fingers around his. "Reggie and I were civil but estranged until a year ago. He was playing deep and losing badly. I decided that it was a perfect revenge to take as much money from him as I could. To take what he valued most as he had done to me."

"He told me that he won far more from you than he ever lost."

"Because I soon realized that I was taking money from you as well."

She shook her head and looked away but still held his hand. "You mean that you lost on purpose?"

"Yes. How I wish Reggie were here and I could push his face in that. He trumpeted his victories often enough. I tell you, Summer, it was a true test of my pride."

"I'm so sorry, Stephen."

"What do you have to be sorry for?"

"For not listening to you. For thinking the worst." She gave him her full attention. "Reggie may have lied, but I did not trust our love enough. The truth is I was afraid of the way you made me feel. I was afraid that if you were a part of my life there would be nothing I could deny you. Your power over me would be complete."

"The passion was mutual. The same was true for me."

"Was it? That day I would have given myself to you without consideration of the consequences. When I thought about it later, it was horrifying that I came that close to losing control."

They were facing each other. "What a silly girl I was." She put her arms around his neck, fully expecting to feel like a harlot. Instead it felt right, as right as kissing him. "The very next step is making love as we should have then." It was as honest as she could be.

With a laugh, Stephen swooped her up into his arms and went to a wooden gate at the corner of the maze. On the other side was an outdoor room with a bed growing from a garden of flowers. Its posts were a tree at each corner, its canopy the tree's flowers.

He turned her around, undid the buttons

of her dress, slipped it down her arms, and began to unlace her stays. "I am shy of you, Stephen. I have had a child. I am not so young anymore."

"Neither am I. Is it not a relief that love endures beyond the physical?"

Clad only in her shift, she turned and helped him undress. His body was so fine, welcoming and arousing. Aroused.

Summer had known the marital act from virgin to alienated wife. Had she ever made love? Not until this moment, when she and her lover sank down onto the bed and lost themselves in sweet words and sweeter kisses. Time was suspended. They were living in the present, in a moment without end. Her body fit to his and he held her to him, his hands stroking her back from neck to hips, drawing her closer, against his arousal, and finally slipping into her with a slow, sure move. She arched her body to him, taking all he could give, giving him all that she had. Pleasure surrounded her, as she surrounded him. He moved until she was frantic with need, her hands splayed, gripping the sheets, begging for more while she wished it would never end. The shuddering pleasure that broke the rhythm was a truth all its own; his release, a joining that bound them together.

She lay in his arms. He smoothed the hair from her face. "I have loved you from that moment to this. I am sorry if that is more than you want, but it is the truth."

"Stephen, it is what every woman dreams of, but —" She kissed his chin as she felt him tense. "We hardly know each other. I do not know if you eat breakfast, prefer dinner early. Do you think girls should be educated beyond needlework and music? As a matter of fact, you must agree first that the answers to those sorts of questions are as important as being happy in bed together."

He pushed her onto her back and kissed her until she laughed. "I love how practical you are. It is so very exciting that I think I must make love to you again. But first, let me assure you I will not speak of marriage yet. You will take all the time you need to find out how well we are suited, to answer all your questions with as much honesty as we share here. I promise."

He began to nuzzle her neck and work his way down to her breast. She was breathless and all but gasped. "Wait. I have one more question. Do you think the man must always be on top?"

He answered her without words, showing her exactly how imaginative he could be.

# NINE

"Stephen, you said before, at least a hundred years ago . . ." She laughed as she spoke, for it felt even longer than that as she sat up in the bed, with the sheet drawn over her breasts. She turned to look at him over shoulder. ". . . you said that you wished there was a way to confront Reggie."

"That was small of me. He is dead and I was thoughtless."

"You *can* tell him." She spoke in a rush, turning to him, hoping he would not think her mad. "In this room we have chosen only to speak the truth. He is still on earth. As a ghost."

His doubtful expression compelled her to add, "Is it any harder to believe in a ghost, than to believe in a room furnished from your memories?"

"No, I guess not." He drew her down so her head laid on his chest. "That time I went to his room after he died, that day you came back from the country?"

She nodded.

"I felt almost as though I was having a conversation with him. Except for an exceptionally cold draught there was nothing odd."

"Yes." She sat up and faced him, delighted that he was open to the idea. "Cold is exactly how he feels, like he is cold and empty. I do not know if that is because it was his life or that is the way all ghosts feel to us." She slipped from the bed, not nearly as shy about her nakedness now. Pulling on her shift, she lifted her stays in place. "Please help me with my stays, will you, and then put your clothes on and come with me. Reggie insists that he has wrongs to right and that he cannot move on until he does. That's why I paid the rest of the gambling debts, the money he owed to people who really need it. But he is still here. Perhaps he must talk to you as well."

"If it were not for the wonder of this dream, I would not believe you, Summer." He laced the stays and then buttoned her dress. "Now I must admit that anything seems possible."

Summer picked a rose from the garden and tucked it in his lapel. He kissed her and they promised each other to let this bit of magic live forever in their hearts.

They held hands and laughed as they ran down the hall to the steps and met the porter at the front door. He smiled and bowed them out, refusing the generous tip that Stephen offered. "Your happiness is reward enough. Live well, my lord."

Summer curtsied to the porter. He bowed in return, blushing with embarrassment at her gesture.

The coachman assured them they had not been gone above a minute and was sorry that they had not found what they came for. With as solemn a nod as they could manage, Stephen and Summer climbed into the coach and asked to be taken to Challoner Street, discussing what other phenomenon might exist: witches, fairies, perhaps even unicorns.

Reggie moved from window to door, from chair to bed, sailing through the air with a force fueled by anxiety. Twice he ran into the wall, his spectral form flattening into an unbecoming mass. He was desperate to know what had transpired at the Bennetts' party.

Reggie knew that if Summer and Stephen ever grew close enough to talk sensibly about what had happened five years ago they would make mincemeat of the tale he had told them. Brilliant as it was at the core, his story was all lies.

No one understood that he knew better than anyone else how his life was supposed to unfold and he had found a way to tailor it to his wants. They called it lying; he thought of it as a gift. One that had served him well.

Now he faced a greater challenge — to come up with a way to tell the truth so that they did not know that he had used them. He felt darkness overcome him and did his best to move away from it. It followed him. All right, he had done more than use them. He had lied. The darkness eased.

Understanding that he had lived a life of lies was part of his newly acquired spectral knowledge. But the ability to act on that knowledge was not one of the spectral gifts. He wasn't stupid. He had figured that out weeks ago. Honesty felt as awkward as a badly tailored coat. It did lighten his aura and that was a wondrous feeling worth the discomfort.

He had felt truly marvelous when he told Kitty that he was meant to move on. He had comforted her as best he could when she cried. From somewhere came the idea that he would visit her in her dreams. He told her. Her smile and the lightness of his being convinced him that it was possible. By the time she had gone off to her friend's house she had been resigned. In time he was sure she would be relieved.

Honesty had not been as difficult as he thought it would be. He stretched out his form over the bed and waited to see if he would be told how soon he could visit his daughter in her dream world. Before any ideas came to him, he heard a sound from belowstairs. He flew up from the bed and sailed across to the door. "Summer, is that you? Why did you come in through the kitchen? Come here immediately and tell me what happened at the Bennetts'."

The house was dark and Summer used her key to go in the front door. As she stood in the open doorway and the familiar scents assaulted her, she felt her confidence fail.

Did Stephen sense it? He turned her to him and put his hands on her shoulders. He'd done that before. When he had something important to say and wanted to be sure he had her attention. He was her light and love. How could he doubt it?

She raised a finger to his lips. "Yes, I am a little frightened about the unknown, about what is going to happen. But I promise you this. Even if we cannot find a way for him to move on, I will never let him come between us again. He will not be a part of our lives after tonight, even if I must walk away this evening with nothing but the clothes I am wearing now. I promise that I will trust you."

Moonlight shadowed his face. He slid his hands down her arms, warming her all over. He kissed her fingers and then her lips. The moonlight seemed brighter all of a sudden and she knew that from that moment on they would be inseparable in spirit. This was what it was like to love someone. Joy over-shadowed her anxiety and she straightened her shoulders, ready to face Reggie's ghost and any other specters that thought they could haunt her.

Draping her cloak on the nearest chair, she nodded for Stephen to do the same as she lit the candle Mrs. Rawley had left for her. They hurried up the stairs after sharing one more kiss for luck, love, and a future without Reggie.

She could hear voices coming from his room and stopped abruptly on the top step. "How could Carroll have allowed Kitty to go in there?"

"I thought you said that both of them were away from home tonight?"

"Yes, but who else could it be?" Determined to answer her own question, she slammed the bedchamber door open. Ghostly Reggie and his visitors were startled. In the next instant, the three people — a man, woman, and child — disappeared from the room. Summer saw game cards spread out on the floor and shook her head. "Were you gambling with some new ghost friends?"

"Not precisely. They came in through the kitchen and showed up quite unexpectedly. While the man rested, the woman and the boy taught me this amazing new card game. It's called poker. Tell Stephen, Summer. He will be quite envious."

"I can hear you and see you Reggie."

"You can? You mean the first time you called, you were playing a trick on me? Not your usual style, old fellow."

"No, I did not see you the first time. I felt as though you were here, but I could not see you." Stephen walked into the room ahead of Summer. "I am not sure I want to now. It stretches credulity."

"I tell you two, this is the most annoying part of the ghost business. No one believes you at first. Except my itty-bitty Kitty. She said that she knew all along I would be waiting for her. It is vexing to have to explain yourself every time someone new appears."

Stephen reached out to touch Reggie. His hand passed through his hazy arm.

"Pretty personal of you, Stephen."

"Convincing though, even if I could not see you before."

"No one else could either. But after Kitty came to me, it seems everyone could." He nodded. "The wizard, one of my visitors, told me that I am not visible until one comes who believes before they see."

"That could be the truth, Stephen. Kitty talked about wanting to see her father's ghost at almost the exact time he came back to us." Summer moved into the room to stand beside Stephen. "You have haunted us long enough. We have come to send you on your way."

"Actually, I am wondering if that is such a good idea, *wife,*" Reggie said. He emphasized the last word, obviously aware of the rapport she and Stephen were feeling. "There is no guarantee of heaven. At least she did not say that I would be rewarded if I told the truth, only that I must do it to move on."

Stephen gestured to Summer who nodded and turned to her dead husband. "You have a choice, Reggie. You can tell the truth and take a chance on what is to come or we will walk out of this house and leave you."

Reggie floated to the window.

"Admit to us that you deliberately lied to keep us apart," Stephen insisted.

Reggie's aura darkened before he spoke. "All right, all right." His aura lightened.

"Who are you talking to?" Summer wasn't sure she really wanted to know the answer to that.

"No one. It's only that sometimes my aura weighs me down and other times it lightens." His spectral presence sagged a little. "It all depends on whether I am telling the truth or not."

"Then tell the truth and be done with it, Reggie."

Summer hoped Stephen never used that tone when he talked to her. It was withering.

"Yes, I lied to you." He sailed very close to them but could not fit even himself between them. If Reggie thought to ease Stephen's anger, he failed. Truth seemed to fuel it.

"If I could call you out, I would, you lying excuse for a gentleman."

"Don't be ridiculous, Stephen. You resent me because I won Summer and you did not."

"Which shows what an empty heart you

have. I loved her then. I love her now. All you cared about is that you won her. Then you compounded the insult by treating her like every other prize, with disregard of her value, with disdain. You fool."

"That is not —" He stopped and then nodded. "Actually, that is probably true."

"Why? Why was I so important to you?" Summer asked, more confused than angry.

"I loved you." Reggie flew up to the ceiling and seemed surprised at the force of movement. "The truth. All right," he said to the presence she could not see.

"Stephen Bradley. Lord Stephen Bradley," he spoke the words with venom in his voice. "You had a title, an estate that you were set to inherit, more money than any man I knew."

Reggie sailed over to the window.

"I would be damned if you were going to win the girl, too. I loved that I won. I always loved the victory more than the prize." He came down to float before them. "The truth can hurt. Did anyone ever tell you that?"

Stephen put his arm around Summer. With his love encompassing her, Reggie's words did not wound her as much as he'd intended.

Reggie was drawn back to the ceiling. He flailed his arms but could not slow the ascent. The mist around him was a dull gray. "One more thing. If I am to speak the truth then I must say that I would not have done anything differently. It may damn me to hell forever, but I had a good run of luck while it lasted, a wife to warm my bed, and a daughter who is the light of my life."

This time when he reached the ceiling he began to move through it. "I guess this is good-bye. I told Kitty not to miss me, that I would visit her in her dreams."

He continued to fade through the ceiling, so it must have been the truth. "I love that child, maybe the only person I love more than myself." With that last truth, he disappeared.

Summer and Stephen stared at the ceiling. The room warmed considerably and morning sounds came to them from the street.

Summer heard Carroll clomping up the stairs. Thank goodness Kitty was still at her friend's house and would not be home until after dinner. They had left the door to Reggie's room open and Carroll came in, then stopped suddenly, as though she had run into a wall. She averted her eyes. "Oh, I do beg your pardon, madam and Lord Stephen."

"It's all right, Carroll. We have sent the

ghost away."

She risked a look at them and relaxed. "He is gone, isn't he?" She walked around the room, looked behind the furniture and even opening the clothespress. "The room is so much brighter now, as though a great burden has been lifted, but Miss Kitty will be so disappointed." Carroll went back to the door. "I imagine that in time she will grow up and convince herself that it never really happened. Won't that be sad?"

Summer could feel Stephen doing his best not to laugh. "Did you want something, Carroll?"

"Oh yes." She held out a coin. "I found this on the floor near Lord Stephen's coat. Does it belong to you, my lord?"

"Yes." He turned to Summer. "Shall we give it to Kitty?"

"Oh, you *both* are going to give it to her. Does that mean you are planning on marriage?" Her question was more earnest than coy. Before they could answer, she crossed her hands over her heart, one hand still holding the coin. "Oh, I wish you will let me stay on. I would not even mind if you moved to Kent."

"You do not need to wish for that, Carroll." When had she realized that Carroll was as loyal as she was fey? "You are my maid for as long as you wish to be."

"Oh thank you, Mrs. Cassidy." She beamed at them as though she was going to be the mother of the bride. "Then I wish you and Lord Stephen a lifetime of happiness together, I really do." Carroll set the coin on the table near the door and left.

"I do not think I could have wished any better myself," Stephen Bradley said as he bent to kiss the woman who was his past and surely his future.

■ ■ ■ ■

# COLD CASE
# RUTH RYAN LANGAN

■ ■ ■ ■

# ONE

Sam Hunter cursed under his breath as he peered through the windshield. The wipers couldn't keep pace with the rain that pelted his car as it inched along the dirt road.

For a man who prided himself on a keen sense of direction, it wasn't easy to admit that he was lost. He'd begun feeling like he'd dropped into an alien landscape. It had started when he'd turned off the highway to find the covered bridge he remembered from a long-ago college semester spent in Vermont.

There should be road signs. Or at least lights from shops and houses. Instead there was only pitch-blackness.

Everything would have been so easy if his reservation had been honored in the hotel that had sprung up near his old college campus. In the online brochure, the hotel boasted a Jacuzzi, a sauna, and an excellent workout facility. Just what the doctor ordered. Except that when he'd arrived he'd been informed that the room he'd reserved, Suite 606, was occupied and there was no other room available anywhere in the town due to the college's homecoming game.

He detested messy situations. But that seemed to be the way his life was going these days.

So here he was, driving blind in the middle of a storm, looking for an old inn he remembered from earlier times. It was far enough from town that few would want to stay there.

He'd been so certain of the location. A covered bridge, a narrow dirt road, and then the inn, set amid acres of sugar maples. But he'd already driven across the covered bridge, and so far there was no sign of the inn. No sign of anything.

In the misty glare of his headlights he saw something dart in front of his car. He blinked. Was that a woman, hands outstretched, eyes wide and terrified? What woman in her right mind would be out on such a night? There was no time to ponder as he hit the brakes and turned the wheel sharply, hoping to avoid the impact. The car shuddered, skidded, before slamming into a ditch, activating the airbags, which exploded with such force he was knocked breathless.

For long minutes he could do nothing more than breathe in and out, relieved that he was still conscious.

Gingerly he probed his ribs. If a few of them weren't broken, they were definitely bruised, as was his head, which had snapped back against the headrest with such force, his ears were still ringing.

He sat very still, struggling to get his bearings.

The driver's side door was jammed up against the ditch. He inched across the seat and opened the passenger door. Cold air slammed into him as he slowly, painfully pulled himself from the oddly angled car.

He muttered a few rich, ripe curses when he realized the extent of the damage. The rear driver's side tire had blown out on impact. The car was leaning so far to one side, it was nearly tipped over. There would be no way to get out of this mess without a tow truck.

And the woman? Had she escaped injury?

He peered about hopefully. "Hello. Anybody out here?"

The only sound was the rain.

"Hello. I'd like to help. Can you hear me?"

He trudged through mounds of sodden leaves that lined the road. Though he scoured the area, there was no sign of the woman. Where could she have run to?

Was that a light in the distance? He blinked against the rain and saw only darkness. A second later, he saw it again. A faint flicker of light.

Praying it was the inn, or anything that resembled civilization, he hunched deeply into his jacket and started walking. Icy needles of rain soaked his clothes and settled deep in his bones. And still the flickering light seemed no closer.

Sam scrubbed at his eyes. When he looked up the light seemed nearer. Or was it just because he wanted it to be so?

He started forward. By now he could no longer feel his feet as he walked,

What in hell was he doing in this godforsaken place? If he hadn't chosen Vermont in November he could be back in his New York walk-up, chugging a beer and watching the Giants stomp the Steelers. After he'd spoken his mind to Captain Chase, he'd wanted to get as far away from the city and his former job as possible. Wasn't that why he'd made this choice?

*"I talked it over with Dr. Kresge, and he says you're making progress, Hunter."*

*"That's shrink speak, Captain, for 'Let's put him on some pills for a while and see if he can put away the past long enough to be any*

good at his old job.' "

"The pills can help level things out."

"I don't want to level things out." Sam dropped his gun and badge on the captain's desk and stared at the floor, avoiding his eyes. "I plan on walking away and never looking back."

"Wait, Hunter." The captain lowered his voice. "You ask any man on this force, he'll tell you that losing a partner in the line of fire is tough enough. But losing a partner who took a bullet meant for you, now that's as tough as it gets."

"That's why I'm walking."

"Like hell you are. Don't you understand that it will go with you, no matter how far you travel?"

"Maybe. But at least I won't have to be surrounded by people who know my history. I won't have to see that look in their eyes."

"They care about you. I care about you. You're the best detective we've ever had on this force. You and Vince solved more cold cases in the past ten years than were solved in the previous twenty. You have an amazing talent as an expert witness, Hunter. You see things others can't."

"Thanks. I appreciate it." Sam turned away. "I'll be in touch."

"All right. All right." The tough-talking police

captain stood and rounded his desk, laying a hand on Sam's sleeve. "I'll accept your badge and gun, but I'm not accepting your resignation. I'll consider this a leave of absence. When you've worked things out, I expect you back on the force. I need you. This department needs you."

Sam had walked out the door without another word.

So here he was, on his own for the first time since leaving law school and joining the New York State Police force, and wondering what in hell he was doing in the middle of nowhere. Hadn't Gordon Belski warned him? Belski — balding, paunchy, his eyes sad as a hound dog's — was the most vocal cynic on the force. The one who'd seen it all.

"You think getting away is the answer to a cop's nightmares? Mark my words, Hunter. You'll see endless little towns and villages, all looking like the last one, and you'll drive for miles without seeing a single burned-out building or a sign of gang graffiti, and wonder why you can't settle in and enjoy yourself. Want to know why?" Without waiting for a reply, he'd added, "Because cops are different. We're not hardwired to be tourists. Everywhere we go, we're looking for that one little thing that spells trouble. Everybody else sees a blur of people.

*We see a face in the crowd that resembles a murder witness who went missing, or a drug dealer who slipped bail. So go ahead and plan a leisurely life in Vermont. Don't blame me when you wake up in some quaint little village feeling miserable as hell, seeing a killer in every stranger you meet, and wishing you were back at work in this dump, where at least there are others who share your suspicions."*

*Sam looked around at the peeling paint, the ugly metal desks littered with foam cups of lukewarm coffee. Heard the ringing of endless phones. "Gee, thanks for those words of encouragement, Belski. I have no intention of thinking like a cop, or being one, ever again. Now, if you don't mind, I'm out of here for good."*

*"In your dreams. You'll be back here in a week. Two, tops."*

*Hunter reached into his pocket and slammed a bill on the desk. "Ten says I won't."*

*"Easiest money I ever made." His buddy tossed down two fives and grinned like a loon as he slid them into his drawer. "Want to go for double or nothing?"*

*He and Belski looked up at the odd trio who suddenly appeared in the squad room. The man was well over six feet tall, with long blond hair, wearing some sort of medieval costume. The dark-haired woman with him was staring* around with deer-in-the-headlights eyes. A boy in his early teens in a Pirates hoodie seemed more annoyed than curious.

Sam flicked them a glance and rolled his eyes. "Just one more reason to get away from all the crazies in New York."

"Oh, I don't know. They look just like your average, run-of-the-mill nutcases we get every day here. I'm betting you'll see something even stranger than this in Vermont, even if, at first, it appears harmless enough." Belski was grinning as he started toward them. "Something I can do for you folks?"

"I am afraid we made a wrong turn. Come along, Marie. Hugh." Wizard-robe was already herding the woman and boy out the door.

Only in New York, Sam thought.

His reminiscences of his last day on the force slipped away as he stopped dead in his tracks and stared. Looming out of the darkness was something shimmering through the rain and fog like fairy lights. He could make out the shape of a building. It appeared to be a farmhouse. And none too soon. He was so cold he wondered that he could still feel any part of his body.

As he drew nearer something thudded in the darkness and he reached for the gun in his shoulder holster, only to remember that

278

it was back in New York, along with his badge. He swore when he stumbled over a rickety pole lying at an angle. Dangling from the pole was a rusty sign reading STORM HILL. It creaked and sighed with every gust of wind.

Storm Hill. An apt name, he thought. The storm was so much worse up here than it had been down on the roadside. Wind a howling monster. Hard pellets of rain and sleet raking the flesh like shrapnel.

He noted his empty pocket where he kept his cell phone. Where had it gone? More than anything else, it was his lifeline. Frantic now, he knelt in the icy slush, snagging leaves and branches and stones until, after a long, fruitless search, he was forced to admit that it was gone. It could have fallen anywhere along the path he'd just taken, and he was too cold to retrace his steps.

He moved numbly forward until the building was directly in front of him. He climbed several steps of a wide front porch and lifted a brass door knocker. Within minutes he heard footsteps drawing near. The door was opened.

A woman lifted a lantern to his face, nearly blinding him. He blinked, and she lowered the lantern to her side.

"Sorry. I didn't expect to see anyone out

on such a night."

"I was coming up the road and a . . . something raced past. I thought it was a woman, but I couldn't see what it was in this rain. I ended up in a ditch."

"Ah." She took in his sodden clothes, his pinched face. "You're soaked. Please, come in."

She stepped back and Sam moved past her, grateful to be out of the cold and sleet.

Though the woman seemed startled by his appearance, she quickly took charge. "You're half-frozen. There's a lovely fire in the parlor. Follow me."

As he trailed behind, he realized that she was much younger than he'd first thought. Probably the drab housedress made her appear older, or at least old-fashioned. He didn't think women wore such things anymore. Despite the clothes, the body beneath was slim as a willow. Her dark hair fell around her shoulders long and loose. Her eyes, when she paused and looked back at him, were the bluest he'd ever seen.

She indicated a wooden rocking chair pulled in front of the fire. "Sit here."

As soon as he was seated, she dropped an afghan over his lap. "Warm yourself while I find you something hot. Would you prefer tea or soup?"

"You wouldn't happen to have any whiskey, would you?" He had to fight to keep his teeth from chattering.

She thought a moment. "I'll see what I can find."

Then she was gone, leaving him reaching out his hands to the warmth of the fire while he stared around.

The room looked like something from another era. A rag rug covered the center of the wooden floor. The sofa was faded. The portraits hanging above the mantel were ancient. He ran a hand over the rough, curved wood of the rocker. Even this chair looked as though it may have been hand-carved.

"I've found some whiskey to warm you." The young woman paused on the threshold before crossing to him.

"Thank you." He accepted the tumbler and wondered at the sudden rush of heat as their fingers brushed. "My name is Sam Hunter."

"I'm Mary Catherine McGivern. What brings you out on such a night, Mr. Hunter?"

"Sam." He couldn't help smiling at her formal tone. "I'm just passing through. I spent a summer here in Vermont during my college days and . . ."

The grandfather clock in a corner of the room sounded the hour.

Hearing the outer door open, Mary Catherine frowned and turned away. "That will be Hoag, home from the fields and wanting his supper. I'll come and fetch you when it's ready."

"Thank you. That's very generous."

"Not at all." With a swirl of skirts she was gone.

Sam stretched out his feet to the fire, but not even the warmth and the whiskey could ease the pain in his ribs or the throbbing in his head. He leaned back, eyes closed. Dr. Kresge was wrong. The captain was wrong. And so was Belski. He was through with police work for good. Nothing would change his mind. Let someone else muddle through dusty files of unsolved cases. Let someone else put their life on the line to see that justice was done.

He thought of Marina Marinelli, his partner's wife of thirty-five years. The pain in her eyes at her husband's funeral was enough to break even the most hardened heart. For Sam, knowing Vince had died in his place just made it worse. He'd escaped the funeral as quickly as possible, but there was no escaping the lingering guilt. His partner shouldn't have died. Wouldn't have, if Sam had been an instant faster on the draw.

He looked up as a shadow fell over him.

Mary Catherine gave a shy smile. "Sorry. I didn't mean to wake you."

"I wasn't asleep. Just thinking."

"Supper is ready. If you'll follow me."

He trailed her along a narrow hallway until she paused in the doorway of the kitchen.

A big bear of a man was seated at the head of the table, his sleeves rolled to his elbows, revealing muscles hardened by years of farm chores. His hair, wet from the rain, gleamed silver in the light of the fireplace. He fixed Sam with an icy stare.

"Hoag, this is Sam Hunter. Mr. Hunter, my stepfather, Hoag Slade."

When Sam started around the table to offer a handshake, the man pointed his fork the way a killer would take aim with a pistol. "Sit at that end."

Belski's words played through Sam's mind. There he was again, thinking like a cop. Hoag Slade was holding a fork, not a gun. The man was simply cold and hungry and tired after a day of farm chores, and not some crazed killer.

*Thank you, Belski, for planting that seed in my mind.*

As he took his seat, Mary Catherine nodded toward the girl beside her. "Sam, this is my sister, Anna."

The girl, a younger, coltish version of her older sister, gave him a shy smile. Seeing her stepfather's frown, she lowered her gaze as she carried a platter of food to the table.

Without a word, Hoag helped himself to fried chicken and garden beans, mashed potatoes and gravy, and biscuits warm from the oven. When he'd filled his plate, Mary Catherine and Anna passed the food to Sam before taking their places at the table and filling their own plates.

While he ate, Sam glanced at Hoag. "Do you think you might be able to give me a lift to town after supper?"

From his position at the head of the table, Hoag glowered. "Nobody's going anywhere tonight. In case you haven't noticed, the storm's getting worse out there. Rain's turned to sleet. Fields will be iced over by morning, I'm betting."

"Well then." Mary Catherine poured tea and passed it to Sam. "You can spend the night in the spare room off the kitchen. It isn't very big, but it'll do for one night, don't you think, Hoag?"

The older man's frown deepened and he looked as though he might protest before giving a grudging nod. "I don't see we have a choice."

The look on his face said much more than words. Sam had the distinct impression that given a choice between putting him up for the night or tossing him out in the storm Hoag Slade would gladly choose the latter.

The two young women were watching the older man with matching looks of unease.

Now wasn't this a fine way to spend the first night of his new life as a former cop turned civilian?

But it was only one night, Sam assured himself. By tomorrow he'd be on his way, happy to leave this dreary place in his dust.

With that he bent to his food, too weary to appreciate the perfectly fried chicken, the smoothly mashed potatoes, the garden vegetables. Too weary to care about anything except getting through the meal and into a warm, dry bed. It couldn't come too soon to suit him.

# Two

Sam had to work hard to swallow back his disappointment. It was obvious that he wasn't welcome in Hoag Slade's home, but there seemed to be nothing to do but accept the inevitable. He was stuck here until morning.

He kept his features perfectly bland as he turned to Mary Catherine. "Thank you. I appreciate your hospitality. I'd be grateful for the room off the kitchen."

"It's no trouble." She looked over at her sister. "After supper, would you mind fetching Mr. Hunter a set of sheets for the bed, and that afghan from the parlor?"

Her stepfather turned on her with a fierce glare. "You can take care of it yourself, girl. I need Anna's help in the barn."

"Of course." Mary Catherine exchanged a sympathetic look with the girl who would be forced to leave the warmth and comfort of the house for the chill of the barn. "You'll need warm gloves, Anna."

"I won't forget."

They finished their meal in silence. As soon as Hoag mopped up his gravy with the last of the rolls, he shoved away from the table and got to his feet.

Without a word Anna followed him from the room.

When the door closed behind them, Mary Catherine visibly relaxed. "More tea, Sam?"

"Thank you." He held out his cup and watched as she poured. "That was a fine meal."

She flushed. "Such praise. I'm not accustomed to compliments."

"Really? You ought to be." He glanced around the tidy room. "Your house sparkles. It's obvious that you've put a lot of love into it."

"I do love keeping house. Like my mother, I enjoy cooking and cleaning. And baking. Oh, I do love baking. Cakes and pies and fancy cookies." She glanced away. "Listen to me going on. According to Hoag, that's nothing but vanity, and we have no right to indulge in it."

"There's nothing wrong with taking pride in your work."

"What is it you do, Sam?"

"Police work. Or rather, I did. At the moment I'm not sure just what I'll be doing next." He shrugged, clearly uncomfortable talking about himself. "I'm taking some time to . . . sort through things."

If Mary Catherine recognized his discomfort, she gave no indication as she began gathering the dishes. She poured hot water from a kettle into a basin and began to wash.

Sam enjoyed watching her. The economy of movement. The way her hair curled damply around her cheeks as she dipped her hands into the basin. The obvious enjoyment she took in her work. Without a word he picked up a towel and joined her.

She was clearly surprised and pleased by his help. "You've no need to do this."

"You cooked. The least I can do is lend a hand with the cleanup. Especially since you're forced to work with no power. Lucky you have an old woodstove and some lanterns."

"Doesn't everybody?"

Her question had him chuckling as he reached over her head to hang a cup, and then another.

Up close she smelled of soap and water, with just a trace of cinnamon.

She teased his memory, and he found himself thinking about the recurring dream he'd told Dr. Kresge about. In it, a beautiful, mysterious woman pleaded with someone bent on doing her harm. Sam had been forced to stand by helplessly while she was killed before his eyes. Dr. Kresge had dismissed it as nothing more than lingering guilt over the death of his partner.

*"Acute trauma can manifest itself in many ways."*

*"It's a dream, Dr. Kresge."*

*"Of course. But in your case, a dream based on reality."*

Why was he remembering it now? And why did he feel that he knew this woman?

"You're quiet." She smiled up into his face and handed him a plate.

"I was thinking that this all seems somehow familiar. Yet I know I've never been here before."

"I'd remember if I'd met you."

"I know I'd never forget meeting you." He returned her smile, and had to fight the urge to touch a hand to her cheek. Up close her skin was as fine as porcelain. Her full mouth made for kissing.

She blushed and looked down. "We don't get to meet many strangers here."

"Why?" He dried the plate and set it carefully in the cupboard.

"We're far from town. But even if we were closer, Hoag wouldn't approve. He discourages friendships with the folks from town."

"For what reason?"

She shrugged. "He's suspicious of strangers. And with good reason."

When Sam arched a brow she took her time drying her hands on a towel before adding, "When Hoag married our mother, he made many demands. One was that we change our name to his."

"And you and Anna refused?"

She nodded. "It was too painful for us. We were proud of our family name and felt by giving it up we would be betraying our father."

"I should think Hoag would understand your feelings."

"He said it was false pride."

"Didn't your mother come to your defense?"

"Yes, but gently, so as not to hurt Hoag's feelings. She told us privately that she would have found a way to keep us from doing as Hoag asked."

"What was your birth father's name?"

"Morgan. Morgan McGivern." Her eyes lit with a radiance that seemed to animate all her features. "Oh, he was so fine and handsome. And such fun to be with. My mother used to say that he made her laugh at least once every day of their years together."

"He sounds like a fine man. How did he die?"

"When he didn't come home for supper, my mother found him lying in a freshly plowed field, the plow horse standing nearby. She said that it was probably his heart. His father was near that age when he died in much the same way."

"Did the doctor agree?"

"There was no need to call on the services of a doctor all the way from town. It was obvious that our father had been dead for hours."

"How long after that did your mother meet Hoag?"

"Oh, she'd known him for some years. Hoag used to help my father at planting time and harvest time. Once she was alone, Hoag came by and offered to help my mother with the farm chores. She was grateful for his help. Within a year they were married. At first my sister and I were puzzled and hurt, but we decided to put aside our feelings and try to be happy, since our mother seemed pleased to have a man handling the farm chores once again." Her voice lowered. "It was hard on all of us after our father died." She paused, considering how much to say. "One day Hoag hired a drifter to help with the chores. Things seemed to change shortly after that. Hoag became angry and suspicious. And, it turns out, with good reason."

She glanced over at Sam. "With no warning, our mother ran off with the farmhand. Hoag said that's what came of trusting a stranger."

"I'm sorry. Did Hoag try to go after your mother to change her mind?"

"Oh yes. He went off in a high temper, and was gone all night. When he returned, he said nobody had seen Mother or the farmhand. He alerted the authorities, but there's never been a single report of them anywhere."

"Didn't your mother leave any clues that she was leaving?"

"None." Mary Catherine shook her head. "Even now I find it so hard to believe. It just wasn't in my mother's nature to do such a thing. She was devoted to us and to this home. Oh, she may have thought of leaving Hoag a time or two. They'd had their arguments. Sometimes really heated." Her voice lowered. "You've had a taste of his temper."

Sam nodded.

"When I told him that Mother wasn't the

type of woman who would run off in the night, he reminded me that there are dark, secret places within each of us."

Sam would know a thing or two about that. "But to leave two daughters." He fell silent before saying, "Did she show any sign of depression?"

Now where did that come from? It galled him to realize that after all his time in counseling, he was beginning to sound like Dr. Kresge.

"Oh, no. Even when she and Hoag fought, she was always sweet and gentle and forgiving. And though life here was hard, she was devoted to Anna and me."

"Have you never heard from her since she left?"

Mary Catherine sighed. "Not a word. Not a card or letter. It was especially hard because it altered all our lives forever. At the time she ran away I'd been planning to leave home to take a job in town."

"Doing what?"

Again that sweet animation in her eyes. "There was a lovely inn where I'd agreed to oversee the housekeeping. It was what I'd dreamed of. A job that would satisfy my love of keeping house, and a chance to be on my own." The sadness returned to her eyes and her voice. "But with my mother gone, I wasn't able to leave. As Hoag pointed out, Anna needed me."

"Was there no one who could help? A relative? A housekeeper?"

Mary Catherine nodded. "I suggested that Hoag hire a housekeeper from one of the neighboring farms, but he said he'd never again allow a stranger in his house. He accused me of being selfish for wanting to spend his hard-earned money on hired help when I was perfectly capable of doing the job myself. He said only a spoiled, pampered princess would put her own future ahead of the family's comfort."

"Anna seems old enough to get along without you now."

Mary Catherine paused, and Sam could see her carefully considering before she decided to take him into her confidence. "For some time now Anna and I have been making plans to talk to Hoag. We're hoping he'll give his consent for us to move to town together."

"What will you do there?"

Mary Catherine looked away. "I'll find a job. And Anna can live with me and get the art classes she's been desperately wanting. Until now Hoag has insisted that she learn her lessons here at home. But I can't teach her what she needs to know. I'm not an artist. She's gone beyond my knowledge. Besides, she deserves to be with others her own age."

Sam folded the damp towel over the edge of the sink. "As I understand it, you're of legal age and still waiting for your stepfather to give his permission for you to leave?"

"I know it seems silly. He's . . . overly protective."

"Or controlling."

She nodded. "I know it has to do with the fact that my mother left him. But I've stayed on as long as I can. Certainly longer than I'd planned. It's time for me to move ahead with my life."

*It's time for you to move ahead with your life, Hunter.*

Sam brushed aside the chill that raced up his spine. "And if he refuses to give his permission?"

She stared down at the floor. "I could always do as my mother did, I suppose, though I'd rather leave with his blessing. I'd actually planned on talking to him tonight."

"Maybe it would be better to wait until the storm passes and I'm gone. He didn't seem happy with the fact that he had to put up a stranger for the night. Now that you've explained the situation, I understand a little better what he's going through."

She touched his arm. Just a touch, but he felt the heat rush through his veins as though she'd lit a match to his blood. "I'm sorry you had to see that side of him, Sam. But he'd be the first to tell you that his bark is much worse than his bite."

Sam looked down into her face and couldn't help but smile. There was a sweetness, a goodness in her that called to him. "If you say so."

What was wrong with him? He'd only just met this woman and right now, this very moment, he had an almost overpowering urge to hold her. To kiss her. A single touch from her and he was burning for more.

"Well now." With effort he stepped back from the heat that shimmered between them, determined to keep his distance. "If you'll show me where those sheets are, I'll make up my bed."

"Of course. You have to be exhausted. Why don't you fetch the afghan from the parlor while I get some sheets?"

She climbed the stairs and returned with an armload of bed linens.

Leading the way to a small room off the kitchen, she proceeded to help make up the bed. She stood on one side, he on the other. As they smoothed the sheets and added the warm afghan, they glanced across the space and shared a smile.

"This is nice." Mary Catherine gave a sigh. "Isn't it odd that it seems so easy, so natural, to be working this way together? As though we've been doing it all our lives." She shot him a questioning glance. "Do you feel it, too, Sam?"

"Yeah." And though he couldn't deny it, it puzzled him. He'd always been a loner. He liked it that way. For all his adult life he'd avoided relationships. It certainly made life easier, as he'd been told dozens of times by his fellow cops. The toughest part of their jobs was soothing the very real fears of their wives and children. He had no such problems to deal with. No one to worry over him, to fuss over him, to complicate his life.

"Do you believe in fate, Sam?" Her words were little more than a whisper.

"Sorry, I've always just believed in myself."

"And the things that happen in your life? Are they all mere accidents?"

"They are what they are. We make choices, and live with the consequences." Hadn't he said that very thing to the shrink?

*"If I'd been a second quicker. If I'd taken out that bastard before he could aim his gun, we wouldn't be having this conversation. Now, I just have to live with my mistake. And, no mat-*

297

ter how you try to spin the facts, it was my mistake that cost my partner his life."

Mary Catherine stared at the floor. "I've always believed that everything that happens is just one tiny piece of some great unknown plan."

"When do you get to see the whole picture? Or is that some grand, mystical secret of the universe that has to be kept from mere mortals?"

She glanced up. "I believe you're laughing at me."

He shook his head. "I don't mean to. But I can't buy into the theory that we're nothing more than puppets on strings being moved by some cosmic puppeteer."

"Such fine, big words. You make it all seem silly. But it's the truth, Sam. Life is never a straight, smooth road. It's marked with ruts and twists and turns, with no way of seeing what's up ahead."

"I see there's a temper beneath all that gentle charm." He enjoyed the quick flash of anger that came and went in her eyes and wondered at the things he was feeling. This strange female had him thinking about her in his arms. Lying with him in this bed, lighting his fire. And what a bonfire they could ignite.

Which of her moods would win out?

Solemn or sweet? Temper or humor? The woman intrigued him. She tempted him.

She was trouble.

He was the first to break the silence. "Thanks again for the hospitality. After all I've been through, I'm sure I'll have no trouble falling asleep."

She paused beside him, and once again touched a hand to his arm. "I'm sorry if I've been rambling on about my belief in the fates. It's been such a long time since I've had anyone to talk to."

"You're easy to listen to, Mary Catherine." Despite his weariness, his body reacted in a purely masculine way to her touch, and he had to struggle to bank the sudden surge of desire that raced through his veins. "Even though we agree to disagree, I'm glad you felt comfortable enough to take me into your confidence."

He was feeling smug about keeping the conversation light. In another second she'd be gone, and he could get his testosterone under control.

"Good night, then, Sam." She lifted her face and smiled up at him, her mouth mere inches from his.

That was his undoing. That and the fact that her eyes held an invitation that was impossible to resist.

"Good night, Mary Catherine." Without a thought to the consequences, he lowered his head and brushed her lips with his.

He saw the sudden slash of lightning outside the window moments before a crash of thunder shook the very foundation of the farmhouse. The storm outside seemed to match the storm being waged within him.

Startled, Mary Catherine clutched his waist. His arms came around her, pinning her to the length of him. He'd intended to merely hold her, but the minute they came together, mouths fused, bodies straining, they were lost.

"Stay with me." The words were out of Sam's mouth before he'd even given them a thought. "Come to bed with me, Mary Catherine."

There had been plenty of women in his life. Too many to count. But he had never in his life had anyone affect him like this. The touch of her, so clean and fresh, the feel of her, soft and pliant in his arms, had his brain scrambled and his blood so hot he wondered that he didn't burn to ash.

"I . . . Oh, Sam. If only I could."

There was another heart-stopping crash, and Sam tightened his hold on her.

This time it wasn't thunder. On a rush of cold air, Hoag stomped into the kitchen and strode across the floor until he stood in the open doorway of the little room.

His voice was a roar of absolute fury. "I should have known better than to leave you alone with this stranger. The apple never falls far from the tree. Damn you to hell, woman. You're just like her."

# THREE

Mary Catherine's head came up sharply. She pulled away from Sam with a guilty look before facing her stepfather. "We didn't plan on this happening. It just . . . did."

"Do I look like a fool?"

Sam stepped in front of Mary Catherine, shielding her with his body, hoping to give her time to compose herself. "I apologize, Hoag. This was entirely my fault."

Hoag's arm snaked out and caught his stepdaughter by the wrist, tugging her away from Sam and shoving her roughly through the open doorway. "Go up to your room."

"But, Hoag . . ."

"Now, woman." He turned to Anna, who stood wide-eyed by the back door. "You, too, girl. Get."

The two young women hurried up the stairs.

At the sound of their doors closing, Hoag turned back to Sam. "I'd put you out now, but you'd never make it the thirty or more miles to town in this storm. Not that I'd care if you froze to death. Good riddance, I say. I want you gone at first light, do you hear?"

Sam nodded.

Without another word the old man turned and stormed up the stairs.

Sam closed the door to the tiny room and jammed his hands in his pockets before turning to stare morosely at the sleet falling outside the window. The sound of it, like knives being flung against the pane, set his teeth on edge. He had the feeling that his entire life was unraveling, and he could do nothing more than stand by and helplessly watch.

What was he doing here? Of all the places he could have landed in a storm, why had he settled for this miserable, gloomy farm?

"Fool. Look at you," he muttered. "Career in the toilet. Change of scenery nothing more than a nightmare. A lost reservation, a freak accident, an isolated farmhouse, and an old man with an explosive temper. Could it get any worse?"

And then there was Mary Catherine. Had she bewitched him? It was the only explanation he could come up with. He didn't believe in love at first sight. Didn't believe that a single kiss from a pretty woman could make him lose all common sense. But there it was. One kiss and he'd been lost and ready to make a fool of himself. And for what? In the morning he'd be sent packing and she'd be left to face her stepfather's wrath. There was no way the old man would let her go off to town now. Sam knew that his reckless behavior had just killed whatever chance she'd had of starting over.

Starting over.

Wasn't that what this trip had been about? A chance for him to have a new life, in a new place, where nobody knew about him and the tragedy that marked his past.

And now his bad luck had rubbed off on this innocent young woman.

He turned away from the icy view outside the window and kicked off his damp shoes before stretching out on the bed. After all he'd been through, he expected to fall asleep instantly. Instead, the events of this strange day played over and over in his mind, keeping sleep just out of reach.

Sam lay in that twilight state between sleep and wakefulness, when he became aware of someone moving about in the dark. He sat up, and saw a woman standing beside the window, staring out at the rain and sleet.

"Mary Catherine?"

At the sound of his voice she turned her head. Her hair was long and dark, her body slim. But though she resembled Mary Catherine, he knew instinctively that this woman was a stranger to him.

"What do you want?" He started to get out of bed but she held out a hand, palm outstretched, and he sank down on the edge of the mattress. He blinked. "Aren't you the woman I saw on the road? The one who caused my accident?"

She gave him a mysterious smile.

"You think it's funny that I was nearly killed?"

She moved closer and he scrambled to his feet, hoping to use his height to intimidate her.

"You were never in danger." She reached a hand to his cheek and he jerked back when he felt something cool and misty brush his skin.

His eyes narrowed. "Who are you?"

Her gaze remained fixed on him. "You'll soon know who I am."

"Sorry. I'm not a mind reader. Now tell me what this is all about."

"I chose you as the witness."

"Witness to what?"

"To what you know best." In the blink of

an eye she seemed to glide across the room to stare once more at the falling sleet.

"Look. I don't know what kind of a trick this is but . . ." He started toward her, but she disappeared from view. One instant she was there, the next she was simply gone.

He felt a rush of cold, damp air. When he peered through the window he thought he saw a shadowy figure drifting across the icy patch of lawn. But that was impossible. She'd been here. Right here.

Now there was nothing. Only the sound of the icy rain against the windowpane.

Sam didn't believe in ghosts or otherworldly things. He was a cop. Trained to believe in facts. In things he could touch or taste or see. Yet he had absolutely no explanation for what he'd just seen and heard and felt. He touched a finger to his cheek.

He did know one thing. He believed in evil. And he sensed it in this place.

He thought about leaving. Now. While the rest of the household slept.

But that spooky woman's words were playing with his mind. A witness? Witness to what?

What a sick joke. Some witness he'd make. Just ask his partner.

Vince.

The pain was almost more than he could

bear. He pressed his fingers to his temples to ease the throbbing and tried to think about something to get his mind off his troubles.

At once a name came to mind: Mary Catherine.

He'd stay until morning. But not because of this creepy nighttime visitor. There was another, more important reason to stay.

Mary Catherine.

She was playing with his mind, too. Though he knew he had no hope of any future with her, he wasn't quite ready to walk away. He could still taste her. Could still feel her body pressed to his.

Dear God, right this minute he wanted her desperately.

He stretched out on the bed, eyes wide open, ears attuned to any sound. He lay that way for what seemed hours. Sometime before dawn, sleep finally overtook him.

Sam woke to morning sounds and smells. Booted feet stomping in from the barn, then out again. A heavy pail being set on the kitchen floor. Voices calling. Meat sizzling in a skillet. The wonderful aroma of cinnamon rolls being lifted from the oven.

Itching for a shave and a shower, Sam ran a hand over the stubble on his cheeks and chin before slipping into his shoes. At least they were dry, as were the clothes he'd slept in.

He opened the door, prepared to face Hoag's wrath. Instead, there was only Anna in the kitchen.

She looked up from the stove. "Good morning."

" 'Morning." Sam glanced around. "Where are your stepfather and sister?"

"Out in the barn. Mary Catherine left me to keep a watch on her biscuits while she helped Hoag with the chores."

Sam stared out the window. The countryside had become an ice palace. Every square inch of ground was sheeted with it. And still it fell, coating everything, making even the short walk from the house to the barn a dangerous undertaking. He saw a rope stretched from the back porch to the barn. Obviously intended to keep them upright while maneuvering across the ice.

How in hell was he supposed to get away from here now?

"Would you like some coffee, Sam?"

He pulled himself back from his bleak thoughts. "Yes, thanks. I'll get it." He crossed to the stove and filled a cup before glancing over. "Would you like some?"

Anna shook her head. "I prefer tea." She

picked up a pretty cup and sipped, regarding him over the rim. "You're going to take Mary Catherine with you when you leave, aren't you?"

He nearly choked on the scalding coffee. "Now what makes you think I'd do such a thing?"

She gave a knowing smile. "I saw the two of you last night. That didn't look like a friendly peck on the cheek."

Sam managed a laugh. "Just how old are you, anyhow? What would you know about kissing?"

"I'm not a baby. I'm sixteen. I may not know as much as I'd like, but I do know about my sister. She loves you, Sam."

"Love." He gave a wry laugh. "She doesn't even know me. We just met yesterday."

Anna saw the barn door open, and Hoag step gingerly on the ice-slicked ground before grabbing hold of the rope.

She began to speak faster. "The minute my sister saw you, she changed. She knows you're the one."

"The one?" His hand holding the cup paused in midair.

"The one she's been waiting for."

"Is this something she told you?"

"She didn't need to tell me." Anna looked at him and Sam felt his heart do a slow, strange dip. This girl had the oldest eyes he'd ever looked into. Old and wise and so very sad. Like the eyes of the visitor he'd had earlier. Or had he only dreamed her?

"I know my sister. She's made up her mind. Just like Mama. She's going to go with you when you leave, Sam."

The door opened on a rush of cold air and Hoag stepped inside, followed by Mary Catherine. When she spotted Sam she flushed and looked away. Hoag merely glowered and pushed past Sam without a word.

He turned to his younger daughter. "Breakfast had better be ready, girl."

"It is." Anna took the basket of eggs from her sister's hand and began breaking them into a sizzling skillet. "I didn't let the biscuits burn. They're perfect."

Mary Catherine tousled her hair. "Thanks. So are you."

The two sisters shared a nervous laugh and within minutes began to carry plates of meat and eggs and potatoes to the table.

Hoag sat in his usual place at the head of the table, and his stony silence left no doubt that he had no intention of inviting Sam to join them.

Mary Catherine glanced over her shoulder. "Sit down, Sam."

"No thanks. I'm not hungry. I'll take my coffee out to the porch."

He opened the back door and stepped outside, where he was instantly buffeted by a blast of icy wind.

He stared around, trying to get his bearings. He could see the fallen pole where he'd tripped. It was deeply embedded in ice. Far below the hill he thought he could make out the ribbon of road, though it, too, was covered with ice. How far away was his car? Not that it mattered. There would be no way to get it out of that ditch without a tow truck. And by now his cell phone, buried somewhere under a coating of ice, would at minimum need to be recharged. Even if he had his phone, and it worked, who could he call in this desolate place?

He sipped his coffee and tried to remind himself that civilization was just miles away. But it may as well have been at the end of the earth. He'd never felt as isolated as he did at this minute.

The door opened and Hoag pushed past him. "When the storm lets up, I want you gone."

"That's the plan."

Sam watched as Hoag grabbed the rope and made his way to the barn. Sam continued watching until the old man disappeared inside.

Mary Catherine stepped onto the porch with the afghan wrapped around her shoulders. She lifted a corner of it. "Want to share?"

"Thanks." Sam huddled close and held onto the edge, before offering his cup. "Want some coffee?"

"Thanks." She sipped, then handed it back. "Come inside, Sam. Hoag will be busy in the barn for hours."

"I think it's better if I stay out here."

She glanced at him in surprise.

He grinned. "What I mean is it'll be safer for you if I stay outside."

"And what if I don't want to be safe?"

His smile fled. "Don't say that. You don't want to tempt your stepfather's temper."

She shot him a puzzled look. "What's wrong, Sam?"

He shook his head. "I don't know. I . . . had a visitor last night."

"A visitor? In this storm?" She touched a hand to his forehead. "You're a little feverish. I suppose that would explain it."

"I didn't imagine it. I wasn't hallucinating. At least I don't think so."

She smiled, the way a nurse would smile

at a very ill patient. "Tell me about this visitor."

"She looked like you. She told me I was here to be a witness."

"What are you supposed to be witnessing?"

"She didn't say. Only that I would do what I do best."

"What do you do best?"

"At the moment I can't think of a thing. I've never felt more useless."

"Did this visitor tell you her name?"

"She said I know her."

"And do you?"

He stared down into her eyes. "I'm not sure." He leaned closer. "Right now, I'm not sure of anything except this." He brushed his mouth over hers and absorbed the jolt of pure sexual pleasure. Even though he'd tried to prepare himself, it caught him by surprise. Against her mouth he whispered, "What have you done to me?"

"I was about to ask you the same. I know you must think me a wicked woman, but I swear to you I've never known feelings like these before, Sam."

"Feelings?"

"As though we were meant to meet. As though our lives are somehow intertwined. Don't you feel it, too?"

Something flickered across his face before he composed his features. He didn't like this. Any of it. "Look, Mary Catherine. No matter what we feel, you have to understand that we can't act on it." He caught a strand of her hair, whipped by the wind, and watched as it sifted through his fingers. "We're two calm, sensible adults. We know better than to act on our impulses."

"You mean the way my mother did."

"I didn't say that. You're not your mother, Mary Catherine."

"But I'm like her. I have her dark hair and blue eyes. I love the things she loved." Her voice lowered. "And now, suddenly, I'm afraid of my stepfather's anger."

"Was she?"

Mary Catherine nodded. "Just before she disappeared, she told me that she was afraid."

"Of him?"

"She didn't say. But now, seeing him like this, I remember how he was just before she disappeared. His temper would explode over the simplest thing. And when it did, there was no telling what he might do."

Like kill a wife who was attracted to a stranger? Sam thought of Belski's warning. Typical cop's reaction. He tried to brush it aside, but it was there, gnawing at the edges of his mind.

Hadn't he seen the fury in the old man's eyes last night? Was it enough to drive Hoag Slade to kill?

"When this storm lets up and I'm able to leave, would you and Anna like to go with me?"

"Don't say that, Sam. Don't even think it. He'll never allow it."

"You're old enough to make your own decisions. He can't stop you."

"But he can insist that Anna stay. She's only sixteen." Mary Catherine blinked back tears. "I could never leave her alone with him. I guess I've known that all along. I kept making plans to leave, but they were just silly dreams. Until he gives Anna permission to go with me, I know in my heart I'll never leave here."

"Are you willing to sacrifice a few more years of your life just to keep her safe?"

"Wouldn't you?"

Sam had no need to reply. The bleak look in his eyes said it all.

Mary Catherine drew the afghan around her shoulders and stepped away. "It's time I got started on the day's chores."

She walked inside, leaving Sam standing alone in the bitter wind and sleet. The frozen countryside matched the sudden chill around his heart.

# FOUR

"Sam." Anna looked up from the stove when he stepped in from the porch. "Mary Catherine asked me to save you some breakfast."

"I'm not hungry." Sam glanced around the empty kitchen. "Where are the others?"

"Hoag will no doubt spend the day in the barn." Ignoring his protest, the girl set a plate of eggs and potatoes and crisp bacon on the table and indicated the chair. "As he always likes to say, not even a storm can stop the need for farm chores."

"Hoag doesn't seem bothered by the chores."

"Mama used to say he embraces them because it gives him an excuse to be alone. She suspected that he loved this farm more than he loved her."

"What do you think?"

"I think Mama was right." Anna poured a fresh cup of coffee and set it in front of

Sam, pleased when he sat and began to eat.

"Where's your sister?"

"Mary Catherine went down to the cellar to dig up some vegetables to make soup for tonight's supper."

Homemade soup. Sam doubted he'd ever tasted it. Even the restaurants that claimed to have homemade actually bought most of the ingredients from vendors. "Your sister told me she enjoys keeping house."

Anna nodded. "She's like our mother." The young girl looked away, studying the sleet against the window. "I wish she weren't."

"What a strange thing to say." Sam paused, fork in midair.

"You'd understand if you knew what happened to our mother."

"Mary Catherine told me she ran off with a stranger."

"She told you?"

He gave a barely perceptible nod of his head.

"And now you're here." She gave a long, deep sigh. "And it's happening all over again."

"Anna, Mary Catherine isn't your mother. And I'm not the hired help."

"So you say. But it's just like before. The longer you stay here, the angrier Hoag will get. You need to go now before . . ." Anna shivered and fell silent.

Sam looked up. "Before what?"

"Something bad is going to happen."

"How do you know?"

"I don't know how I know, I just do."

Sam shoved aside his plate, his appetite gone. It was this storm, he knew. It was getting to him. To Anna. To all of them.

He deliberately kept his tone light. "I know that Mary Catherine enjoys keeping house. How about you? What do you like best, Anna?"

"I like to draw." She gave him a sad smile. "Mary Catherine says I'm like our uncle, our dad's brother, who lives in Boston. He's an artist."

"Is he good?"

"Really good."

"What does he think of your work?"

She shrugged. "He's hasn't seen it in years. He stopped coming around after our mother married Hoag. I guess he didn't approve. He stopped writing to Mama. But when I was younger he used to bring me paints and canvas and encourage my talent."

"Do you have any of your paintings?"

She looked down. "I keep a few hidden.

319

Hoag doesn't want them cluttering up the house."

"I take it he doesn't approve of your talent."

"He said it's vanity to think I have talent."

"There's nothing wrong with taking pride in your work."

"You don't think I'm vain?"

Sam gave her a gentle smile. "I think you're a fine young woman. I'd love to see some of your paintings. As for Hoag, he ought to be proud of you and your sister."

"He finds fault with everything we do."

"That sounds to me like a very angry man."

"He is. I suppose he has a right to be." She lifted pleading eyes to Sam. "He's especially angry that you're here. You need to leave. Soon."

"What about you and Mary Catherine?"

"I'm going to leave this farm whenever I get the chance."

Sam decided to humor her. "Where will you go?"

"To New York. London. Paris. Rome."

"What will you do there?"

"Paint. And show my paintings to people who will appreciate them."

"That's a fine goal. What about Mary Catherine?"

Her voice took on a note of fear. "I worry about my sister." She shook her head. "Something is going to happen. I feel it."

Something in her tone had Sam standing and heading toward the little room off the kitchen. Inside he paced, mulling the girl's words, and those of his nighttime visitor. If, in fact, he'd actually had a visitor. With all that had happened, he was ready to accept Dr. Kresge's explanation of the recurring dream. That scene last night could well have been an extension of it. Isn't that what all the experts had said? He'd suffered an extreme trauma. His mind was searching for a way to deal with it.

But that didn't explain what was happening here and now. He could feel the hostility from Hoag Slade, and could even understand it. He hadn't exactly conducted himself like a gentleman in the old man's house. And that was another issue. He was puzzled by the depth of feeling he had for Mary Catherine. It was true that she was beautiful, but so were dozens of other women who had been in and out of his life. Yet he couldn't recall a single time when he'd felt completely taken over by passion.

He was out of his element. As though his emotions were dangerously out of control and taking him down a path he wouldn't normally choose.

He wasn't alone in those feelings. Mary Catherine obviously returned his passion. And Anna had made it plain that she knew what her sister was feeling.

If Anna could sense it, so could Hoag. A dangerous thing for a man with a history like Hoag's. After being abandoned by his wife, he had a right to be wary of strangers.

Sam crossed the room and stared dejectedly at the icy world outside the window. For now he had no choice but to stay. Since Hoag was occupied in the barn, he would look around the house and find some work. He'd always liked to putter around his apartment. There must be something here that required his attention.

"Thinking about Sam?" Anna paused in the doorway of the bedroom she shared with her older sister.

Mary Catherine turned from the window with a guilty look. "Is it so obvious?"

The younger girl sighed. "I can't remember the last time I saw you staring out the window in the middle of the day, looking completely lost and confused."

"Am I that transparent?"

Anna crossed the room to catch her sister's hand. "It's just that I know you so well."

Mary Catherine sighed. "I wish I did."

"What's that supposed to mean?"

The young woman sat on the edge of her bed and studied her hands. "I've never felt like this before. All hot and cold and nervous as a cat in a room full of snarling dogs."

Anna saw the misery on her sister's face and dropped down on the edge of the bed beside her. "Are you saying that this is how Sam makes you feel?"

"Not Sam. But the feelings I have for him. This is all too sudden. I don't know what to do about what I'm feeling."

"What do you want to do?"

Mary Catherine looked over, her cheeks pink. "I'm not sure I can say it out loud."

Anna wrapped an arm across her sister's shoulders and rubbed her cheek to hers. "Oh, Mary Catherine. You don't need to say a thing. It's there on your face. In the way your mouth curves whenever Sam speaks to you. In the way your cheeks go all pink whenever Sam looks at you. And the way your eyes go all soft and dreamy whenever you look at Sam."

"Am I wicked?"

"You could never be wicked. But you need to take care. Think about Mama."

"I'm not Mama." Mary Catherine pulled away and studied her younger sister's face. "I know I'm like her in many ways. But I'm not going to run off and abandon you."

"You once said that about Mama. And look what happened. In all this time, she's never once tried to contact us. Why?" Anna's face crumpled, and tears filled her eyes. "How could she just run off and leave us without a word?"

"I don't know." Mary Catherine stood and gathered her younger sister into her arms. Against her cheek she whispered, "I don't know why she left, baby."

The two young women remained locked in one another's embrace, tears falling silently.

It was Mary Catherine who finally drew away a little. "But I know this. Mama loved us, Anna. She would contact us if she could."

"Then why hasn't she? Do you think she's afraid of Hoag's temper?"

Mary Catherine shrugged. "What other reason would she have for staying away so long?"

"She could be hurt or lost or . . ."

"Shhh." Mary Catherine stilled her sister's words with a finger to her lips. "We've been over this so many times. I can't bear to think about Mama being lost or . . . hurt. You just have to let it go, Anna."

"But I'm afraid. There's another stranger here, and I see the way you look at him."

When her sister opened her mouth to protest, Anna stopped her. "I know what I see, Mary Catherine. You have the look of a woman in love."

Mary Catherine sank back down on the edge of the bed and buried her face in her hands. "I've tried so hard, but I can't help what I feel."

Anna sighed. "I knew it. Have you told Sam?"

"I wouldn't dare. We've only met. It would be too bold of me. Besides, what if he doesn't feel the same way?"

"I guess you'll never know unless you ask him."

Mary Catherine clapped a hand to her mouth. "I couldn't."

"All right. Then just wait until the storm passes and let him leave, without ever knowing how you feel."

"You're thinking that's what Mama should have done, aren't you?"

The two sisters fell silent.

"I suppose I could . . . show Sam how I feel."

"Now who's talking about being bold?"

Mary Catherine swallowed. "It's just talk. I could never do it. How would I feel if he rejected my . . . advances?"

"It would hurt. But at least you'd have your answer." Anna squeezed her sister's hands. "If you want my opinion, Sam Hunter isn't the type of man to lead a woman on. If he returned your advances, it would be because you matter to him. Of course," she added, "if that were the case, he would want you to leave here with him when he goes."

"Without you?" Mary Catherine caught her younger sister's hand. "You know I could never do that. I'll never leave you alone here with Hoag, Anna."

"That's what Mama said."

"When?"

"Just before she left. She gave me her word."

"You never told me." Mary Catherine blinked back tears. "I'm not Mama."

"I know." Anna kissed her sister's cheek. "Why don't you go downstairs and start that soup."

Mary Catherine drew a little away and studied her younger sister's face. "What about you?"

"I'll tidy up our room. Go." Anna shooed her toward the doorway.

When her sister was gone, the younger girl walked to the window and stared at the storm. It was growing worse out there. And it mirrored the storm brewing in this household.

Anna frowned. She hadn't been completely honest with her sister. She was afraid. Not for herself, but for Mary Catherine.

Anna saw things that others didn't. Dark, frightening images that didn't make sense. But though she didn't know exactly what they meant, she sensed danger. She'd had visions just before Mama vanished. Dark, haunting nightmares that had left her trembling in the night.

She'd seen blood, and heard cries of terror and howls of rage. Black, blinding rage.

And now all those nightmarish visions were back.

# FIVE

"Oh, Sam. You've fixed it." Mary Catherine paused with her hand on the doorknob. "It's been loose for months. Hoag kept saying he'd get around to fixing it one of these days. But he claims that the farm chores take all his time and energy, even though Anna and I know the truth. He'd rather spend all his time in the fields than see to anything in the house."

"Just needed a couple of screws." Sam tucked the screwdriver into the ancient tool belt he'd found hanging from a nail on the porch. "I think I can get rid of that squeak on the bottom stair, too."

"Oh, that would be grand." She gave him a smile that was bright enough to melt all the ice that had fallen outside the window. Just seeing it had his heart feeling lighter. He'd been wise to handle a few household chores.

She watched the muscles of his back and

shoulders bunch and tighten as he knelt at the bottom of the staircase and began to gently pry at the warped board. Why did the sight of him affect her this way? "I had no idea you were so handy."

"I need to do something to pay you back for your hospitality." He struggled to keep his mind off her and on the business at hand as he sanded the wood smooth. Satisfied, he glued the strip of board until it was level with the others, before adding several screws to make it solid.

"Let's see if that worked." He indicated the stair and Mary Catherine stepped up.

"No squeak." She saw her little sister watching from the top of the stairs and gave a laugh. "Now Hoag won't be able to hear you when you sneak into the kitchen late at night for a last cookie or piece of chocolate cake."

"Really?" Anna hurriedly joined her sister on the stair and the two began to giggle as they danced up and down without hearing the annoying squeak.

"This is great." Anna looked at Mary Catherine. "Why don't you have Sam fix that drawer in your bureau? You've been complaining for years about the way it sticks whenever you use it."

Mary Catherine glanced over. "Would you

mind doing it, Sam?"

"I'm happy to." He tucked away the hammer. "If you find me some sandpaper and a little oil, I ought to have it working as good as new in no time."

Mary Catherine sailed out of the room and returned minutes later with the things Sam had asked for.

"Follow me." She led the way up the stairs to the bedroom.

Sam took his time looking around, more than a little curious to see where she and her sister slept.

Like the rest of the house, the bedroom was spotless. The dark wood of the floor was brightened by an oval braided rug. Two small four-poster beds stood on opposite sides of the room, covered by handmade quilts. Pretty embroidered pillowcases covered the mound of pillows resting against each headboard. A stone fireplace ran the length of one wall. On the hearth stood a stack of firewood.

Anna crossed the room and opened a closet door before holding something behind her.

Sam glanced over. "What've you got there?"

She blushed as she turned to reveal her painting. The face staring back at him from the crudely framed canvas was Mary Catherine's. It was so perfect, so lifelike, all he could do was stare.

Anna's mouth turned into a pretty little pout. "You don't like it."

"Is that what you think?" He stepped closer. "Anna, I love it. You have an amazing talent."

At that the girl dimpled. "I'm so glad you think so. Of all my work, this is my favorite."

"If you can do this, with no lessons at all, think what you could do if you took some art classes."

"Oh, wouldn't that be grand?" She glanced at her sister, then away. "Maybe someday." She started out of the room, then paused and looked back. "I think I'll hide this down in the cellar. Just in case."

When she was gone Sam looked at Mary Catherine. "In case of what?"

She shrugged. "Hoag hates her paintings. He says she sets too much store by them."

"She has a right to be proud of her work. I wasn't just trying to flatter her. She has real talent."

"I wish Hoag would agree. When he found the last of her paintings, he tossed them in the fire. She was in tears for days."

Sam had to bite down hard on the oath that sprang to mind. He couldn't wait to get away from Hoag Slade and his vile temper for good. Considering that he'd only been here since yesterday, he wondered how these two sisters could stand living here day after endless day with such a man.

Needing an outlet for his frustration he pointed to the dresser. "You'll need to empty the drawer."

Mary Catherine worked quickly to remove the contents, and Sam was aware of the delicate underthings she was trying to conceal as she carried them to her bed.

If she were any other girl, he'd have teased her about her extreme modesty. But with Mary Catherine it seemed the most natural thing in the world. He decided to keep his jokes to himself.

When it was empty Sam slid the drawer out and carried it downstairs to the kitchen table. Covering the table with an old cloth, he carefully sanded the wood until it was smooth. An hour later he returned the drawer to her room. After testing to make certain it opened and closed easily, he gave her a smile. "Anything else that needs my attention?"

"Only one thing I can think of." With a little cat smile Mary Catherine sidled up beside him and slid her hand along his arm.

He knew she could feel the tension in him

as she brought her hand to his shoulder, and then to his neck. His voice was gruff. "Don't play with me, Mary Catherine."

"I'm not playing, Sam."

"The hell you're not." He caught her hand, his eyes fierce. "You know Hoag's temper. What you don't know enough about is me. I'm not some neighboring farm boy who'll be satisfied with a few stolen kisses. You may have lived a sheltered life out here, but you're smart enough to know you're a woman. And I'm a man. Don't play with fire, Mary Catherine, or we're both apt to get burned."

At his outburst a mix of emotions crossed her face. Surprise. Embarrassment. And then, slowly, a hint of a sly smile. "I can't think of a nicer way to die. Can you, Sam?"

He'd had every intention of ordering her to back off. To use his best cop voice to keep the situation from getting out of control. But her lips were already brushing his, her breath mingling with his until all he could taste was her. It was as potent as any drug.

He kept his eyes steady on hers as he dragged her against him and savaged her mouth.

If he'd thought to frighten her, he was mistaken. This was all the invitation she needed. She wrapped her arms around him

333

and held on tightly as he took them both on a wild ride.

He could hear the hum of excitement in her throat as his mouth left hers to explore the soft hollow between her neck and shoulder. Her head fell back, giving him easier access.

"Mary Catherine, you know this is madness."

His words, whispered against her throat, had her shivering.

"I don't care, Sam." She caught his face between her hands and brought her mouth to his. "I don't care about anything except you. Except this."

He knew they were crossing a line, but it no longer mattered. There was a demon inside him demanding that he take what she offered. Here. Now. And to hell with the consequences.

He kissed her long and slow and deep, before pressing his mouth to her throat. His lips burned a trail of fire to her breast and he felt her tremble and sigh. It only inflamed him more as he drove her back against the wall. Her body was so deeply imprinted on his he could feel her in every part of his being. His body, mind, heart, soul.

His woman, he thought fiercely. His. Hadn't he known since he'd first seen her?

"Sam . . ." At her cry his head came up and he struggled for breath.

He saw the stricken look on her face an instant before he heard Hoag's voice bellowing from the doorway.

"Again? And in her very room?"

"Hoag." Mary Catherine struggled to calm her ragged breathing. "This was my . . ."

Sam turned, silencing her as he thrust her behind him. "I'm sorry, Hoag. I realize that I have no right. But your daughter means the world to me."

"The world, is it?" The older man's hands were fisted at his sides. The fire in his eyes gleamed hotly. "Let's see how you like the world beyond these walls. You'll leave now."

"Hoag, the storm . . ." Mary Catherine's words died at the look in his eyes.

"Now!" Hoag shouted. "If this is the way you repay our hospitality, you've no one to blame but yourself for being turned out in this storm. Go. And I hope to hell you freeze to death."

Without a word Sam turned and touched a hand to Mary Catherine's cheek. Tears spilled from her eyes and he wanted desperately to comfort her. Instead he whispered, "I'm sorry. This was my fault. I'll come back for you, when things have calmed down."

"When the storm has calmed? Or Hoag's temper?"

There was no time to reply. He heard the hiss of fury from the man in the doorway and turned away. As he crossed the room and passed Hoag, he could feel the white heat of an out-of-control anger emanating in waves.

Police work had taught Sam to gauge instinctively when a man had reached his limit. Hoag Slade had passed that point long ago, and was now ready to explode. Sam knew that the least little thing could set him off.

As he descended the stairs he saw Anna standing in the kitchen. From the look on the young girl's face, Sam knew she'd heard everything.

"Good-bye, Anna." He stepped into the spare room and retrieved his jacket. "I'm sorry for the way things worked out."

"You'll never survive in this storm." She hurried to the door and clutched his sleeve.

"You, too?" At Hoag's growl of fury Anna looked up.

Her stepfather stood on the stairway, shaking with impotent fury. "You're all alike. You, your sister, your mother. Get away from him, girl. Right now."

"I'll come back for her. For both of you,"

Sam muttered.

"No. Not for me." Anna wiped away a tear. "You'll both leave me."

"Get out!" Hoag's voice was a roar of fury.

Without a backward glance, Sam opened the door and stepped out to the porch.

Hunching deeply into his jacket, he faced into the raging wind and sleet.

Needles of rain laced with shards of ice stung Sam's eyes. Eyes already blinded by the endless glare of the landscape that stretched as far as the eye could see.

He struggled to identify any landmarks that might lead him to the road. Once there, he reasoned, he could follow it to town. If he didn't freeze to death first.

He strained for a glimpse of his car, but all he saw was ice. When he could no longer feel his feet, he forced himself to keep walking anyway.

He knew what it was to keep going against all odds. Hadn't he kept his wits about him when he'd watched his partner take the bullet?

*The bullet meant for me.*

Sam was satisfied that he'd done everything by the book. He'd taken down the punk with a single shot. He could have killed him, but he'd made a conscious decision to disable him until backup arrived. He'd wanted the gunman to pay, not with his life, but with an endless lifetime behind bars.

He'd caught up his fallen comrade. Had cradled Vince in his arms and used his most commanding tone to urge him to hang on and fight.

*"Stay with me, buddy. You have to live. You can't let that bastard win."*

But Vince was beyond fighting.

Was that when Sam had started down that slippery slope of guilt and shame?

Shame?

That was a word he hadn't thought of until now. Guilt. Hell, yes. He'd carried around a heavy burden of guilt for the death of his partner. But shame?

He went very still. With the wind howling like a pack of mad dogs and the sleet blinding him, he drew inward and realized that it was, indeed, shame that had been driving him to the very depth of despair. It shamed him that he hadn't been quick enough to see what Vince had planned. It would have been there in his partner's eyes, if only he'd looked. Would have been apparent in the sudden stiffening of his spine as he'd stepped directly in front of Sam. Directly into the line of fire.

And even now it shamed Sam that, though he loved his partner, he'd loved the rules more. Everyone would have forgiven him for bending the rules and killing the man who'd shot his partner, sparing Vince's family the unspeakable horror of a trial.

The reporter who'd filed the lead story had called him a man without emotion. A man so cool that, even in the heat of battle, when most men would have hungered for vengeance, Sam Hunter had calmly disabled the shooter before offering aid and comfort to his fallen comrade. The press had picked up on it and dubbed him The Iceman.

A robot incapable of passion.

What stung the most was that Sam knew it to be true. At least until coming here. He'd spent a lifetime playing carefully by the rules, never letting his emotions get in the way.

Mary Catherine had awakened enough passion for a lifetime.

And look where it got them. He was out in the cold. And she would be forced to endure the wrath of her stepfather's fury alone.

Alone. Without anyone to protect her. Without anyone to witness the punishment Hoag would mete out.

Hadn't his nighttime visitor suggested that

very thing?

*You were never in any danger. I brought you here to be a witness.*

Thunderstruck, he turned directly into the howling storm, determined to retrace his steps to the farmhouse. But with the wind screaming around him, and the sleet biting deeply into his flesh, he had no idea where he was. He could be scant yards from Storm Hill, or miles off course.

He thought he saw the faintest of light flickering up ahead, and despite the fact that he could no longer feel his hands or feet, he forced himself to keep walking.

Was it truly a light or just his imagination? No matter. He had to keep moving, or risk freezing to death.

He nearly bumped into the barn before he realized where he was. Shoving open the door, he stumbled into a plow horse's stall and dropped into the hay.

Warmed by the heat of the animal, he fell into an exhausted sleep.

# Six

Sam heard the scrape of the barn door as it was forced open. Sleet swept in on a rush of wind, beating a tattoo against the walls before the door was pushed closed.

Sitting up in the hay, Sam watched as a lantern was hung on a peg. The slim shadow flitting across the lantern's light had him sighing with relief.

"Mary Catherine." He scrambled to his feet, wondering how long he'd been asleep. There'd been no light in the barn to judge the time of day. It could be daylight, or the middle of the night.

"Sam. Oh, Sam, you're safe." She flew into his arms and hugged him fiercely. Against his throat she muttered, "You'll never know the things I've been thinking. In my mind I could see you lost and alone out there, with nowhere to turn for shelter. I was so afraid. Afraid for you."

Something twisted in his heart. He

341

couldn't remember the last time someone had been afraid for him. Had actually worried about his safety. "I'm used to taking care of myself. I was more concerned about you. I should never have left you alone."

"You had no choice. You've had a taste of Hoag's temper. There was no telling what he might have done if you'd refused to go."

Sam brushed a quick kiss over her lips and absorbed the jolt. "I'm safe now. We're safe. As long as we're together, we're going to be just fine."

Mary Catherine stepped back. "I don't dare linger, or Hoag will be suspicious. I have to get back to the house. I was just coming out here to ready the animals for the night." She picked up a bucket and began filling a trough.

Sam caught her arm. "What can I do?"

"They'll need enough hay and oats to last until morning."

Sam forked hay into each stall, and at her direction, shook oats from a bucket hanging on a peg. That done, he walked with her to the barn door.

She stood on tiptoe to brush a kiss over his mouth. "As soon as I'm sure that Hoag is asleep, I'll come back with food and a warm blanket."

She shoved open the door and stepped

out into the night. On a swirl of stinging, icy raindrops she was gone.

"Did you miss me?" Mary Catherine, afghan draped over her head and shoulders, danced into the barn and quickly closed the door, shutting out the storm.

"I've been missing you for hours."

"Sorry. I had to be certain Hoag was asleep." She tossed aside the blanket and walked to a scarred wooden worktable where she set down a platter covered with a linen towel. "You must be starved. I've brought you beef and biscuits and gravy and . . ."

Sam turned her into his arms and gathered her close, burying his face in her neck. "It's not food I'm hungry for."

He'd had hours to lie in the dark and think of her, only her, and the things he wanted to share with her. Now that she was here in the flesh, he forced himself to move slowly. To touch, to taste, to savor. And so he cupped her face in his hands and pressed slow, soft kisses to her cheeks, her chin, the tip of her nose.

"I'm not sure just when you began to matter so much to me, Mary Catherine. Maybe from the first moment I saw you."

She sighed and he continued raining soft,

wet kisses over her temple, her eyelids, the corners of her mouth.

"I didn't plan any of this. It just happened."

"I know. It was the same for me, Sam." She raised herself on tiptoe to brush his mouth with hers.

That sweet gesture, at once loving and giving, had the blood pumping hot through his veins as he filled himself with the taste of her, the sweet fresh smell of her.

It had been his intention to go slow and easy. But passion had him by the throat. His hands were suddenly rough, almost bruising as they moved over her, burning a path of heat along her spine.

This wasn't his style. Or hadn't been until Mary Catherine. He'd always thought of himself as a patient man, a gentle lover. Now there was a fire simmering inside that had him taking her with him on a wild, dizzying ride.

"I want you, Mary Catherine. Just you. I need you. Now."

"Yes. Oh, yes." She stepped back and began unbuttoning the front of her simple dress, keeping her eyes steady on his. The fabric parted, slipped from her shoulders, and pooled at her feet.

"It's the same for me, Sam." She opened

her arms to him and he dragged her close, kissing her long and slow and deep, until they were both groaning with need.

He tore aside his damp shirt before lowering her to the afghan. And then he was touching her everywhere. Kissing her everywhere. She returned touch for touch, kiss for kiss, until their two hearts were racing, their breathing ragged.

"I've never wanted anything as much as I want you." He wondered that he could speak over the need that had him by the throat, fighting to be free.

"Not nearly as much as I want you. I've been waiting all my life for you, Sam. Just for you."

It was true, she realized. Everything that had happened in her young life had been preparing her for this moment, this man. She'd seen him in her dreams. Tasted him on her tongue whenever she'd opened her mouth to raindrops or snowflakes. And the moment he'd walked through her door, she'd known him. Her heart had responded to him, as well as her soul.

"I didn't realize it until now, but it's the same for me, Mary Catherine. You're the woman I've waited a lifetime to meet. To love."

And then there was no need for words as

they took each other on a wild, dizzying ride, climbing high, then higher still. At the very pinnacle he paused a moment, aware that the beast inside him had slipped beyond his control. He'd wanted to be easy with her, to be gentle, but there was no holding back now.

He looked down into her eyes and could see the fierce emotions that were driving her.

"Don't stop, Sam. Love me. Just love me."

"Mary Catherine."

Whispering her name like a prayer, he drove them both up, up to the very edge of a high, steep precipice. They teetered for a heartbeat before stepping over the edge, waiting for the fall.

Together they soared.

Mary Catherine's tears spilled over, dampening his cheek.

"God, I'm sorry. So sorry." With his face buried in her hair he could feel his heart still racing, his blood still pounding in his temples. "I was rough."

"No. You were wonderful. This was . . ." She sniffed. ". . . incredible."

She tipped his face so that he could see her smile. The sight of it had him settling. His heart, his mind, his soul were suddenly at peace.

"I don't know what's happened to me. Ever since coming here, meeting you, I've been a different man."

"How so?" Her fingers absently played with the thick mat of hair on his chest.

"I've always been . . . careful. Controlled. In fact, my nickname on the force was The Iceman."

"Tell me about yourself, Sam. About your family." She wrapped her arms around his neck. "I want to know everything about you. What you like to eat. What kind of boy you were. The kind of man you've become."

"My father died when I was ten. My mother went back to work as a high school English teacher and told me I needed to be the man of the house. I guess that's the day I left my childhood behind."

"Is your mother still teaching?"

He shook his head. "She had a chance to enjoy retirement in Florida with her sister before she passed on almost five years ago."

"I'm sorry."

He shrugged. "I'm used to being alone."

"What brought you to Vermont?"

"I guess I was hoping to find a simpler way of life. I kept remembering a time during my college days when my heart felt so light at the autumn foliage, and the pastoral setting. A covered bridge. A lovely old inn. Acres of sugar maples."

She was watching him intently. "Why did your heart seek such solace?"

"I was sick and tired of solving crimes of passion and violence." His voice nearly broke. "There was an accident. Someone special died, because of me."

She sat up, her eyes wide. "You caused a death?"

"My partner took a bullet meant for me. He stepped directly in front of me, and before I could stop him, he was gone."

Hearing the pain in those words, she touched a hand to his cheek. "Your partner must have cared deeply for you."

"I'm sure he did."

"Did you care as deeply for him?"

"Of course I did." His voice was gruff with emotion.

"And if you'd been given the chance, would you have taken a bullet for him?"

"Without a moment's hesitation."

She fell silent for a moment. When she spoke, her voice was little more than a whisper. "What a splendid thing for two people to love so deeply, either would be willing to die so the other might live."

"I never thought of it that way."

Seeing that her words had a profound effect on him, she gathered him close.

He clung to her. "You're an amazing woman, Mary Catherine. I can't count the number of times I've heard those feelings expressed, and refused to really consider them. But now, coming from you, they make sense."

"I'm glad." She snuggled closer, and brought her mouth to his throat, sending heat spiraling through him.

His arms tightened around her, and he could feel the passion rising. He wanted her again. Now.

She brought her mouth lower, to trail hot, wet kisses down his chest. "Because you're a very special man, Sam Hunter. I truly have waited all my life for you. I knew you'd come for me. And if I'm ever given the chance, I'll gladly die for you."

His tone was suddenly fierce. "Don't say that. Don't even think it."

She lifted her head and brushed her mouth over his. "All right. But I've already said the words. I can't take them back."

And then there were no more words as they came together in a storm even more fierce than the one raging beyond the walls of the barn.

By the flickering light of the lantern Sam

studied the face of the woman asleep in his arms. Watching Mary Catherine sleep, he'd never felt such peace. As though all that had happened in the past was now nothing more than a dim memory. Her unselfish lovemaking had unlocked something in his heart. He no longer felt alone. She was his, he thought fiercely. His. She was the most perfect woman he'd ever met. Kind and gentle, yet strong enough to carry on even after the loss of both her parents. Patient with Anna, and tolerant of a cruel stepfather. And, despite all the odds, capable of clinging to a dream for independence and a future beyond this farm.

Her love had washed him clean. Now, finally, he truly believed that he could put the past behind him and look to the future.

He smiled. And what a future. There was nothing he couldn't do, with Mary Catherine beside him.

She stirred. Her eyes opened and she traced a finger around the curve of his lips. "Is that smile for me?"

"Yes. Only for you. And do you know why?"

"Why?" She stretched, loving the feel of his arms around her.

"Because you've made me so happy. I never expected to feel this way. In the past months I've known only misery. But ever since meeting you, things have changed. I don't know how it happened, or why, but I do know this. You've given me back my love for life. Right this minute, I feel as if I could take on the whole world and win."

"You can, Sam. Always believe that."

"We can. Together." He bent to brush her mouth with his. At once the fire began, heating his blood, causing his heart to race. "As long as we're together, Mary Catherine, we can own the world."

She drew a little away, her eyes steady on his. "I just thought of something comforting that my mother said to me shortly before she ran away." She spoke the words with fierce concentration. "Even if I can't always be with you, my spirit will be."

He shot her a puzzled look. "How odd that you should find that comforting. To me it just proves that she was planning on leaving you and Anna."

"I don't know why." She smiled. "But her words give me a great deal of comfort. I like knowing that her spirit will always be with me. I want you to know that it's the same with you and me, Sam. My spirit will always be with you."

He frowned. "You make it sound as though you're saying you won't be leaving with me in the morning."

"Never think that. I want, more than anything in this world, to spend my life with you."

"Then don't talk about your spirit. I want you, woman." He gave her a wolfish, heart-stopping grin. "In the flesh. Which, I might add . . ." He began nuzzling her neck, her throat. ". . . is some of the finest flesh I've ever tasted."

She gave a throaty laugh and threw back her head, twining her fingers in his hair. "I'm so glad you approve. Just for that, I'm about to give you a great deal more flesh to enjoy."

Their laughter mingled with the sounds of the night. Oh, it was so grand to be able to laugh together. To feel their hearts soar with newfound joy. Gradually the laughter turned to sighs, and the sighs to murmurs of plea-sure.

Caught up in the passion, they wrapped themselves around each other and rolled in the hay, feasting, sighing, whispering words of endearment as old as time.

# SEVEN

Mary Catherine snuggled against Sam's chest, loving the feel of his strong arms around her.

All night they'd loved and dozed, then awoke to love again. Sometime in the wee hours they had donned their clothes before digging into the meal she'd brought from the house. Now, replete, content, they burrowed deep into the hay to guard against the raging wind outside.

Tracing the curve of his mouth with her finger, Mary Catherine gave voice to the thoughts that swirled through her mind. "Why is it that a passionate man like you never married?"

"Passionate?" He gave a roar of laughter. "I told you my name on the force was The Iceman. That applies to my personal life as well as professional. Before meeting you, I thought a woman would complicate my life."

"Complicate?" She sat up. "Am I a complication, Sam?"

"Yeah. Definitely." He softened his words with a long, heartfelt kiss. "The very best kind. You, lady, are a beautiful complication."

She purred her approval. "Why the name Iceman?"

He shrugged. "I've spent a lifetime playing by the rules. I've always been proud of the fact that I never let my emotions get in the way of my job. And it worked well for all these years. But everything changed when I met you. Suddenly I don't care about the rules. I care only about you. I want you safe and protected and happy. I guess what I'm saying is, I want to take you with me and see that Hoag never bullies you again. You know . . ." He paused, considering. "I never meant it to go this far."

"How far?"

"Honestly? I wanted you. But I wasn't expecting to feel the depth of passion I feel for you." He saw her color with pleasure and thought about admitting all the feelings that were inside him. But they were so new, so surprising, he found he wasn't ready to talk about love. And so he added quickly, "Until you, I was content to be alone. I never even knew what I was missing. Now you, on the other hand." He tucked a stray strand of hair behind her ear, loving the feel of the softness against his flesh. "You're the most passionate woman I've ever met. It all seems so easy and natural for you."

Mary Catherine smiled. "Until meeting you, I was never even tempted by passion. You've changed me. I've no doubt that you're my destiny, Sam."

Her words had him going very still. He stared deeply into her eyes. "Until now, I never believed in such things. Meeting you has changed my life completely, Mary Catherine." It was still too difficult for him to say the words, and so he simply lowered his head and brushed her lips with his to show her.

At once the passion flared as they came together in a fierce embrace.

The rasp of the barn door being torn open had their heads coming up sharply.

On a rush of frigid air, Hoag stood framed in the doorway. With the inky darkness behind him, and the dim light of the lantern glinting in his eyes, he looked like the very devil himself. His scowl deepened as he took in the sight of them.

"I knew it." His words were torn from a throat clogged with rage. "The minute I saw you, Hunter, I knew you were no good."

Sam stood facing the man's anger, and thought about the punks and bullies he'd stared down during his years on the force. Hoag had that same look about him. A look of absolute determination mingled with desperation. A dangerous combination.

"This isn't about Sam, Hoag." Mary Catherine scrambled to her feet, clutching the afghan about her. "You would have blamed any man who dared to cross your path. If you want someone to blame . . ." She tossed her head defiantly. ". . . blame me."

"Oh, I do." He turned on her with a sneer. "I knew when I wed that mother of yours that her spawn would be just like her. There's no loyalty in your kind. You'd lie with any man just for the pleasure of it."

"You know that's a lie. Sam isn't just any man. He's the man I love."

"Love!" Hoag spat the word like a curse. "The way your mother loved me? You dare to give in to your lust and try to call it love? I'll tell you what love is. It's giving all that you own, your land, your home, your spawn, to the man who saved you from a lifetime of back-breaking labor."

"Is that what you offered my mother? Your labor in exchange for all that she had?"

"What if I did?" His eyes narrowed. "She

sealed the bargain with a vow."

"If that's true, she paid too high a price." Mary Catherine faced Hoag, her eyes bright with unshed tears. "No wonder she fled. I'm glad she escaped this prison."

Something flickered in Hoag's eyes. Something so hot and dangerous, Sam forcibly took Mary Catherine's arm and drew her behind him. Then he stood between them, facing the man whose fury emanated from him in great, black waves.

"This is no longer between you and your stepdaughter." Sam's tone was dangerously soft. But there was no denying the steel beneath the words. "I've asked Mary Catherine to go with me in the morning."

"She'll never leave this farm."

"You have no legal hold on her. The choice is hers."

"I'll give her the same choice I gave her mother." Hoag glanced from Sam to the woman who stood slightly behind him.

"I've already made my choice, Hoag. I'm going with Sam."

"Then you're a fool, just like her." Hoag gave a cruel laugh. "And now you're going to spend eternity right next to her."

"What's that supposed to mean?" Sam studied the man whose too-bright eyes and clenched jaw made him resemble a monster.

"She tried to leave me. Just like this one." Hoag gave a high, shrill cackle. "I told her then that she'd never leave this place and bring the authorities back to lay claim to what was mine."

"Yours?" Mary Catherine's voice betrayed her shock. "This farm will never be yours. It belongs to our family."

"Bloody fools. All of you. I own this place now. Every acre of land, every animal, and every person on it."

Mary Catherine shook her head. "You forget one thing. Your name isn't McGivern. This land has been in my father's family for generations."

"When your mother married me, it became mine. I poured my sweat into these fields, and that makes them mine. When she told me she wanted out of the marriage, I let her know that I was never leaving."

"Is that why she ran away?"

Mary Catherine's words had him throwing back his head and giving a high, shrill laugh that scraped across their nerves. "Oh, yeah. She ran, all right. All the way to the barn, hoping the new handyman would keep her safe from my fists and get her and her brats to town."

Mary Catherine gave a cry. "She wanted to take us with her?"

He huffed out a breath. "You think she'd ever willingly leave the two of you? I put an end to her plans. I slit her throat and buried her right here in the barn, along with the hired help. I knew he was an itinerant worker who had nobody to miss him. It was an easy matter to tell the authorities they'd run off together."

Sam felt Mary Catherine's sudden hiss of pain as she struggled to breathe. "You . . . killed my mother?"

Hoag merely laughed. Just as suddenly, the laughter faded, replaced by a look of intense hatred. "Think you're going to take what's mine?" Hoag reached for something just out of Sam's line of vision and turned, swinging his hand in a wide arc.

Pain crashed through Sam's head, sending him to his knees. Through a shower of blood and stars, he caught sight of the shovel in Hoag's hand a second before it slammed against his temple a second time, sending him sprawling in the hay.

Struggling to his knees, Sam shook his head to clear his vision. When Hoag pounced, he ducked and brought his fist into Hoag's abdomen. Using those few seconds of distraction Sam scrambled to his feet.

The two men faced each other, their

breathing labored, fists clenched. When Hoag attacked, Sam was ready. He managed to avoid the first blow, while catching Hoag in the face. Blood spewed from Hoag's nose and stained the front of his shirt. Grunting in pain, Hoag lowered his head and drove Sam back against the stall door. The body blow had Sam staggering. Hoag used that moment to land a blow to Sam's chest that had him going down on one knee in the hay.

From some distant part of Sam's mind, he heard Mary Catherine's cry and looked up to see Hoag reach for the pitchfork resting against the wood of the stall.

Seeing it, Sam struggled to his feet, steeling himself for the vicious attack he knew was coming.

Hoag drew back his arm, prepared to hurl the pitchfork. In the same instant that he released it, Mary Catherine gave a cry and darted forward, pushing Sam aside and taking the blow meant for him. The triple prongs of the farm implement bit deeply into her chest, driving her back against the stall door. When Hoag withdrew the weapon, a river of blood spilled from her chest.

At Mary Catherine's strangled cry, all the fight went out of Sam as he crawled to her and gathered her into his arms.

"Why? Oh God, why?" It was all he could manage to whisper against her ear. "This wasn't your fight. It was mine."

"I warned you." Her words were raspy, halting. She lifted a hand to his face. "I love you more than my life, Sam Hunter. Without you, nothing would matter. Everything in my life would be empty and meaningless."

"What about my life? This can't be happening. Not again." He buried his face in her hair and struggled to breathe, in and out, in and out, as the pain of loss washed over him in a series of crushing blows.

Sam saw the blank look that came into those soft blue eyes, and heard the rattle of fluid in her lungs. His words were a cry of desperation. "Hold on. Don't leave me, Mary Catherine."

*"Hold on. Don't leave me, Vince."*

His own words echoed through his mind.

"Please, Mary Catherine. I couldn't bear to lose you. Don't let this madman win."

"He'll never win. You'll see to that, Sam. Don't you understand yet? Your life has to go on so that monsters like Hoag can never win. You're the witness to what has gone on here."

"I don't care about that. I don't care

about anything except you."

"I'll always be with you, Sam. Just remember that. My spirit will always be with you."

He could feel her slipping away. Her breath was shallow, her clammy flesh the color of chalk.

He clung to her and watched as her life slipped away.

He'd seen death so many times. His father and mother. His partner. But this . . . this was so much harder than anything he'd ever endured.

Without a word he lay her in the hay and pressed a final kiss to her mouth.

Almost blinded by the pain, he found the strength to stand, despite his wounds. "You've killed her. That beautiful, sweet, gentle woman. You killed her."

"My, my. So dramatic." Up close Sam could see the madness Hoag could no longer hide.

"I warned you." Hoag swung a shovel, catching Sam squarely in the temple. Pain radiated in waves of nausea so great that Sam brought his arms up, cradling his head in his hands as if to keep it from separating from his body.

Just as he thought he'd go mad if he had to bear another moment of the deep, searing pain, Hoag swung the shovel again and

Sam was hurled into a deep, black pit of unconsciousness.

Death. Sam had smelled it often enough in his line of work to recognize it, even with his eyes shut. Was he dead then?

The pain radiating through his entire system gave him his answer. Death would be preferable to what he was enduring. There wasn't any part of his body that didn't scream as though burning in the fires of hell.

Maybe that was it. Maybe he was beyond dead. Maybe this was to be his fate. To live with this pain forever in hell.

He opened his eyes and stared around. He was lying on the hardpacked earth that formed the floor of the barn. By the light of a lantern hanging from a post he could see Hoag scattering fresh hay over a mound of dirt in the stall.

The pitchfork stood against a wall between the stalls. The prongs had been carefully cleaned until they gleamed in the lantern light.

The bloodstained hay had been forked into a wagon along with dung from the stalls. By morning it would no doubt be spread over a distant frozen field, where all trace of the blood and death that had occurred here would be washed away.

"Mary Catherine." Pushing through the pain, Sam lifted his head.

Hoag tossed the last of the hay and led a horse into the stall before walking over to stand, legs apart, grinning down at him. "Looks like she won't be going with you. She decided to stay here with her mama."

"You're . . ." Sam pulled himself up along the rough wall until he was weaving like a drunk. "You're mad."

"Yeah. Crazy like a fox." Hoag's fist smashed against Sam's temple, dropping him to his knees. Dragging him up by the front of his shirt, he brought his face within inches of Sam's. "Just so you understand who's in charge here. I want you out of my sight." He reached around Sam and tore open the barn door. With a shove he sent him staggering into the dark, bitter night.

Sam turned, praying he wouldn't keel over. "Why don't you just kill me, too?"

"Oh, don't you worry. The weather's going to do that for me." Hoag's high-pitched laughter sent chills down his spine. "But I couldn't resist keeping you alive long enough for you to see your lady love dead and buried. Just a little extra kick, don't you know?" He pointed to the stall, where the horse stomped and blew, already flattening out the soft mound of earth beneath the hay. "Come morning I'll lead the authorities to the frozen body of the murdering bastard who lured my sweet stepdaughter away from her happy home. They'll spend weeks going over my land, searching for her body, before they give up the way they did last time." He threw back his head and roared at his private joke. "And then there'll be only one standing between me and the land I deserve."

"Anna." Sam's voice was little more than a whisper over the howling of the wind.

"Sweet, stupid Anna." Hoag threw back his head and cackled. "She doesn't have the backbone that her ma and sister had. She'll stay. She'll do my bidding. Or she can join the others in the barn. It really doesn't matter to me."

"Why?" Sam hoped that by keeping Hoag talking, he could find a way to distract him and, hopefully, overpower him.

Instead the barn door slammed shut and Sam was left alone, bloody and battered not only by his injuries, but also by the realization of what had happened to Mary Catherine.

The weight of the guilt he suffered was almost more than he could bear. He'd been unable to save the woman he loved.

*The woman he loved.* It was a phrase he'd never used, and one he'd never expected to say in his lifetime.

The pain was too great. He no longer cared about himself. It didn't matter whether the storm killed him or if he should die of his injuries. Death would be welcome.

The thought of living without the love he'd only just discovered was impossible to fathom.

But there was one last thing he could do for Mary Catherine. He could free her sister from this hellish prison.

Sam stood shivering in the darkness, staring at the light in the upstairs window. Hoag had not only locked the door, he'd jammed a chair against the knob to assure that Sam couldn't break in.

As Sam watched, Anna's face appeared at the upstairs bedroom windowpane, her arms along the sill, a sad, haunted look on her face. Was she already believing that he and her sister had run off together, just as she believed her mother had, leaving her alone with Hoag?

He had to warn her of the danger. It was the only good thing he could do before the storm snatched his life.

"Anna! Down here! Anna!" He shouted

her name into the howling wind and waved his arms like a madman in a frantic attempt to get her attention, but the wind snatched his voice and carried it away.

When she didn't respond, he knelt in the ice and felt around for stones to hurl against the windowpane.

Before he could toss them she got to her feet and Sam could see a dark shadow behind her. Numb with cold and dread he watched as Anna turned and faced Hoag standing in the upstairs doorway.

Whatever words he spoke had her covering her face and weeping before running from the room.

The old man walked to the window and peered out. Spying Sam standing below in the frozen yard he threw back his head and laughed before blowing out the lantern.

And then there was only the darkness and the wind and the cold.

On a wave of desperation, Sam turned away and stumbled down the frozen hillside, praying that he could make it back to his car before the cold that permeated everything turned him into a solid block of ice.

# EIGHT

Sam stood at the top of a hill, buffeted by wind and icy sleet, wondering if he had the strength to go on. While he watched the rain turned to snow. Fat white snowflakes swirled about, the blizzard nearly blinding him. He'd never known such cold. His bones felt brittle enough to snap like twigs. He had long ago lost all feeling in his hands and feet.

He'd experienced so many moods since leaving the farm. Heartbreaking sadness at the loss of his beloved Mary Catherine. Worry over the fate of innocent Anna. Hatred of the madman who had shattered a family's trust. And finally a fierce determination to remain alive, if only to tell the authorities what he'd witnessed.

*You're the best expert witness this department has ever had, Hunter. Your uncanny ability to calmly, dispassionately fit together the intricate pieces of even the oldest crimes has helped solve more cold cases than any-one in the department's history.*

Didn't this family deserve the testimony of an expert witness?

Far below, Sam thought he saw something familiar shimmering under a layer of ice. Or was it just wishful thinking? No. There was a glint of dark through the ice. His car. He was sure of it. Now, at last, he had a goal. If he could make it there, he could find shelter from this bitter cold.

Stumbling, falling, slipping, sliding, he skidded his way down the hill until he'd reached the car. Tearing open the passenger door, he shouldered his way inside, past the shredded airbags, past the shards of safety glass that had rained down from the broken windshield, and, exhausted, slumped in the seat.

Fumbling with the key that was still in the ignition, he turned it, desperate for some heat. The engine coughed, sputtered, chugged for the barest moment before going still.

He turned the key again. Nothing. Not a sound. It was completely dead.

With an oath of disgust he gave in to yet another mood swing. He was overcome with an overwhelming sense of despair. What a fool he'd been. He was so certain that reaching the car would somehow save him, and in turn condemn Hoag. But now he had to admit that he was no better off than he'd been at Storm Hill. Though the vehicle offered him meager shelter from the storm, the broken windshield allowed the wind and snow to continue their relentless attack. And since the car was no longer mobile, he was trapped inside, waiting for death to claim him. It would simply take a little more time.

His lungs filled with the acrid odor of burning rubber from the spent airbags as he leaned his head back and closed his eyes. He was so weary. Weary of the fight to do the right thing. Weary of hanging on while those he loved were taken from him. Weary of trying to make sense of all the things that had happened in his life.

"I'm sorry, Mary Catherine. You were right all along. I was angry at my partner, Vince, for making the ultimate sacrifice, even though, given the chance, I'd have done the same for him. And now you. As painful as it is, I do understand. It was, quite simply, love. Though I didn't deserve his love or yours, I'm grateful, with all my heart. I never thought I'd find that kind of love in my lifetime, because I never felt worthy. But please know this. I loved you. I truly loved you. How I wish I'd told you."

He heard a roaring in his head and blamed it on the blows he'd endured at Hoag's hand. There was no doubt he'd suffered a concussion, or worse, a skull fracture. He was so dazed and confused he actually thought the roaring was growing louder. The sound of it had him pressing his hands to his ears, but he couldn't shut out the ear-splitting sound.

"You all right?" A woman's voice sounded from outside the window.

He tried to answer, but couldn't seem to make his mouth work.

He felt a great torrent of ice and wind as the passenger door was yanked open. A beam of light blinded him and he closed his eyes against the stab of pain. When he opened them, a woman's face was peering at him in the darkness. He couldn't see her face, only a halo of light around her.

"You're pretty banged up. Here." She caught his arm and began sliding him across the seat. "Your car's on its side. You'll have to exit from this door."

"Can't move." He looked down and saw that his seat belt was fastened. When had he done that?

"That's all right. Don't exert yourself. You're bleeding. You just sit there." She reached over him and unsnapped the seat belt, then, working quickly, eased him out of the car.

"Can't make it in this storm." He leaned heavily on her as the wind howled like a beast. "We'll both freeze to death."

"Don't you worry. We'll be fine." She settled him on her snowmobile and fastened the seat belt before taking the wheel.

With a roar they took off across the icy, snow-laden hills, leaving the ribbon of road far behind.

Sam wrapped his arms around her waist and pressed his face to her back while he struggled to keep his teeth from chattering. He was beyond cold. Beyond numb. Beyond feeling or thinking or even responding.

He knew that this wasn't really happening. He'd seen enough accident victims to know that he was hallucinating. Still, he closed his eyes and allowed himself to drift. Even if the woman wasn't real, it gave him a small measure of comfort to pretend to be heading toward safety.

The roaring stopped as suddenly as it had started, and in the eerie silence, she helped him stand.

"Just a couple of steps." She lifted his arm around her neck and eased him up, one step at a time. On a porch she nudged open a door and helped him inside.

Warmth flooded him, and he nearly collapsed with blessed relief.

Real. It was real. He sank to his knees.

"Wait. Don't stop." She kept him moving along a hallway until they reached a large room. "Sit here."

She lowered him into an easy chair set in front of a blazing fire and draped an afghan around his shoulders.

She turned away before pausing on the threshold. "I'll be right back."

He heard her footsteps recede and sat, head down, blanket up to his chin, as he absorbed the warmth. By the time she returned, his teeth had stopped chattering, and he could actually feel his fingers and toes.

She held out a tumbler of amber liquid. "Here's some brandy. Drink."

"Thanks."

He took a long pull, then waited as the warmth snaked through his veins. He took another drink, and then a third, before setting aside the glass.

"Thanks. I actually think I'll live, but for a while I wasn't so sure of that. I figured I'd only dreamed you."

She smiled. "Oh, I'm real enough."

"My name's Sam."

"Hi, Sam. I'm Kate. Welcome to Storm

Hill Inn."

"Storm Hill?" He wondered if his shock was evident on his face. "I've been here."

She grinned. "I wouldn't be surprised. It's been here for over a hundred years."

"No. I mean today. I just left here."

She gave him a gentle smile. "That's quite a bump on your head. The doctor won't be able to get through this storm tonight, but if you're not feeling better in the morning, I'll give him a call. I'll also phone Phil Liggett in town and tell him to bring his tow truck by whenever this storm lets up. Your car's practically totaled."

"You don't understand." He looked around, trying to get his bearings. Was this the same place? The furniture was definitely more modern, with a pair of sectional sofas in deep chocolate, and two taupe chairs pulled up in front of the fireplace. The hardwood floors had been polished to a high shine, and instead of the old rag rugs, there was an expensive Oriental rug in shades of beige and caramel and brown, with a border of deep green and burgundy.

"It doesn't look the same, but I was here, with Hoag Slade and Mary Catherine."

Kate smiled. "Mary Catherine. Wow. Now there's a blast from the past. She was my great-great-aunt. She caused an enormous scandal in her day when she ran away with a stranger, just the way her own mother did. Nobody ever heard from either of them, but everyone around here talks about the ghost who travels these roads after dark. They say the sadness in her eyes is heartbreaking."

Sam pressed his fingers to his temples. "I'm going to tell you something. I know this will be hard to believe but . . ." He saw a wisp of smoke from the fire begin to shimmer and glow, before taking the form of a woman. For a moment, he simply gaped while the woman blew him a kiss.

His heart took a hard, swift jolt. "Did you see that?" He pointed.

"What?" Kate glanced at him, then to the place he indicated.

"I thought . . ." Sam gave a quick shake of his head, but the vision had faded and disappeared. ". . . I saw her. Out there on the road, and just now. She's the same one who visited me while I was here these past two days."

Kate's voice gentled, as though she were speaking to someone addle-brained. "Not half an hour ago I was looking out the window at the storm when I saw your headlights swerve off the road. I knew at once you were in trouble. It may have taken me ten minutes or so to get out to the barn and get the snowmobile started, and another ten minutes or so to reach you, but you weren't in your car more than twenty minutes to half an hour tops."

He took another long drink of the brandy before closing his eyes. "Are you telling me it was all a dream?"

She shrugged. "You've suffered a really nasty blow to your head."

"But what about the fact that I know Hoag and Mary Catherine?"

"Everyone around here knows their story. It's common folklore."

"I'm not from around here. And Anna?"

"My great-great-aunt?"

Sam realized he had Kate's complete attention.

She shook her head, as if to deny his words. "Not many people know that Anna McGivern is from around here. She pretty much rewrote the family history to deny her heritage."

"That may be so, but I saw her. I knew her."

"She lived here back in the nineteen-thirties, Sam."

"I wanted to take her with me. To keep her safe. I tried to get her attention, but Hoag won. I saw his face at the window. He had the last laugh."

She touched a cool hand to his forehead. "You need to rest. Are you a history professor?"

"Cop. Ex-cop," he amended.

"But you don't deny that you've read the history of Storm Hill."

"Never." He shook his head. "I can't explain. I know it sounds crazy. It does to me, too." He leaned his head back and closed his eyes, fighting the vicious headache that had begun at the base of his skull. "What do you do here, Kate?"

"I run this bed-and-breakfast." She crossed to the fireplace to poke at the logs, sending up a fresh blaze. "I've always loved housekeeping. It's a passion of mine. After college in Boston, I got a job as a concierge at one of the top hotels. But what I really dreamed of was running my own place. My parents made it all possible when they left Storm Hill to me." She stood and offered a hand. "Enough about me. You need to lie down." She helped him to his feet. "Let me show you to a room upstairs."

Sam's head was throbbing. "I'm not sure I can climb any more stairs."

"Don't worry." She draped his arm around her shoulders. "No need to climb. There's an elevator."

They stepped into the small cubicle and

Kate pushed a button. Moments later they stepped out and walked several steps along the upper hallway.

Sam stared around with sudden interest. He'd been here. Despite the architectural changes, and the modern furnishings, this was the same upstairs where Mary Catherine and Anna had shared a room.

He felt light as air as he moved slowly beside Kate. It didn't matter if anyone ever believed him. He'd been here. How else to explain all this?

"Ah. Here's your suite."

When she paused outside a closed door, he couldn't hold back his sudden shock. "606?"

She glanced from him to the hammered copper numbers on the door. "Aren't they a treasure? I found them in one of the fields here when I was in college. They were the work of my great-great-aunt, who was quite the artist. I thought they were perfect for my dorm room, since I lived in Number 909. But when I brought them here with me, they kept flipping down. Finally I gave up. Now they're 606. But I still like the way they look." She opened the door. "Welcome to Suite 606. I call it the Mary Catherine Suite."

He spotted the portrait on the mantel.

"Mary Catherine."

Kate walked over and touched a hand to the painting. The resemblance between her and the woman in the portrait was amazing. "That's right. This was one of my great-great-aunt's early, primitive works. This is the only known picture of Mary Catherine, painted before she ran off with her handsome, mysterious stranger."

"She didn't . . ." Sam halted. How could he possibly explain? "And Anna? What happened to her?"

Kate seemed surprised by his question. "Happened?"

"Did she also disappear?"

Kate chuckled. "According to family lore, her stepfather, Hoag Slade, refused to allow her to take the art classes she desperately wanted, so she waited until he was working in a distant field before she walked the thirty miles to town. From there she hitched a ride with a traveling preacher all the way to her uncle's farm in Boston. He was something of an artist himself, so he taught her what he could, and then sent her to a fancy women's boarding school in New York."

"Did Slade try to find her?"

Kate shrugged. "Apparently all he cared about was this farm. He died here all alone. Since he had no heirs, the land reverted to the McGivern family."

"So Anna inherited the farm after all?"

Kate shook her head. "Anna wanted no part of it. It held too many bittersweet memories for her. She was already an acclaimed artist living in Paris."

At that, Sam found himself grinning. "She made it to Paris."

Kate smiled. "She repaid her uncle's generosity by deeding the farm to him. My great-great-grandfather raised six children here. His oldest son worked the land, and left it to my grandfather, who in turn left it to my parents. When they were ready to retire, and realized how much I loved hotel work, I was the logical one to take it over." Kate smiled. "And here we are."

Sam nodded, feeling slightly dazed and bewildered. "Here we are."

"Well." She turned away. "I'll get a fire started in here. The shower is through those doors. If you'd like, you can eat up here in your suite."

"I will if you'll join me."

"I'd like that."

Sam glanced toward the door. "Are there any other guests?"

She shook her head. "I don't have another guest booked until Thanksgiving. I'm sorry to say that you and I will have the place all to ourselves."

He might be recovering from a blow to the head, but he wasn't imagining the invitation in her smile, so like the inviting look he'd seen in another's eyes. He had to admit that she was the prettiest, sexiest concierge he'd ever met. And one with a tantalizing, mysterious heritage.

For an out-of-commission cop who specialized in cold cases, it was exactly the vacation the doctor had ordered. And maybe, just maybe, he'd extend his time here indefinitely, if Kate McGivern proved to be as passionate, as spontaneous, as her great-great-aunt had been in that . . . dream.

The thought had his blood heating and his pulse racing. Or had it been just a dream?

Whatever had happened out there in that storm, he was a different man than the one who'd left the city bowed and broken. He had a new zest for his job, and for life.

Belski was going to owe him big-time. If things went as he hoped, he might never leave Storm Hill.

He found himself wondering if the nearby town had need of a seasoned cop. It was time he got back to doing what he loved, and, he thought with a grin, loving what he did.

It looked as though his frozen heart had just defrosted. Love, he sincerely hoped as he made his way slowly to the shower, was definitely something to look forward to in this Iceman's future.

■ ■ ■ ■

# WAYWARD WIZARD
# MARY KAY
# McCOMAS

■ ■ ■ ■

For my longtime pals,
Nora, Mary, and Ruth —
friends don't come any better.
Thank you for letting me add
my two cents to your dollar.

And Brandy Loy, my son's German tutor.
Danke!

# ONE

Marie Barnett loved her son. She really did.

"Hugh, if you don't settle down I'm going to rip your arm off and beat you over the head with it." He merely looked at her, unfazed. "Okay, but I *will* take you home."

"Good. Let's go." The twelve-year-old turned abruptly into the flow of pedestrians, toward the main entrance of the museum. "I'll drive."

She grabbed the back of his black hoodie and brought him to an awkward halt, saying, "Excuse us," twice to the people who bumped into them. She warned him through her teeth, "We have a deal, remember? You don't embarrass me in public and I won't embarrass you. You're pushin' it, pal."

"What. Like it's not embarrassing just *being* with you?"

That hurt. It was meant to. But the knowing didn't diminish the stinging pressure of tears behind her eyes; tears she refused to shed — she'd wasted enough time crying.

"I get it . . . that you feel that way. I'll take you home now if you like."

"What I'd *like* is for you to go and leave me alone."

"Can't." She looked down the wide museum corridor that was filled with people almost shoulder to shoulder, shuffling slowly in the direction of the "America and Baseball" exhibit in the next chamber. *A traveling showcase of artifacts, pictures, and other "over the fence" memorabilia commemorating our nation's favorite sport,* the brochure said. And it better be *waa-ay* over the fence memorabilia or she'd never hear the end of it from Hugh. "Your dad . . . and your . . . Laura would call leaving you here alone irresponsible behavior and I," — she looked down at his face — "I think I've been irresponsible enough for one lifetime, don't you?"

"Two lifetimes."

She gave him a weak smile and a nod. It was true.

"Three lifetimes."

The sin she had committed against her son was unforgivable and she deserved every bitter jab and tearing barb he could deliver. But the mother in her wanted Hugh

388

to grow into a man with a generous spirit and a forgiving heart and it was frustrating that she wasn't in a position to teach him such things.

Looking into his face, she once again marveled at the scramble of features that meshed so perfectly to make him one of a kind — her almond-shaped eyes and thick wavy black hair that needed a haircut, his dad's near-perfect nose, and his grandmother's wily smile . . . when he chose to use it.

"Right. I'm sorry I asked." She exhaled and tried to start over. "So what's it going to be? Are you going to stay where I can see you and stop wedging people aside and wait your turn so we can stay? Or are we leaving? It's up to you."

She watched her son turn sniper before her eyes, reloading, taking aim; he opened his mouth to fire . . . Quickly, she held up her hand to ward off the next shot. "It's a simple stay or go question, Hugh. One word. One chance. Choose wisely."

A tiny part of her wanted to laugh at the mental war playing itself out across the gentle hills and soft slopes of his still mostly boy face. His green-hazel eyes were defiant. He really wanted to zing her again but not quite as much as he wanted to see the first catcher's mask . . . or seventy-five of the 278 bronze plaques from the Baseball Hall of Fame . . . or Babe Ruth's bat.

"Stay." It cost him but he kept his head high, his expression sullen, and the angle of his narrow shoulders resentful and insolent just the same. Her sweet baby boy had a real aptitude for animosity.

"Good. I've been looking forward to this."

She waved him back into the river of what could only be devout baseball fans, taking in the Mets' blue, orange, and black colors on sweatshirts and the orange, black, and white of the Baltimore Orioles on T-shirts and jackets; the familiar red, white, and blue of the Phillies — their hometown team — and the black, gold, white, and red of Hugh's beloved Pirates . . . Pittsburgh being where his hero, Honus Wagner, was born and raised, and taught himself to be the all-time greatest shortstop in the history of baseball . . . according to Hugh.

Well, according to most baseball history books, as well. She checked. It was important to her to know what a person had to do, who a person needed to be, to be someone special in her son's eyes.

Her heart ached to be one of those people again.

She followed at a discreet distance, knowing he wouldn't enjoy any of the displays if he could feel or even sense her breathing down his neck. She assumed the equivalent of a ten-foot pole would suffice, and wondered if he'd be up to exploring the Dead Sea Exhibit later. She slowed down and craned her neck to catch a glimpse of something — anything — as she passed by the entrance. Maybe she'd come back another day . . .

The milling crowd bottlenecked into an orderly line, sometimes two abreast, to view the artifacts presented behind walls of glass or in brightly lit display cases . . . and even out in the open, uncovered, like the first Major League Silver Bat presented to George Kell who won it by two ten-thousandths of a point over Ted Williams in 1949 — or so it said on the plaque underneath it.

Marie couldn't claim a profound attachment . . . or even much interest in baseball. The year she allowed Hugh to play five-year-old T–ball was, perhaps, the longest and hottest summer known to mankind. She was sure her brain would fry in its shell under the hot sun as she waited endlessly for one child after another to hit a small ball off the top of a plastic stick, while the other children grew terminally bored and restless in the outfield and their parents exchanged nacho cheese dip recipes or developed short, uneven tempers as they waited for the four innings or two hours — whichever came first — to pass.

Of course, that was the spring after the car accident. All her big bruises and small lacerations had healed, so had the shattered right clavicle and broken humerus. She no longer wore the body brace that protected the three compression fractures in her spine but she kept it, in her closet, for *just in case*. The doctors still had sympathy for her pain then and were ordering reasonable doses of Percocet for it so . . .

She heard her son utter a soft, enthused, "Oh," up ahead and tried to stretch her neck around a husband and wife to see . . . a glove and an autographed ball. But she couldn't see whose, couldn't share the moment with him. She glanced at his young face, it was rapt, and she sighed.

So . . . maybe the heat and the boredom, the pain and the drugs blurred her awareness of the exact moment in which Hugh fell in love with baseball that summer. Perhaps if she'd witnessed that flash of satisfaction, that instant of pure glee that ignited his unremitting delight in the game, she might have formed a vicarious passion for it of her own, but . . . Well, she had hadn't, she had missed it, as she'd missed so many other pivotal moments in his life.

She inched herself along the line until she stood looking through the glass at the glove and ball. Her pulse jumped and she smiled. It was the little miracles in life that she loved best.

"Look at that. Ty Cobb's glove." She glanced briefly at the wavy black hair on the back of Hugh's head and then at the elderly man beside her like she was speaking to him. "The Georgia Peach. He was kind of a jerk, you know, but he sure could play baseball. He once collected sixteen total bases — three homers, a double, and two singles — in one game, setting an American League record that has yet to be surpassed."

Perfect. Almost verbatim from the book.

"Yes, I know," said the old man kindly, looking distracted.

"He was also the very first Major League player to win the Triple Crown for batting."

"That's true, too." He leaned and looked pointedly beyond her at the large empty space between her and the people she was following.

Moving slowly, she skimmed the next few displays. Mel Ott, New York Giants. Ryne Sandberg, Chicago Cubs. Ted Williams,

Boston Red Sox. She couldn't remember them, but she could remember Ty Cobb. *Everybody* could remember Ty Cobb.

"He played center field for the Detroit Tigers for twenty-four years." She turned her head in time to see Hugh turn his face away from her . . . her one-man audience was waiting for her to finish. "I think loyalty is undervalued sometimes."

The old man nodded, the expression on his wise, blotchy face telling her that while she had a valid point, it was clear she had no place to stick it. He turned back to the slightly younger couple he was with and Marie moved on alone.

Once again, she'd over-taught — a syndrome of the insecure teacher in which she explains beyond boredom, instructs to the point of disinterest. A newly acquired disease she found extremely frustrating.

The rain the weatherman promised started with a loud clap of thunder and on its heels lightning and then thunder again. It was a sudden hard rain that came with a wind that blew it against the tall, opaque windows, making it sound like pebbles against the panes.

She passed the glove of outfielder Enos Slaughter's 1942 season and the hat worn by Lou Gehrig, The Iron Horse, who played in 2,130 consecutives games for the Yankees. What she saw was Hugh's back when it came to attention with interest or bent to read or stretched restlessly when the crowd slowed down. She especially liked watching the curve of his cheek swell when he smiled in amazement or happiness. He'd completely forgotten about her and was behaving like the polite, inquisitive, easily pleased boy she'd always known him to be.

The moment she'd been hoping for came with another flash of lightning and immediate thunder so loud she almost didn't hear it. It passed through her mind that the building might have been struck, but the thought didn't stay long enough to divert her from her son.

"Oh man!" His voice was what she wanted to hear; it was tight with restrained delight, thick with joy. He turned to her, his smile as bright as a thousand suns. "Mom. Look."

Instantly she was beside him, but she wasn't sure if she skipped or floated over. It was hard, but she tore her gaze from his face to look at his discovery. A yellowed and unnumbered Pittsburgh jersey, a ball with a faint inscription, and a small card maybe two inches by three in a glass box. The image on the card — the most valuable baseball card in the entire world — looked almost like a caricature, but there was no denying who it was.

"Honus." They said it at the same time, with the same reverent tone in their voices. No words came to describe the look on Hugh's face as he examined every inch of each artifact through the glass. She suspected every stranger in the room could guess what he was thinking — that he wanted to meet Honus or watch Honus play or *be* Honus or at the very least be *like* Honus. His yearning was a palpable thing.

"Do you think that's really his jersey? It doesn't look very big, does it?"

"Not by today's standards, I guess, but he was what . . . five-eleven and two hundred pounds? He was considerably bigger than the average man of his time." She bobbled her head. "And I think they're pretty careful about labeling what stuff belonged to who in museums." She could have stopped there but . . . "I mean, I think it's a rule or something that museums have to be as truthful as possible. There must be people whose job is to make sure all the exhibits are what they say they are." Her lips just kept flapping. "They run tests on everything, take pictures, catalogue it, and preserve it. I'm sure they have enough of his stuff that they don't have to put a fake jersey on display." She watched his head turn slowly toward her. It was too late to hide. "I . . . I wonder if the card belongs to this collection or if it's on loan from someone else's. It's not very big either, is it?"

He gave her that look — the one that read she was the stupidest, dumbest, ugliest moron on the planet — and walked away. Her eyes closed and her shoulders drooped as hopeful winds abandoned her sails and she went dead in the water.

For two marvelous, miraculous minutes, he had forgotten that he hated her; he had called her *Mom* and asked her a question that didn't necessarily have to end in an argument. And what did she do?

Outside the museum, nature raged violently — inside her head, the weather wasn't much better.

She shuffled by "Shoeless" Joe Jackson's shoes and baseball's most treasured relic, the Doubleday Ball, from the mythic first game in 1839 with barely a turn of her head. Her mother, her sponsor, and even Bill, her ex-husband, kept telling her that Hugh just needed time. He'd come around. He'd learn to trust her again and eventually he'd forgive her . . . in time. But how much time?

She picked up speed and bypassed the

bats from the Mark McGwire–Sammy Sosa home-run chase of 1998 and the record-setting bats of Babe Ruth and Roger Maris to catch up with Hugh, who was finished with the show and heading for the front door without her.

"Hey. Wait a second. What do you think?" She pointed to the sign for the Dead Sea Exhibit. She raised her brows and spoke like she was offering him a cookie. "Mummies maybe."

He read the sign and was thoughtful for a moment. He glanced at her, trying to gauge her desire to see it — to which her purely indifferent façade gave nothing to measure.

"Whatever." His shrug expressed apathy in a thousand different ways. He flipped the hood of his sweatshirt over his head and scuffed the soles of his shoes across the marble floor as he walked toward the arid-looking display at the entry.

Lightning exploded outside the giant windows.

The Dead Sea presentation consisted mostly of pottery and jars and some remarkably well-preserved tender artifacts like leather sandal soles, pieces of rope, and basket fragments that might otherwise have deteriorated to dust but for the special climate conditions of the area.

This site, an excavation just a few short miles from the caves in which the young Bedouin boy found the first of the two-thousand-year-old Dead Sea Scrolls in 1947, was considerably younger, dating to the thirteenth century — a small forgotten town, or more likely a military encampment. Christian not Muslim, they decided from the writing on the plates and lamps and the silver coins. Crusaders perhaps.

She viewed each bowl and intricately carved wooden comb in awe, as if each piece . . . well, like the miracles they were for having survived so long. She wondered about the people who used them, who owned them, and why they continued to exist when all else had perished long ago: What made these pieces so special?

Lightning crashed on the roof of the museum. The building reverberated and the lights quit and returned in a heartbeat. Marie's gaze automatically hunted for Hugh — and found him just as the electromagnetic latch on the pedestal showcase he was standing beside failed. The safety glass top popped open on its own and the security alarms let out an ear-piercing blast . . . that quickly turned to a sick whine and went silent.

Everything after that seemed to happen in

slow motion.

She watched it register on Hugh's face that the container was open. In his eyes she saw the warring intention of calling for help and the lure of touching something older than even his granddad's Korean War souvenirs. That's when she noticed that his right hand was already inside the case.

"Hugh. No!" She started toward him, her legs felt stiff and heavy like tree stumps. "Don't touch anything." He didn't seem to hear her. "Everything is very fragile in here."

He carefully withdrew his hand. In it was an odd-looking object that reminded her of the old-fashioned cast-iron ice tongs people used to use — only it was a high-polished silver, it was three inches long, three more wide, and fixed at the fulcrum was the most amazing stone she'd ever seen.

Plump and circular, about the size of a juicy plum, the stone was colorless and clear but for a wispy cloud of blue that appeared to hover *above* the stone or skim across the top of the stone when the light changed. She'd never seen anything like it.

It captured Hugh's attention as well. With one gentle finger, he tried to push the blue haze off the rock without success, though he didn't look at all disappointed.

Short seconds had passed since the power

surge and she was making progress but it was like her signature nightmare of running madly to prevent or ward off one horrendous calamity after another . . . through lime Jell-O . . . barefoot . . . and despite her every effort to ignore the little chunks of pear getting stuck between her toes she *just* misses thwarting every single disaster. Just misses.

So she wasn't surprised to feel the distinct sensation of déjà vu prickle the skin across her shoulders as she watched Hugh experiment with the two prongs below the stone . . . which even to her looked as if they ought to open and close like a clasp.

"Don't break it, Hugh. Put it back in the case." He looked up at her then and for the second time that day he smiled at her and raised the ornament for her to see — dislodging in that moment a minute patch of ancient rust that had held the two prongs constant for eight or ten centuries or more. "Oh God."

"Uh-oh." With the unerring accuracy of a prepubescent male, Hugh knew he'd broken it and immediately tried to fix it, closing the two blades beyond their original position and causing the two end points to touch. The stone lit up like a nova, causing them to squint against the smarting in their eyes.

Marie reached out blindly and grabbed Hugh, determined to be with him. The light faded somewhat and cast a soft, luminous blue light spiraling around Hugh.

"Mom? What's happening? It's tingling. I can feel it vibrating in my fingers."

"Give it to me, sweetie. Quick." She waved her arms through the pale blue light, trying to make it dissipate like smoke. She took the decoration from him, felt the warmth of it against her palm as she turned to put it back in the display case. "It's warm but I don't feel it vibrating." The lid came up easily. "I can't count the number of times I've told you not to touch things that don't belong to you, young man." The toggle settled neatly in its black velvet nest. "Don't worry, honey. We'll get this all straightened out. There. Now we'll find someone and just explain to them . . . the power failure and the latch popping open . . . but I don't think we need to mention our touching . . . Hugh?" She scanned the room with eyes like a hawk's; she hadn't looked away from him for more than a few seconds. "Hugh?"

# Two

She turned left and then right in a panic, hoping someone would come to her aid — the elderly couple or the young father with the toddler and the first-grader. She just wanted someone to point in the direction Hugh ran, she could take it from there.

It took several blinks and a good long stare before it registered that the people in the room with her weren't moving. But she was moving because . . . why? . . . because she'd been touching the . . . whatever it was?

The urge to scream stuck in her throat like she'd swallowed a hard-boiled egg, whole. She covered her face with both hands, then pushed them through her hair in one desperate motion.

Fine. She'd find Hugh alone. She'd tear the museum apart, brick by brick, if she had to.

But even before the thought could settle solidly in her mind, she knew he was no longer in the building . . . no longer in the state . . . quite possibly no longer on the planet. Seeing him again was not going to be as easy as simply finding him; she was going to have to follow him first.

Theoretically, the shorter the head start he got the sooner she could catch up to him. Feeling the need to hurry, she turned back to the pedestal display and the beautiful clip thingy inside. Once again she put both hands inside the case, ran a finger over the clear, colorless moonstone, and watched the blue haze hover and settle over the surface. Amazing. It was the key to Hugh's disappearance, her shocked and muddled brain was certain of it, and she didn't care if she had to shatter it with a hammer, it would give her back her son.

And yes, it did occur to her — a couple of times, serially — to check her mental status. She knew that ancient artifacts tend not to glow and vibrate, and that young boys are not predisposed to evaporate in curling clouds of blue light. They just weren't. But she hadn't spent the last eighteen months in a recovery program without going through some serious reality checks and this felt as real to her as anything she'd ever experienced . . . clean or wasted.

She picked up the ornament, a thumb and

an index finger pinching the bottom of each prong. "If I don't disappear, too, I'll have to explain all this to Bill . . . like he'd believe one word of it. God, make it work. Please. Take me to Hugh."

Pulling the tongs out and up, they caught for an arresting moment over the rusty patch that had held them stationary for so many centuries, then opened fully. She remembered the look on Hugh's face when he realized he might have broken the clasp, tried to calibrate the timing, and closed the two blades beyond their original position, causing the two end points to touch.

The stone came to life once more and cast a soft, billowing, pale blue light curling around her.

"Thank you, thank you, thank you," she muttered. Then, "Oh God. Oh God. Oh God," as her two most basic animal instincts, maternal and survival, clashed like the wind and the rain outside.

Her hands shook and her fingers were clumsy while she reset the prongs to their original position and settled the silver toggle in the display case. She wanted all to be as it had been for Hugh, the exact same way if possible, and maybe they'd end up in the same place . . . wherever that was. Oh God.

The blue light swirled. She stooped and

reached for the handle on her hobo purse, clutched it close to her chest, and squeezed her eyes shut tight as she braced herself for whatever came next. Abruptly it came to mind to leave Bill a note so he wouldn't worry about Hugh, but by the time she opened her eyes it was too late.

She was standing in a cavernous . . . well, cave seemed like the only word to describe it and yet the stone walls were straight and the corners were sharp and true. It was dark, dank, and drafty. Like a cave. Instinctively, she looked up for bats and suddenly realized that she was *seeing* because there was light somewhere.

She pressed a hand to her chest and the half-laced opening of a simple, super-sized linen gown and the soft woolen over-tunic that covered it. The borders and hem of the gown were decorated and it wasn't nearly as unpleasant to wear as she might have imagined. So . . . she'd followed Hugh to a medieval festival?

Where the hell was her purse?

In a swift sweep of the room, she took in the large, heavy table in the center and that each of the longer walls had several stools and four rough-hewn chairs lined up neatly with a smaller, less cared for utility table on the fair end. Behind her, on each side of the room, was an open entry to a passageway or another compartment and between them was a door that looked thick and dusty.

And the light? It was soft and low and might have been candlelight had there been any candles, reflective natural light had there been any windows. As it was, it would be difficult to read by but it was more than adequate to move around in.

So she did.

The heavy wooden door was first, of course, but she gave up on it quickly when it refused to budge. Peering into the absolute blackness inside the tunnel on her right, she hastened over to the other only to find it equally opaque and impenetrable — visually anyway.

Hugh had to have gone somewhere, she thought, hoping against hope that they were both still in the same universe. She slipped her right foot forward like a searching tentacle, feeling for the edge of the abyss she was sure she was about to topple into. She did the same with the left foot and then the right again before she realized that in spite of the pitch-black at her feet she could see the walls on both sides of the wide passage. The walls, a cold fire sconce up high — the light was traveling with her.

But before that fact could sink in and tip

her world yet again, she caught sight of a door about sixteen feet ahead of her. It was ajar and firelight flickered invitingly. Best of all, the closer she got, the more certain she became that she could hear Hugh's voice — Hugh's and the adult male voice of someone else.

"Yes. I understand the point of a sporting event. We have the hastilude, which includes many kinds of martial games though I would suspect you are most familiar with the tournament and the joust, which is my favorite."

"The joust?" She didn't need to see Hugh's face to know he was impressed. "Like knights? Do you joust?"

"Exactly like the knights, and no, I do not. My interests sprout and grow in the realm of books and learning, study and invention . . . exploring. But I did once attempt it in a lesser form at a quintain and I can tell you it is not for the faint-hearted, my friend."

His *friend?* The voice was deep and kept low like the rumble of the earth settling. It had an English-sounding accent, a fringe of amusement, and not a single note of *un*friendliness to it.

"Ah." It was a satisfied sound. "We will speak more of this . . . and of baseball later.

But for now, perhaps you should open the door for your mother. She has arrived."

Had she made a noise? Was her heart hammering too loud?

Someone in the room sounded pleased, but then Hugh grumbled, "We've got doors at home. She knows how they work."

That, apparently, was her cue to swing the door open and step into the room — with the low-glowing light! — as if she planned to all along. Hugh was the first and only thing she saw — across the room in an odd-looking chair staying warm by a huge open hearth fire. He looked fine — despite his fawn-colored tunic and brown leggings and the weird little shoes with the curled-up toes. He looked just fine.

"Excuse me. Hello. My name is Marie Barnett and I've come for my son." She wasn't sure if she actually spoke the words because her tongue felt stuck to the roof of her mouth. She was terrified. "I hope his being here hasn't caused you any inconvenience."

While a broad-shouldered man rose from a large X–frame chair across from Hugh's, she quickly glanced around the room for exits and weapons, should they be needed. There were four X–frame chairs in the room — three around the fire, one against the wall across the room — also two oak benches, a sizeable chest, and a large worktable with candles shining on top to reveal several scrolls and many books, in many different sizes. Books everywhere, in fact. There were tapestries on the wall, a landscape and a tale of some kind with the same character showing up multiple times across the hanging.

In fact, if this wasn't a sound stage somewhere in the twenty first century, then she was standing in a thirteenth-or maybe fourteenth-century castle with some wealthy baron or earl or something judging by his clothes — a long, pale, mossy green tunic and a thick, full-length cloak of . . . cyan — not turquoise, not quite aquamarine — cyan, like the blue of the light, with white fur trim. Certainly not the heavy, rough wool worn by the peasants in Robin Hood movies.

"He has caused me no trouble, madam." His voice resounded in the room. He turned and between the glow she came in with, the candles, and the fire . . . he looked golden. His skin and long blond hair certainly did but even his brown eyes looked more the color of fine bourbon than horse chestnuts. Somewhere in his early thirties, he was tall — six foot three or four and so powerfully built . . . so larger than life-looking he made the echo-filled room feel small. Only the truly insane would joust with him, she decided.

Facing her more directly he looked . . . taken aback, startled possibly, by her appearance and tried to hide it, but not before his gaze raked her head to toe and back again. She glanced down at the emerald green over-tunic and the russet embroidery around the linen hem and wondered, *Why?* She thought she looked quite elegant — considering.

"We have been discussing . . ." He looked over at Hugh for confirmation. ". . . baseball and the many exhibits at the . . . museum. Fascinating." He was picking up vocabulary words left and right, and was obviously intrigued. Recalling his manners, he quickly added, "Madam, please permit me, my name is Nester Baraka of Viator. I am at your service."

He bowed at the waist.

"Great. Thanks. How's it going?" She stretched out her hand in friendship and took a step forward so he could reach it more easily — no telling how well he got around in his bolts of robe. She spotted a flat oval stone mounted on a clasp similar to that in the museum fastened at his left shoulder — it was striking, a tan stone with colored dots, like the skin of a leopard. "I appreciate your kindness toward Hugh. I do. But we need to get back to the museum right away. I have to have him there by five o'clock sharp or I'm toast because, believe me, Bill's not going to believe this one . . . for one thing."

"Toast?" he asked, his big warm hand still holding hers, she noticed.

"Serious trouble. And for a second thing this is just, well, we wouldn't do well in this environment. We need electricity and running water and . . . vaccinations." She was about to slip her unshook hand from his when he tipped it, bowed over it gracefully, and brushed a wispy kiss on the back. "Oh. Thanks." Was her face on fire? Discreetly, she slipped her hands behind her and pressed her lips together — they were tingling.

"Man, Mom." Hugh squeezed between the third chair and Nester to shrivel her with a grow-up-and-don't–embarrass-me look that worked very well. To Nester he politely explained, "Most people in our time don't kiss hands anymore and the ones that do are really old or they're really weird."

"Really weird?"

"Yeah, you know . . ." He bobbed his head

and strained his expression. "Strange."

"Ah." He looked to her instantly, then back at Hugh. He was nervous, too? "I suspect we will have many of these miscommunications on our journey. You have but to speak of them and I will strive to adjust."

"What journey?" she asked, pleased with the strength in her voice.

Nester and Hugh looked at one another, then her, then back to each other again.

"Hugh, do you recall the way to the kitchen?" Nester asked and Hugh nodded. "Please go there and return with bread and cheese and ale for your mother. I am sure she is hungry and tired from her travels."

"She can't drink ale or wine. She's allergic. Do you know 'allergic'?"

Surprised, Marie glanced at her son to see if he was mocking her, but his face in the firelight was nothing but earnest and young, which led her to believe, because she very much wanted to, that he was trying to protect her.

"It does not sit well" was his guess. "Fresh cider then."

Hugh rushed off . . . almost, until Marie caught him, parked him in front of her, and clamped her hands on his boney shoulders. She gave him a quick, motherly once-over — something akin to a Goodwrench On-

Star Multi-Point Vehicle Inspection but faster and more accurate. Was he afraid, drugged, hypnotized, brain-washed, traumatized, or body-snatched? Her hands slid closer to his neck so she could cradle his head in her hands and look into his eyes.

"I'm okay, Mom." His words were soft and kindly spoken, as if he understood her fears, as if he appreciated her concern. "Really."

She held him several more seconds because he hadn't allowed her to in over a year. She nodded and released him, and then watched as he ran from the room — the low glow of light slipping away from her to follow him.

At least that's how it looked to her, but who would believe it?

"He seems very comfortable. How long has he been here?" she asked as she turned back to Nester.

"Two days."

"But I followed him immediately."

"He said you would."

"I couldn't have been more than three minutes behind him. He did? He said that?"

"You are his mother, are you not?" She nodded, speechless. "When a boy is lucky enough to know his mother, he knows his mother well."

"We've been having problems lately. He's angry with me."

"Yes, I see him making great efforts to distress you, but he finds no joy in it. Please," he motioned to the third chair, then extended his hand farther to several straw-filled pillows on the floor closer to the fire to give her a choice. "Be at ease. It has been a long time since I had visitors; I have forgotten my manners. Please, sit. We will talk."

The chair was heavy indeed but not as big as it seemed at first; cleverly made, it took its X–shape by crossing the front and back legs. The woodwork was rubbed smooth and the seat was made of loose cushions resting on webbing between the side rails of the frames.

"I don't suppose you'd be willing to try to convince me that I'm dreaming?"

For half a second he looked confused and she was sorry she'd spoken facetiously, but when understanding lit his eyes and his full, lush lips curled and split into an obliging smile, she knew instinctively that they were in no danger from him. He wasn't particularly happy to see them, but he wasn't going to eat them either. She found herself relaxing a little despite the peculiar circumstances.

"I would be willing to do this, madam . . ."

"Marie."

"Marie." He made her name sound exotic and rare. "I should also like to assure you that very soon you will awake and find all as it should be. Unfortunately, I am a poor liar. And frankly, I do not wish to deceive you. I am sorry." He readjusted his position in the chair, leaning casually, confidently on the arm toward her. "I do believe, however, that we can be of assistance to one another if we speak only the truth to each other. I am sure you have a great many questions for me, but I must beg that you allow me to ask mine first."

"Okay. Shoot."

"Shoot."

"Go ahead, ask your questions."

He nodded, looked away briefly like he was cataloging the new meaning to an old word and came back to her. "I believe, were it with you, that it would have made its presence known by now. Still, I am compelled to ask . . . did you bring the Sellithos with you?" Her face must have looked as blank as her brain felt. "The stone, the moonstone on the clasp that sent you here. Did you bring it with you?"

His expression was . . . prediscouraged — disheartened even before he heard her answer. She almost didn't respond.

"No. I'm sorry. I didn't. I didn't know . . ." He lowered his gaze from hers and looked away as panic tightened like a giant python around her stomach. "I wanted to repeat Hugh's actions as close as I could, to increase our chances of ending up in the same place. What's that expression on your face, what does it mean? We can go back, right?"

"Yes, of course." He stood abruptly, walked to the large, open fireplace, muttering something about a boy and now a woman like they were two broken wheels for his wagon, useless. He kept his back to her when he spoke more clearly, "Eventually."

# Three

"What did you say?"

He turned to face her. "I said I will get you and your son home eventually, and I will." He slid his right hand behind the sleeve on his left arm and easily removed a small platter where a golden brown apple was cut in quarter-inch slices and spread out in a perfect circle. She could smell the freshness of it and see tiny beads of juice on the yellow meat. He held it out to her asking, "Are you a patient woman, Marie?"

"Not particularly." She looked at the apple like it was moon fruit even as she took it from him. "And absolutely not where my son is concerned."

He nodded and returned to his chair. "Then let us begin." He looked at her for a full minute. "Do you have questions?"

"Are you kidding me?" She held up a slice of apple as evidence. "I want to know what happened, where we are, who *you* are, what year it is, what the deal with the stone is, how we get home, where my best pair of jeans went, and why there was a light following me until it ran off with Hugh? And that's just to start."

This time his smile was more than just gracious, it was appreciative. "Good. We will begin with the most easy to answer. It is spring I believe in the year 1223. I am Nester Baraka of Viator, as I have told you. Nester is the Greek word for traveler. Baraka is the same word in Egyptian. Viator is where I lived and studied, and in return acted as counsel and guardian to my lord William and, unfortunately, his wife and second son, Lord Mark. I am a wizard." She simply looked at him. Of course he was. "You might say a magician or a sorcerer."

"I might say a lot more in a minute but . . . what if I say witch or warlock?"

He squinted and angled his eyes away. "I *am* of that circle but I do not consider myself to be so occult or as spiritual. I have but one natural ability and the rest I have studied and learned and practiced to make my own. I believe witches and warlocks consider all their abilities to have come to them naturally, even through study." He looked back at her. "A hair's difference, I own this, but trust me it is a disparity that cannot be traversed."

"Okay. The second son, Lord Mark, from the tone of your voice you don't like him. Why? And what happened to the first son?"

"Sir Fredrick. He was a good and fair young man and would have been a proper heir to Lord William had he lived through a riding accident at the age of thirteen. That left Mark — well meaning, I suppose, but reckless . . . and willful and foolish beyond measure."

"Why? What did he do?"

"We will come to that." He paused for a moment as if collecting his answers. He touched the stone at his left shoulder, caressed it, barely looking away. "This piece of leopard skin jasper is called the Petroleon. It and the Sellithos are very old and they have been together since before Homer and Plato, since before King Narmer, who wore Both Crowns of Egypt. They have been passed from priest to priest, shaman to shaman; later from parent to child or wizard to wizard . . . like Moses and Joshua. In my case, I received them from my grandfather as my father had not the disposition or inclination to learn and practice magic — but I did."

"I didn't know wizards got married." She was off the subject of rocks . . . not to mention Moses and Joshua being wizards. Who knew? Who would have imagined . . . any of this?

"We do not as a rule." He cleared his throat and smoothed out a wrinkle in his tunic. "Not that we could not should we wish to, but it is generally not wise . . . to live among the unskilled or to sequester one in this kind of solitude." His hands, resting on the arms of his chair, indicated his surroundings. "One can be dangerous, the other is unkind."

"Dangerous. Because people tend to burn at the stake what they don't understand? Like witches and wizards?"

"Correct, contingent mostly on the level of their own misery, I am afraid."

She was reluctant to tell him how little the human race had changed in eight centuries and turned her mind instead to the seemingly impossible task of procreating small wizard children with so little human contact . . . and then just as quickly turned her thoughts in the opposite direction, sensing the less she knew about wizard breeding the better off she'd be.

"So the stones are magic?"

"In a way, yes, but —"

"They're your talismans, your amulets, and your protection against evil spirits."

"Evil spirits?" There was a brief jerk of amusement around his lips but he went on, entirely serious. "No. But they do protect me from other things. They also help me. They balance me, they complete me. They are . . ." He started to gesture with his hands, looked straight into her eyes, and seemed to have difficulty finding the right words. She could see the pulse at the base of his throat bumping against his tanned skin and his nostrils flared a bit when he inhaled, like he was trying to catch her scent from three feet away. If he were any other man in the universe, she would have snapped her fingers at him and told him to get with it. But this man was . . . well, he was special — even beyond his wizardship, she could *feel* that he was extraordinary and unique. Plus, he'd been very kind to Hugh in a potentially traumatizing situation, so the least she could do was let him stare at her . . . for the seventeen seconds it took to make her so uncomfortable she felt like tearing her skin off.

"They are your rocks, but they're not really magical." She hesitated. "I have to tell you, Nester, that one at the museum —"

"Sellithos."

She nodded. "I think it's been going to charm school. It lit up like an atomic bomb and all that blue light swirling and the motionless people and ending up here . . . it seems pretty magical to me."

"Motionless people, you say?"

"Like statues. Like stone."

His patient, closed-lipped smile said *I get motionless,* but what he said when he spoke was, "I am sure it does seem like magic . . . Marie . . . and the stone is powerful indeed, but it is not magical.

"Magic is a method of initiating or altering circumstances through the manipulation of energy. And magic is *achieved* through the focus of willpower and emotion, which shape and reshape that energy. Therefore, Sellithos would need a brain and a heart, with thoughts and emotions, to be magical.

"As it happens, I do have a brain and a minimum of natural talent." In a blink he was gone and in the next blink he was resting back in Hugh's chair like he'd been sitting there all afternoon. Marie gasped and the corners of his eyes crinkled when he smiled. "Child's play. I have done this since I was seven years of age."

To prove it he quickly disappeared in a lounging position to rematerialize standing beside her chair looming over her. "It is entertaining to be sure. But beyond that it has no purpose, no value, no point at all." He dragged his heavy robes back to his chair with ease and sat down. "Or so I once thought. I cannot express the depth of my disappointment when I realized that my one gift, my skill was to be no more than an excellent party trick."

"A really, *really* excellent party trick." Well, she was really, *really* impressed.

He slanted a look at her, a good look, as if he wasn't sure what to make of her but wasn't averse to giving it a try. That's when she noticed his eyelashes, fully half an inch long, thick and curled at the ends like his hair . . . and totally endearing.

God. Lush lips, golden hair, endearing eyelashes? Fine. He was a head-to-toe thrill of a man that she wouldn't mind getting stranded in a medieval castle with . . . but he was also a freaking thirteenth-century wizard, and while he seemed real enough at the moment she wasn't sure he really existed, period.

"It's more than an excellent party trick, isn't it?"

"I am a traveler. I was born to travel, and not simply about the room as you have seen, but through space . . . and time."

"A time traveler. Then you can take Hugh and me —"

He smoothly cut her off. "I did not know I could travel in any other way until my grandfather gave me the stones and I was sent away to study with the great wizard Pearoline. As it happens, my talent and strength are considerable but alone, without the stones, I can go no farther than half a day's journey in any direction and only as far as tomorrow and yesterday." He paused. "Sellithos and Petroleon magnify my powers . . . immeasurably."

"So you *can* take Hugh and me —"

He wasn't quite done. "For hundreds of years the stones were kept together for a reason. They are a pair. They are two parts of a whole. As darkness and light make the day —" He pumped his hands up and down. "— they balance one another . . . and they balance me. Do you understand?"

She gave a slow nod. "You need the stones to increase your power enough to take us home and you need them for balance, your . . . inner balance, and to keep your power stable and . . . *but,* oh God, but you only have one stone." Suddenly all the dots connected. "What does that mean? That means . . . what? We can't go back? Maybe . . . just one stone is enough to get Hugh back alone. What do you think? He's not as big as some of the boys in his class."

She stood as her voice got higher. "I simply can't allow my son to grow up in the thirteenth century, Nester. I can't. Hell, you guys haven't even invented baseball yet — he'll shrivel up and die here. Plus, he's usually fused to a computer, he has no survival skills, he can't possibly —"

"Madam, please. Marie. All is not lost."

She stopped mid-hysteria. "It's not?"

"I have an idea."

"You do?" Her words echoed above in the cool, empty air. She sat again. "Of course you do. What is it?"

"We're going to journey together," Hugh said, pushing his way into the room while the pale flush of light stayed behind in the corridor. He was excited and made time travel sound like a bus tour of Ipswich, South Dakota — nothing to it. "All three of us will go. Together."

He set two small metal bowls on her lap. One contained a cool, wet towel, which she used on her forehead and hands and was grateful for; the other contained a bit of goat cheese that she sampled with her fingers — twice — and a small wedge of brie, half of a small round loaf of heavy bread, and what appeared to be a small, pointed dagger. She was contemplating the safety factors of Hugh using such a deadly-looking weapon

426

to eat with when he pushed a small stool against her chair for one or more of her plates and sidled into the space between her and Nester to whisper, "You can use your fingers or just stab it with your knife. That's okay here."

He was helping her? Was he trying to spare her the embarrassment of making a fool of herself in front of Nester . . . or was he protecting Nester's sensitivities . . . from her?

She gave him an uncertain smile and said, "Thanks."

But seeing the gratitude in her eyes flipped his switch and cold iron doors slammed down over the light in his eyes before he turned away. Nester wondered aloud if Hugh could warm his mother's cider without scalding himself and he eagerly took up the challenge and moved away, leaving Nester and Marie with their eyes fixed on one another.

She wasn't sure what he could see in her eyes, but his were tolerant and attempting to be passive even though he didn't know her or what she'd done to Hugh.

Or did he? She glanced between the wizard and her son and sat up straighter, hid her thoughts in the cheese bowl on her lap, and tried to remember if she'd ever felt more alone.

"I have lost my thought." Nester said to no one in particular. "Oh yes, our journey to return the two of you to your own time before Marie becomes toast and to retrieve Sellithos." He fingered Petroleon idly. "If only I had them together at present, you could be home in less time than it takes to sigh."

"You said you would tell me how you lost Sellithos," Hugh said. "Is now a good time?"

"It was not lost, my friend, it was stolen. Because I was blind. Because I was thick-headed. Because I . . ." He stopped when Marie looked up at him from her meal. "Because I was careless. Tell me, do you know of the Holy Wars in the East waged to free Jerusalem and the sacred Holy Land from Muslim rule?"

She nodded her head and chewed as fast as she could to say, "The Crusades. We call them the Crusades." She took her warmed cider from Hugh.

"Yes. Five times now the noblemen and knights, and the armies that follow them, have traveled east at the Holy Father's behest."

In a low voice intended to soften the blow, she said, "There are nine Crusades. More really, but officially nine. In that particular region."

He shook his head sadly. "So many. And for what? Brave men and foolish young boys die by their oath for nothing more than what is simply repeated acts of prejudice in God's name. It is wrong." He went quiet, seeking answers from deep in the fire.

"It is no different in our time." He looked up, but he didn't look surprised. "Have you lost people you care for?"

"Pope Innocent III's attempt to invade the Holy Land through Egypt was a mishap of notable extent. My lord William, my friend, was lost," he said. "Though he did hear the victory cry, I am told."

"I'm sorry."

Nester acknowledged her sympathy with a glance, and then turned to Hugh as if he were telling a whopping tall tale. "Thirteen years later, at just twenty years of age, Lord Mark was all heroic excitement and desperate to dash off and follow the crusading forces from Hungary and Austria, to join the forces of the King of Jerusalem and the Prince of Antioch to take back Jerusalem. They were even so bold and brave as to capture Damietta in Egypt on their way. Then the papal legate, Pelagius, was insistent that they also launch a foolhardy attack on Cairo, Egypt's most cherished city. The ruler of Egypt, the powerful Sultan Al-Kamil, made many offers of peace, but Pelagius refused — so Al-Kamil crushed them, but once the army surrendered Al-Kamil agreed to a peace agreement of eight years with his enemies."

"But what about Lord Mark?" Her son was a bottom-line guy. *Why did the farmer's wife cut off the tails of the three blind mice? How come red buttons are* always *the most important?*

"When the soldiers marched on Cairo, Al-Kamil simply opened the dams and allowed the great Nile River to flood. Lord Mark and scores of his companions were killed."

"Is that why you don't like Lord Mark? Cuz he died?"

"No, certainly not. I am sure he felt he was being righteous and noble and both are honorable, but he was . . ."

Automatically she offered up the words Nester was searching for: "Well meaning but reckless . . . and willful and foolish beyond measure."

When the story of Lord Mark didn't begin immediately, she looked up from the scarfing of her meager but delicious and filling fare. Hugh and Nester watched her — rather Nester watched her and Hugh watched him. She waved a cheese-coated crust of bread over the bowl. "That's what you said. Right?"

"It is. Every word, in just that manner." He hesitated briefly. "I know that in the future common women take on work beyond the home and the garden and the lands of their masters —"

"We have no masters." They could discuss common women later.

"So I am told. What is your work?"

"My *job* or my *career*," she instructed. "I'm a teacher."

"A teacher." He sighed and looked pleased. He nodded and gradually climbed back on track. "Lord Mark was young. And indeed he was reckless and willful and foolish, as was his mother . . . leave out her youth. I give way to her misfortunes in losing her husband and oldest son and I grieved with her both times. But when it came time for Mark and his men to leave, Lady Agnes, who knew I would not simply give Sellithos or Petroleon to her, sent part of her guard to take them. I had not imagined . . ." He caught himself and proceeded more clinically. "I failed to protect them as I swore I would. I was quickly overpowered. Sellithos was taken and given to Mark as a charm for his safety, with the further pledge that the stone and a wish would bring him home whenever he wished. Lies and false promises I ponder often as I attempt to fathom the depths of Mark's despair when, at the end, Sellithos did not answer his pleas but lay powerless in his hands."

They all thought about it and the room got silent until it occurred to Marie, "It was powerful in Hugh's hands."

"It vibrated," he told Nester.

"It brought me here when I begged it to and we're . . . unskilled. We have no magic. Why did it work for us?"

"I wondered the same after I tracked young Hugh to the back of my wardrobe. I felt it immediately, through him I think, when he first arrived, but then finding him was another matter." He slipped a teasing look in Hugh's direction. She felt a pang of jealousy.

"Man, I was scared. I didn't know where I was. You would hide, too." Nester agreed good-naturedly and Hugh looked much relieved. But then he glanced at his mother. "You didn't hide." He looked back at Nester. Despite the fact that her arrival followed his by two days, he was positive. "My mom didn't hide."

He tipped his head back and then forward as if that made perfect sense. "She had nothing to fear, for there is no place more terrifying or dangerous than the space between a mother and her child. No wise man would try to detain her."

She sensed that all his benevolent mother talk was for her benefit . . . for Hugh's, to help mend the rift between them, but she wished he would stop. Drawing attention to the one right thing she'd done in seven years only made the glaring light on everything else she'd done that much brighter. What she needed was time, time for them to get reacquainted, to build trust, to show him *and* his father that she had changed, that she could follow the rules — which, by the way, is why she had immediately nixed the idea of hijacking Hugh and remaining in the past to keep him for herself. She was determined to prove herself in their eyes. Well, that and the lack of a Starbucks franchise and the overabundance of pestilence and poverty and . . . no Nordstrom's.

That's why they needed to go back. To prove to Hugh that she loved him and that he could depend on her for anything; to show his dad that she's well and trustworthy and responsible again; to confirm to herself that she could be a good mother to her son once more.

"Well, this mom is ready to hear how we're traveling back to the museum without the second stone. You said it was possible, right?"

# FOUR

"Yes. It is possible." Nester readjusted his weight in the chair and fiddled with his robe a bit — procrastinating. She cleared her throat softly. "For a while, I attempted to find Lord Mark or, failing that, Sellithos. But by the time I finally reached the Holy Land, the king was just a man called Yitzhak Ben-Zvi and there was a soldier on every street corner with a killing machine. I could see nothing had changed."

"So you've been to the future." She pitched Hugh an excited glance and found him leaning solidly into the pillows in his chair, his elbow on the rest, his fist to his cheek, listening intently even as his eyelids grew heavy.

"Several times. If both stones had been with me and these visits had been to places of my choosing, I might have enjoyed them. As it was, I focused my will and all my power on my destination, I hoped for the best and prayed I would not wedge myself inside a mountain or position myself between two battling armies or appear in any European town square between 1450 and 1700 where killing witches and wizards on sight is an accepted way of life."

Her face was a wince of sympathy. "Your last vacation, I take it."

"Vacation?"

"Holiday." He nodded, he knew that one. "Time away from here."

"When I finally returned to this place — several days before I first left, may I add — I decided I would remain here forever if need be and wait for Sellithos to find me. I waited for me to leave —"

"Why didn't you warn yourself not to go? Save yourself the aggravation?" She heard her own words. "Oh, to be a fly on the wall for that one, huh?"

It was becoming more and more fun to watch him silently chew on new words to get their flavor and meaning. He was astute and clever and very bright.

"Traveling forward in time is much easier than traveling back because what is behind us has already happened and to alter it in any way changes what is meant to be in the future," he explained patiently. "If I had stopped myself I would not have discovered how dangerous it is to travel with only one of my stones; I would not have known to cast the spell on my small haven here so that time, within its walls, would slow a day to a single moment; nor would I have been here to receive Sellithos's message and the leads to finding it, namely you."

"How long have you been waiting here?"

"It has been two years since I cast the spell on this small space — one week after I heard of Lord Mark's death, which was four years after Lady Agnes stole Sellithos."

But even as she nodded her understanding she realized something else. "The traveling is dangerous because you have no control over it. We can't leave Hugh safely behind while you and I go find the other stone because we don't know how long it'll take to find it. We could bounce around for years maybe — so the three of us are going to travel together because it's our only chance of ever getting back home and finding your stone *and* it's quite possible that we might be traveling together forever? Have I got that right?"

His expression was a reflection of the anguish in her soul and he spoke softly. "Yes. But I do not foresee this being the case, only a distant possibility to be aware of as you make your decision."

Marie's gaze gravitated toward Hugh, expecting him to be asleep, but instead she found him awake with sleepy eyes watching her. "I say we go," he said, like she'd asked for his input.

"I say we give her the night to decide as she has not had the time to consider as we have." Nester stood and looked down at her. "Not the reasonable amount of time that you might think. Since my spell is now broken, time here is moving forward swifter than I am able to calculate. Your three minutes to our two days? Another risk factor to our journey, I am afraid, but nothing to that of the imbalance of the stones."

This new information barely grazed the numb matter her brain had become over the past few . . . what . . . minutes? hours? days? since she'd left the museum. And now she was to make a crucial decision with it? She reached out for Hugh, grasping air until he felt compelled to stand and moved into her clutch.

"A chamber has been prepared for you or you may stay with the boy if you wish." Like she'd be letting Hugh out of her sight again — ever. Nester saw it on her face. "He knows the way and the light will guide you safely."

"Yeah, the light. Thank you. I . . . so much

to take in." She pulled Hugh close. "Thank you. There doesn't seem to be much choice, but maybe some sleep will make it seem more . . ." She waved her hand. "I don't know. Real? Logical? Possible?"

"Perhaps," he said, stepping aside to give them ample room to exit. The sooner the better; he made no secret of it. Marie knew the look in his eye: He wasn't used to having people around and he'd come to his limit.

Marie trailed Hugh from the room with her hands on his shoulders, dropping them when it became clear that the light would indeed guide them safely to their room.

"So what's with this light, huh?"

"It's cool, isn't it? It's leftover light that no one wants or misses. The last few rays of daylight after the sun sets, the flash of brightness before a candle goes out, the low glow of embers that no one sees. He invites them to come here and be useful. And they do."

"Can you imagine what this guy could do with a refrigerator light?"

"I was thinking solar panel."

Marie laughed, then quickly sobered. "Are you sure you're okay, honey?"

"Sure I'm sure. I'm . . ."

Marie held her breath. What was he going

to say? *I'm better now that you're here. I'm glad you came for me. I'm ready to forgive you.*

"I'm not a baby, you know."

"I know."

The light stopped in front of a large wooden door that Hugh seemed to recognize. He pulled the latch and pushed it open without hesitating. The light followed them in, split into four portions that settled in the corners of the room to make it cozy.

"Nester says that knights are really nice to girls, so I guess you can take the bed and I'll sleep over here by the fire." Two years ago he wouldn't have thought twice about cuddling up in the bed with her.

Of course, he wasn't a baby, so . . .

"I would think, with all this stone, it gets cold here at night. If we were to share the bed, sleep back to back and share the heat, we might actually manage some sleep tonight," she said matter-of-factly, like it was purely a business proposition.

Hugh looked at the elevated bed with the sheets and covers, saw the tiny gray mouse scurry off into the shadows and linger on the cold stone floor in front of the flames. "We could try that for a while. See how it works."

She made herself busy straightening the

blankets over and over while he used the chamber pot . . . and naturally didn't wash his hands, but compared to whatever else could kill him here she decided this ongoing lesson could wait.

Sleep scooped him up in seconds, but she needed to think things through, watch the fire, keep an eye on the rodents . . . She was out at first base.

Later, she lifted her groggy head up to give Hugh more space on the pillow, opening her eyes to see she'd stuffed most of it under her neck and Hugh's head was strangling the blood from her left arm, leaving pins and needles in her fingers.

Not that she cared. She smiled. In sleep they were still mother and son. Instinctively, he would always turn to her. Unconsciously, he would always trust her. Her spirit buoyed until she recognized the rough stone wall beyond the dark curls on his head.

Morning in a medieval cave belonging to a time-traveling wizard who hadn't gone anywhere in eight hundred years because his magic rocks were lopsided, but who was grudgingly agreeable to journeying timelessly through history with them until they eventually returned to the museum where she and Hugh could take up their lives again and he could collect his missing stone . . .

was not a weird dream. It was a nightmare.

She closed her eyes softly and tried to return to sleep.

She felt Hugh's chuckle before she heard it and looked at him. "I tried that yesterday. It doesn't work. We really are here."

"What time do you think it is?"

"I heard a rooster crow a few minutes ago but . . ." She looked at him. "I think it's just Nester calling us to get up. I looked all over for a window into this place yesterday, but the only real light that comes in is through a couple of skylight panels in the keep — that's his main room, where we were last night — that he studies the stars through . . . or sometimes he paints there, he says."

"Seems like there's nothing he can't do." She watched her son flip the covers off both of them and climb over her to pick up his shoes and shake nothing out of them. She planned to do the same. He grinned at her.

"Nothing he can't do except what he's supposed to do." She raised her brows — shrewd observation — and swung her legs over the side of the bed

"So what happens now? We pack and wait for our limo to the airport?"

Hugh cast a stern eye over the cumbersome linen gown she'd slept in. "Well, first off I think we should pull you together. I told you about the men being real nice to girls here, but the girls have to be, like, special, too."

"I'm not playing some damned damsel in distress for this broken magician who may or may not be pulling a fast one on us as neither of us has even seen the world outside these few stone rooms . . . which makes us hermetically sealed, I guess, and that's a good thing if he's the real deal. But I'm still not going to pretend to be some weak fainting thing —"

"I think just combing your hair and not cussing or being so bossy would do it, Mom."

"I've been bossy?" She straightened out her long skirts and over-tunic, tugged at her sleeves, and took the thin wooden pins from her hair — to brush, retwist, and secure it again. Hugh gave up a sigh and sat on the bed while she splashed water on her face and used the wet end of a rough towel on her teeth. "More ladylike?"

He gave her a hard once-over. "Just be nice and don't say dumb stuff."

"I'll do my best."

Oddly enough, the rude advice felt like a balm to her heart. He wasn't being spiteful or deliberately hurtful, just advising and guiding as best he could.

The leftover light stirred in the corners of the room and united much brighter in the hallway to make it seem almost like daylight.

"He could make a fortune off this unused light."

"I think he just wants his rock back."

Nester stood with his arms in his sleeves in the direct sunlight from the skylight above. Both she and Hugh looked up to clear blue sky, but if it was tenth-century sky or seventeenth-century sky, or the sky of the twenty-first century, they couldn't tell.

Breakfast of some darkly cooked meat and eggs and heavy bread with butter and a dark berry jam was set for two on his work table with a ceramic mug of cider for each.

"I hope you both have all you need and that you slept. We exchanged a great deal of information last night and the decisions we make today will be grave. I am sure your hearts and minds are heavy."

"Well, not really." Hugh's voice was high and clear as he speared a piece of meat with his little dagger. Marie turned a blind eye to it and sat down. "It's like Mom said last night, there doesn't seem to be much choice. We can stay here in the unstable time warp that our breaking your spell has created or we can travel with you for as long as it takes to get home."

"And the danger?"

Hugh looked across the table at her. "We're in danger no matter what we do."

There was a strange look in Nester's eye when he looked at Hugh . . . not strange-strange, but unaccountably proud strange, unexpectedly pleased strange. This odd man had no right to be pleased or proud of Hugh, and yet she felt herself warming to the spark, trying to recall the last time anyone had looked at her that way . . . and wishing the wizard would.

"True." Nester relaxed his arms as he turned to the chest behind him and opened the lid. He withdrew a box and a book and dropped them into the sleeves of his great cloak. "I neglected to mention last night that Sellithos, in its softer more subtle ways, generally tends to the finer details of a journey, such as a disguise and arranging to have money and coins in one's purse for lodging and food." Hugh leaned forward to whisper that he wasn't carrying a purse on this trip and Marie reassured him. "Petroleon has a more corporeal, malelike essence and cannot always be counted on for such details. Do you see the balance there between them? Strong and wild, flexible and shrewd — both very powerful, but with different skills. And alone they are . . . whacked."

"Out of whack," a helpful Hugh murmured.

"Yes, yes." He was hard on himself for the silly misnomer and reminded Marie of her father, a terrible traveler who arrived everywhere early and so over-ready for whatever he was there to do he was nearly exhausted. "So we must be ready to be thrown into any circumstance."

She and Hugh looked at one another. *Like this one?*

In the few minutes it took them to finish their breakfasts the sun came directly overhead in the skylight and Nester was down to the last few items he wanted stuffed up his sleeves.

"I have traveled to the east, as you know, but not to the far exotic east that I have read of in the books I brought back with me. And had I the confidence of both stones I would have gone to the New World across the vast ocean and seen the Red Men who dwell there." He sighed. "I could have done so many things."

From the center of the room he made a slow circle, reviewing his choices. He stopped when he faced them.

"One more thing," Marie said.

More of his smile was in his eyes than on his lips. "Always, if there is a woman in the mix. That has not changed with time, I think."

She simpered at him and started to walk toward the far side of the room, keeping her back to her son. "I need your word that if anything goes wrong you'll make Hugh your first priority, you know, your main goal. He has to get back. If you can only save one of us, save him."

"Of course, madam. And if I am the one to be saved?" His expression was guarded and curious at once. She wasn't sure he really wanted her to answer.

"We'll do the best we can. I promise."

"That is enough."

He turned abruptly and clapped his hands together once. Marie watched him take a breath to fill his chest, to make him appear braver than he felt. "Anyone for the privy then before we leave?"

They slowly shook their heads in unison.

"Once again I find myself in unexplored waters, madam, as I have never journeyed with others before, not in the same spell. Quarters may be close, I am afraid."

She'd suffer through it. "We'll do what we must, right, Hugh?"

Nester looked pleased with her answer in

an absent-minded fashion and held out his arms, looking from one arm to the other, gauging the space between them.

"Come, come." He motioned them forward and asked them to take a firm grip on one another's arms. Hands, he informed them, were not as reliable. To accommodate their smaller hands they joined at the wrists in a remarkably strong lock. "Good. One set of hands at my waist behind me, the other set in front, and I will hold you both here." He wrapped strong, purposeful arms around their shoulders. Glancing between them, he tried an encouraging smile. "Good. This is comfortable. This will work."

Marie tightened her grip on Hugh, who increased the pressure of his hold on her, and pulled them both in close to Nester's chest, who readjusted his grasp accordingly.

"This will work better." He looked up into the sky above them and forced them to shuffle their feet to the right slightly. "We face forward in time and push west."

Nothing.

He first opened his eyes, then closed them tighter. Still nothing. He released his passengers and shook the tension from his arms; he touched Petroleon briefly and begging their pardon stepped away, then turned to face them. He sized them up. Then in a sudden fluster of aggravated movement started unloading his sleeves — book after book, small boxes of bottles, and leather bags of roots and herbs. There seemed to be no end to it.

Finally, drained, he turned and took one look at Marie, grabbed a pouch from the table, and stuffed it back in his sleeve before stepping between them again. She'd faced her share of overwhelming temptations before, but not asking about that pouch was . . . harrowing.

She and Hugh joined at the wrists once more, Nester's arms encircling them.

"We face forward in time and push west."

She looked up to see him swallow hard and close his eyes to concentrate. Her gaze fell to Hugh, who was watching her. A small, hopeful smile was all she had to offer him as Nester's power began to throb inside Petroleon, generating a startling bright light that readily faded to a soft, luminous cyan blue beam spiraling around them.

"Look familiar?" She tried to ease Hugh's anxiety.

"Madam, please. Give way and go with the flow of my energy."

She felt no flow, but she was willing to be quiet, look down on the dark, shiny waves of hair on her son's head — that she might never see again, by the way — and offer this rather difficult moment up to her Higher Power. Surely She would be listening in this century, too.

She knew the wizard's eyes were closed; she watched Hugh's lashes slide to his cheeks and then she shut hers.

First, she felt warm heat wafting up her skirts, and then she heard his deep dangerous voice.

"Do. Not. Move."

# FIVE

She knew the meaning of *"do not move"* and it wasn't the same as do not *look.*

Which she did.

Jurassic Park. Steamy, warm air made their skin instantly moist, their clothes clingy and . . . too much. Still as a statue she looked into the distance: The jungle was thick, profuse, and no sky could be seen unless she directed only her eyes as far up in their sockets as possible to observe it cleaner and brighter and bluer than she'd ever seen it before.

She felt Hugh's hands tremble slightly and she secured her grip on his wrists.

She took in every color under the sun as her gaze fell earthward. Lush, glorious, vibrant flowers in the treetops, vital greens and browns expressing the health and exuberance of the planet, reds and oranges and yellows demonstrating the timeless cycles of life and death and rebirth and . . .

All this she absorbed in the seconds it took to open and focus her eyes . . . and to catch movement in their periphery — the slow, graceful, red, orange, and yellow movement of death — the apparent source of the steamy, warm air swinging away and then back in their direction, flinging white foam and clear, foul-smelling spittle in the opposite path and flashing long, sharp teeth at them.

Easily a hundred, maybe five hundred times their size, it was a carnivorous animal the likes of which no paleontologist had ever dared to dream. Not a stegosaurus or a brontosaurus or an allosaurus or Hugh's favorite, tyrannosaurus, but a mostly red, with an underbelly of orange and yellow, meat-eating *aurus* of some kind with a wild eye on them.

She filled her lungs with a startled and fearful gasp and would have deafened the creature with her screams had not the wizard's hand slipped from her shoulder to cover her mouth. Her heart was hammering hard enough to explode. Unnaturally, she heard birds chirping somewhere nearby. The blue light, she was sure, would only draw more attention to them. Over Nester's thumb, she saw Hugh's eyes closed in a tight grimace; a quick glimpse of the wiz and she knew his were, too. *And who wanted to watch themselves get eaten?* she wondered as she shut hers and automatically turned her face in to Nester's neck and chest for safety and comfort.

The dampness and temperature rose noticeably and a dim sulfur smell prickled her nose even as the smell of broken rock — like in the rock quarry where her grand-dad used to take her so long ago on a rare day off, to show her off and to show her *the pit* he called it, almost like it was something evil — filled her senses so completely it dislodged that hazy memory.

This time when his hand fell away in unguarded disbelief, she did cry out in alarm at the molten explosions taking place just three or four miles away, bright as the sun, shaking the earth beneath their feet . . . not earth, but acre upon acre upon acre of barren lava desert, still steaming in the distance where active rivers of liquid rock met water.

She didn't sound nearly as feral as she felt when she loudly pointed out, "Of all the lame, ridiculous, blind, poorly controlled, prehistoric, spit and wind navigation . . . We're going in the wrong damn direction!"

"So I see."

"So you —"

"Mom. It was an accident." The boy had more faith in this impossible wizard than he had in his own mother. She could see it in his eyes. "Let's just baby-step to our left so we don't mess anything up." They started a slow, circular dance to their left. "I saw this movie once where people in the future were selling, like, safari trips into the past and they were always real careful to never leave any evidence that they'd been there, but this one guy took his hat off when they told him not to and he left one hair behind, you know, on a prehistoric trip, and everything in evolution changed. Killer insects ruled the world and —"

"This will do it." Nester broke into Hugh's story. He looked up at stars she suspected had gone nova centuries before either she or Hugh were born, touched Petroleon briefly, straightened his posture, and read-justed his grip on his passengers. "This will do it."

"Do you know the term *doubting Thomas?*" She mumbled the question under her breath, but when she lifted her head she looked straight into his eyes, she got a little drunk on their whiskey color.

"I do, madam, and I cannot fault you for this belief considering my performance so far. I hope to do better."

Hugh nudged her under the wizard's robes, silently chastising her for hurting Nester's feelings. Although, truth told, she suspected the magical voyager was being far harder on himself than she ever could be. She nodded and averted her eyes to signal she was giving him another chance — but to her count, it was already his third.

"Good. Nothing in evidence for the pests to find. We face forward in time and push west."

They repeated the process as before, Nester closing his eyes and concentrating, Hugh shutting his and believing, Marie sealing hers and praying.

This time the wind up her skirt was frigid and the eye in her mind saw polar ice. She refused to open her eyes until she felt Nester's weight lean heavy and tired against her body for a moment, a fraction of a moment really, but long enough to tell her something was wrong.

The skies were bleak with winter, people moving around and by them with their heads down. The smell of oppression hung in the air like a Sunday pot roast. Hugh apparently also detected the wizard's brief falter and she followed the line of his vision to the man's face — weary beyond fatigue, drained. His gaze slid slowly between them, resting deep inside hers.

"I believe three jumps a day is my limit, madam." Something in the words struck her as funny and she chuckled. "I see now what it takes."

"What what takes?" She started looking around for a hotel, got the impression they were in a northern Europe kind of place — cross-country skiing and northern lights, Oktoberfest and the Freedom Monument, Belgian truffles maybe.

"What it takes to get a true smile from you." She didn't know he'd been waiting for one.

And that's when she saw the first one — a red flag with a swastika hanging from a second-story window. Others hung in storefronts and one was draped across the front basket of a beat-up bicycle.

"Holy shit."

"Madam?" Both males looked around, Hugh's eyes getting larger and Nester's getting smaller as he searched for monsters and obvious peril. She wanted to kiss Petroleon, who'd managed to deliver them in gloomy rough wool that might be several decades old but blended with the present styles well enough to keep them unobserved — so far. "Another blunder?"

"No. You did great. We're only about . . .

sixty or so years from our time. Big jump. Big. Just, ah, just not one of mankind's greatest moments here and if you're feeling like you need a little rest, we need to find shelter." She glanced at Hugh's dark features. "A place to hide really."

"An inn." Funny how she could sense him sensing danger without a word spoken among them.

"Yes. The fewer the guests the better." Glacial winds stung her cheeks and they huddled closer together. "What kind of money, coins do you have?" Hugh had to show him where his pockets were and he started to nod like *I would have remembered* and withdrew a fistful of bank notes and coins with German writing on them. They'd just have to trust that they and Petroleon were timely. "We'll have to risk them because staying out here on the street is riskier. Can you walk?"

"Of course." He was a little indignant. "There's a hostel across the way." He started to move.

"Wait, wait. Does . . . does . . . Petroleon provide us with an intergalactic translator or something like in *Star Wars* or do we wing it? Hugh doesn't speak German, and just FYI, I took Spanish in high school." The panic that bubbled in her stomach was creeping into her chest as she noted a man here and woman there with bright yellow Stars of David on their sleeves taking notice of them — the extraordinarily tall, healthy, golden, semi-Aryan man talking in the street to a woman and a boy with a darker influence.

"FYI?"

"For your information." Hugh supplied absently, keeping his eyes keen. "But I think one of those guys over there just said *bonjour,* Mom. Know any French?"

"Éclair, *'Frère Jacques.'* I don't even say *croissant* right." She turned her head to look at the men talking on the other corner. "You need that sort of nasally, talking through your adenoids noise in the middle, you know?"

*"Je parle le français excellent, madame."*

She and Nester stared at one another a full minute. She in awe, he in smug satisfaction — like she wasn't impressed enough that he could propel them through time and space, he needed to further prove himself to her by pulling fluent French out of his ass?

"Hugh reports that I am a geek without a computer but that we have other uses as well, in your time. This is true?"

"Absolutely. Love and geeks make the world go around. Without one or the other it would come to a full stop." This pleased him and she felt an overwhelming urge to hug him. He was so sweet and uncorrupted . . . that thought pinched and pulled at her heart. It hurt. "So Hugh and I will keep our mouths shut and let your do all the talking. An unnatural state for me, you may have guessed, but under the circumstances —"

"Shhhh." Hugh knew her nervous rattling better than anyone, but with the attempt Nester made to hide his amused glance, he was beginning to as well.

Moments later she stood near Hugh behind Nester because . . . well, because that's where she wanted to be. Close to her son and safe behind her wizard.

*"Une chambre pour trois, s'il vous plait,"* he asked the desk clerk as casually as the circumstances allowed. He held up two fingers, then one as if it were a heedless movement as opposed to a visual aid. One room for two with an extra. A family.

*"Ich verstehe."* The clerk spoke in German and nodded his balding head as he pushed the registry toward Nester. Marie craned her neck to see the heading: 22. Februar, 1943. In a lower voice the innkeeper asked, "Sprechen sie Deutsche?"

The wizard squeezed his index finger and

thumb together tightly. *"Nur ein bisschen."*

Chewing on a thumbnail that no longer existed, the short, thin man glanced first at Marie and Hugh and then to the far corner of the lobby where two men in classic Hollywood dark brown overcoats and old Fedoras sat talking. Gestapo officers assigned to local offices? Disguised? Like every man in town didn't know who they were? Or simple wartime travelers like themselves? Didn't matter. Creepy chills raced up her spine.

*"Parlez-moi le français seulement."*

Nester nodded and presented several German bills for the man to choose from, which he did quickly and deftly.

Once, a long time ago, she heard that people who trust other people make fewer mistakes than people who don't — somehow it made more sense then. Now it made no sense at all as they placed themselves in the hands of a semi-hairless, weasely-looking little man with no fingernails and unpolished shoes, she noticed as they crossed the small lobby toward the stairs.

No one detected their lack of luggage. They passed a long table under a mirror with a telephone, lamp, and old, overused newspaper on it. *"E.T. phone home"* flashed in her mind, but what filled it was the top of the newspaper. *Mainz*-something was printed in larger letters and 4. August, 1942 — almost six months since they'd had a fresh newspaper? Less biased, more truthful news came by mouth at this stage of the war, she mused as she walked between the desk clerk and Nester up the narrow stairwell. It occurred to her that perhaps the building hadn't always been a charmingly small hotel but someone's home — maybe the clerk's home, and taking in strangers to either keep them safe or turn them over to the authorities was his means of making money. *Paranoia?*

He took them to a room that held a dreamy looking bed and a low, tidy daybed. Muttering something in French that made Nester lift his brows, the clerk backed out of the room and closed the door.

Nester looked amused. "What is it?" Marie asked.

"One moment, madam. Please. Hugh and I must . . . ponder a possibility and get back to you." He all but pushed the boy out the door and was gone with him long enough to stir misgivings, then distrust and fear, before they chuckled their way back into her presence.

"What the hell have you been doing? This isn't funny." Their smiles were instantly gone. "Anything could have happened to you and I wouldn't have known even which direction to start looking in. I've told you about wandering off, Hugh." Tears stung her eyes. "We're in special circumstances here and I know you hate me but I have to *insist* that you do as I say. I'm the adult. I'm your mother. We can be friends again later. Do you understand?" He nodded once, an oddly pleased light smoldered in his eye. "And you!" She turned on the very tall wizard with her finger in his face. He quickly held up a hand.

"I know. I am sorry. You are rightly frightened and it is my fault. Please forgive me, Marie. I was reckless." No "madam"? No excuse? A truly penitent look the color of topaz? So unfair.

"Oh man." Hugh sent his friend a grudging look of admiration as she felt the hackles on the back of her neck begin to smooth down into place. "Nice save, Nester." The time traveler turned away just then but she caught the wink he aimed in her son's direction. He then directed his full and confounded attention to the buttons on his coat front.

"Sorry, Mom." This was his own apology, casual but sincere, and not a page from Nester's book. She forgave him immediately.

"That guy told Nester we could use the . . . well, he called it a water closet and that really did a number on my man's mind, but it's kinda like a little bathroom . . . only not, you know? A pot to pee in and a pitcher full of water, but it beats going out to an out-house . . . and Nester's got basically the same setup, you know?"

The thought of the wizard inspecting modern-day plumbing and declaring its magic far more powerful than his own entertained her as she tried to keep the heels of her shoes from tapping as she walked down the hall to the . . . water closet.

The chilly water in the basin felt so good on her hands and face she extended the territory covered to her forearms and neck as well. She folded the towel exactly as she found it — killer insects ruling the world and all.

There was a thud on the door and she made a startled sound, held her breath, and wondered if the Gestapo had Hugh and Nester yet, waited for them to rush in and take her, but nothing happened.

In a move so bold she could hardly believe she made it, she flipped the latch on the door and pushed it open with a clammy palm. One of the men from the lobby, trenchcoatless, stood off to one side. Her heart throbbed with the force of ten in her throat; she felt sweat beading at her temples.

He nodded. *"Ecuse ich. Ich bedauere, Sie gestört zu haben."*

It looked like an apology so she took it as one and nodded back, told her feet to move slowly, slowly down the hall. She felt half-dead by the time she entered the room but still managed a soft laugh at the sudden urge to relieve herself again.

She searched for Hugh first, of course, already asleep in the bed. That was the strange thing about traveling in time — they hadn't spent more than a few minutes each at their first two stops and ninety minutes hadn't passed in this one but the sun they used to direct them when they left that morning had passed through the sky and set like any other day . . . and they were bone weary.

Their exhausted navigator sat in the center of the chaise holding an evenly cut and neatly bundled parcel of sticks in his hands. He spoke in a low whisper that he was plainly not used to because the softness, the whisper part kept slipping away.

"Our host brought us these — not enough for a fire." He motioned to the cold, tiled, unused hole in the wall. He handed the twigs to her. "But enough to take the chill from the air. And these . . ." He motioned to the table beside him. Water for all with three glasses, a teapot with steam missing but the hooked end of a tea ball sticking out, and some sort of flat, pale yellow cake divided into sixths. Dinner and breakfast, she suspected. Hugh's portion was already missing.

"You shouldn't have waited. Your tea will be cold."

He shrugged, unfamiliar with tea. "Yours as well."

He slid two slices of cake onto yet another marvel . . . plates . . . while she poured their tea into lovely china cups. Then they exchanged their efforts. "If Hugh's theory about the insects is even remotely possible — and he says science fiction is . . . remotely possible — then I waited to consult you about a fire. For myself I believe it is not a wise idea as the less we disturb as we pass through time the fewer changes we'll make on the future. As it is, I am concerned about the changes that will occur to you and Hugh simply because you are traveling with me." He shook his head and popped a corner of cake in his mouth. "But I could not leave you behind, either of you. There is no way to tell how long —"

"We've been over this. *We* decided.

There's nothing for you to feel bad about." She wagged her head back and forth. "Except maybe those two stopovers this morning."

He was carrying his guilt for those misadventures barely below the surface of his wizardly coolness — which shattered instantly.

"Unwitting as I was of the danger I put you and your young son in, I do beg your forgiveness. You placed your faith in me, charged me only with the protection of your boy on this journey and I —"

"Wait. Wait. I was kidding you, joking. Teasing." That registered. "*I'm* sorry. I lost my temper when it happened and I shouldn't have. Mistakes are made." She finished the last of her tepid tea. "Nobody knows that better than me so . . . so consider yourself forgiven and forget about it."

She pinched three little crumbs of cake off the thin old wool of her skirt by candlelight and ate them. For some reason she was reluctant to leave him so she reached for the glass and the pitcher of water.

When traveling, hydrate, hydrate, hydrate.

"It was kind of him to feed us," she said, sensing his gaze on her. "Only a few of the wrong people have anything in this time, so it was very generous of him. But I think you're right about burning the twigs . . . might be a bad idea."

"Killer insects?"

Embarrassed and ashamed, she nodded. They both chuckled softly.

"Hugh is a fine young man. I am pleased to call him my friend."

"He likes you, too." So did she, but she wasn't sure if she'd known him overnight or for over six hundred years and the timing to tell him felt off. She stood and shook out the little peplum jacket that came with her straight skirt and the white bobby socks that matched her blouse and stood, taking in the proportions of the cot and the man at the same time.

"You sleep in the bed with Hugh. You'll never get comfortable on that thing." He looked at the bed, agreed with her reasoning, and shook his head.

"I insist," she said.

He got that same taken aback, almost startled look he had on his face when they first met and tried to hide it again by looking down and setting the twigs under the cot, but by the swell of his cheek she knew he was smiling. He wasn't used to taking orders, she realized in a flash, or bold, outspoken women — nor was he averse to them as far as she could tell.

Intrigued, amused, confident that he could handle both was what he was . . .

*When a boy is lucky enough to know his mother, he knows his mother well,* he'd told her the day before . . . or yesterday six hundred and eight years ago.

"How old were you when you last saw your mother?"

Still smiling, he looked up at her. "Eleven, when I left to study with the great wizard Pearoline. But I returned to my father's house when I was fourteen, for a short time, to be with her when she took her last breaths." He glanced away to an old wound, then back to her. "She was beautiful, too, like you. Forward, like you, on occasion and always my fiercest protector . . . like you are to Hugh. It does my heart good to see it." He hesitated. "For so many years with only Lady Agnes to inspire me with her schemes and lies and thievery, with her poorly concealed contempt and unfaithfulness to my lord William, with my own solitude, I was beginning to think I dreamed my mother's virtues. I see now I did not."

That was the nicest thing anyone had said to her in . . . ever, it felt like. "If we both sleep in the bed, with Hugh between us, we'll be warmer . . . and safer, if we need to leave in a hurry."

"You foresee this happening?" He stood. The space between the cot and the chair was cramped and the sudden close proximity of their bodies threw them both off balance, in several directions.

"Well, I can't actually foresee things, you know." Just in case he still had the whole super-mother thing on his mind — and she couldn't seem to look him in the eye to tell. Hugh hadn't told Nester about her, or what she'd done, and she couldn't — just couldn't — destroy the hope in his expression when he realized that Lady Agnes was the selfish, scheming exception, and not the rule in mothers.

"I anticipate using the laws of probability, historical facts, and my own tragic struggle with Good Luck," she said, hiding in her sarcasm. "And I invariably see the worst possible scenario coming my way and instead of getting out of its way I tend to step in front of it like the fat kid in a game of dodge ball, to get hit sooner and out of the center of the ring — so the spotlight isn't always on my mistakes and what I'm doing to correct them or . . ." She felt his fist at her chin tilting her face upward. ". . . to make up for them or . . ." He forced her gaze to meet his — it was kind. ". . . to put

469

them in the past."

He shook his head in wonder. "Later I will ask about dodge ball, but now I must wonder . . . what mistakes could you have made? Did the mistakes you made give rise to grisly monsters the likes of which no man has ever seen? Have your errors filled the hearts of those nearest you with such terror that you can feel each faltering beat in your own chest?"

In a flash she saw the monsters and terrors of her addiction and stepped away from him. "Yes. And dodge ball is a horrible children's game," she said, turning away. "There's a hundred ways to play it and they all involve having balls thrown at you by other players and if you're a fat kid and not very fast you get picked last to play and hit first. Then you don't get to play anymore *or* if you only have one ball and you're it, you get hit over and over again and feel like crap all afternoon. My brother, Charlie, was a fat kid and he has dodge ball nightmares to this very day." She stood on the far side of the bed to remove her slender skirt and shoes, threw her long wool coat like an extra blanket over as much of the bed as she could, and crawled in.

She hunkered down and hummed for heat. "The blankets off your bed and that big overcoat sure would feel good over here."

Shadows passed through the flickers of light made by the candle burning by the bed. Each of two blankets settled over her and Hugh adding weight and warmth to their cocoon. The heavy coat made her smile and she looked up at him.

"Do you always get what you want?"

Her smile faded slightly. "No."

Later in the night, maybe still asleep, she opened her eyes to low, warm firelight that was turning the room toasty. Nester must have changed his mind, she thought, coming up on one elbow to see if she could add any leftover twigs to the fire only to observe the flames burning independently, smokeless, without wood or coal or gas.

Her gaze slowly gravitated to the sleeping wizard. Another nice trick.

# Six

The little red coat from *Schindler's List* walked through Marie's dreams all night and when she woke with a start she was sure *they* had gotten her, *they* had her by the arm, *they* wouldn't let go . . .

"Shhh. Do not wake the boy."

*What boy?* Her eyes opened to a steady gaze that was aged and blended with more gold and soft brown than she had originally noticed. He had the male version of an ordinary, nondescript nose but that little ridged space between his nose and his upper lip was fascinating, the way the lip dipped in the exact middle, rose slightly, and slipped perfectly off each side in a soft, sumptuous glide to his lower lip, which was full, supple, and holding the corners of his mouth up in a smile.

*Christ!* Her whole body jerked when she tried to move away from him but her right arm was secure, under the pillows, in his left hand. Once the realization was made, she immediately moved her arm . . . and scowled at him.

He rubbed his thumb against the sensitive skin on the inside of her forearm and used his right index finger against his lips to quiet her. "They met in the night," he whispered hoarsely, speaking of their arms like they were hamsters, "and kept one another warm. A prophesy perhaps."

Okay. He was a thirteenth-century wizard, a recluse living in a delayed time warp, but he was also a grown man in his thirties, so he had to know that was the worst pickup line since cavemen stopped beating their women to death with clubs.

She nodded and her diaphragm stiffened with the effort not to laugh in his face, but then Hugh saved the day by bursting out in supportive snorts and giggles and rising up in bed to face his friend.

"Man, I don't believe you. Were girls in your time dumb enough to fall for that line?"

Nester released her arm immediately and went up on his elbow to face Hugh. "I am not sure. I knew few girls and . . . fewer women."

And that was just a fact, nothing he was proud or ashamed of and that pleased her more than being able to roll out of bed and slip out the door with the least amount of fuss made.

"Well, you've got some things to learn, man, and letting a chick know what you're feeling before you absolutely have to is . . ."

Marie was pretty sure the next word was "suicidal" and wondered how wise it was to leave Nester with Hugh. Nester was plain and straightforward so she could use simple words to explain why a romantic relationship between them would be unwise. A time-traveling wizard and a recovering mother of a son she could never leave again — one of them would have to make an unbearable choice. It wouldn't be her, and she couldn't ask it of him.

Hugh was out the door when she returned. She started to dress once again in the clothes Petroleon had provided. "Don't let Hugh pollute you." Her smile felt awkward. "While this time is one of man's lowest and most disgraceful points in history, the medieval period — when you're from — is considered one of its most romantic. Chivalry, knights, fabulous royal courts —"

"Built off the backs of overtaxed paupers, unreasonable wars, virulent diseases . . . What?" he asked when she chuckled.

"Nothing." Hugh was back and she wasn't

in the mood for a sociology class. "Just sprinkle a little salt on any romantic advice you get from this guy." He looked confused. It was probably the salt. "Beware of it."

He nodded once, blinded her with a smile. "I will take my lessons from you then."

Startled, flustered, not expecting anything quite so bold or so cheeky from him, she sputtered her response as he walked out the door.

"Smooth, Mom. I'm proud to be your son."

They were both bent over tying their shoes, but when she looked at him she could see he was smiling. His remark was in jest, though in no way a declaration of his forgiveness, which twisted her heart like a washcloth.

*How much longer?*

Putting his forearms on his knees, he gave her a serious stare. "He likes you, you know."

She nodded, equally serious. She wouldn't pretend to not know what he was saying, nor could she subdue her stiff, stilted response knowing he cared more about Nester's feelings than he did hers.

"I'll be careful, I promise. He's been nothing but kind to both of us. It would be too much, even for me, to repay his compassion with a broken heart."

He saw immediately that he'd hurt her feelings again, but when it wasn't intentional it wasn't as pleasing to him, apparently, because he instantly tried to eat up his words. She patted his thigh, giving him a dose of Instant Mother Love straight from the jar.

Nester returned and either saw or felt what tension was left between them as he made a jovial show of preparing for their next leap.

"I like seeing limbs in female fashion. I have seen this before, of course. But I hope as we move forward in time and to the west toward Sellithos that clothes for men become less binding." His utter disgust with his thick wool, prepolyester suit slacks was laughable.

"Oh, you are so in for a treat, man." Hugh stood and whacked the wizard on the back. "Limbs is nothin' and we call 'em legs. We'll get you some boxers and saggin' jeans and you won't feel penned in by nothin'."

"You won't be able to run either." She sent a quailing glace at her son, hoping her cheeks weren't pink. "Or walk for that matter. Men's fashions don't get much better than this in the future, I'm afraid." She got up and walked across the room to stand beside them. "Small variations from time to time, new . . . better, much better materials and craftsmanship, but . . . not much change really."

"So often your time seems not so very different from mine, but not in this matter?"

"When I was, like, a junior in college, I collected these brilliant, ingenuous, and oh-so-meaningful sayings and quotes." She stood close to Nester and locked her arms with Hugh's around his torso. They turned as one until Nester stopped. Aware that he was watching her, aware of his interest, she kept her face averted. "One of my favorites went like this: 'Man himself, in his hopes, his desires, his thoughts, and in his emotions seems to be the only unchanged thing in the world,' or something like that." She glanced up to see his eyes were closed. Already the blue light was like an inverted eddy at their feet closing them in. He'd let her go on speaking because he knew she was nervous. She looked at the stony Petroleon on his shoulder, above Hugh's head, and spoke some more. "Give it your best shot, pal, far into the future and *wa-ay* over the sea."

She closed her eyes firmly, swallowed, took a deep breath, and regretted not learning to swim.

"Look!" Hugh's voice cracked with excitement. "Flying cars. Look out the window! That is so *cool!*"

They were standing in a narrow, crowded room, where a woman — one of those women who could wear her hair very short and still look stunning — was lifting her head off a desk. Following Hugh's gawking stare Marie saw that there were indeed what appeared to be oddly built automobiles passing swiftly by a long, narrow window. Her mind became a visual decoupage, vivid and fragmented. Flying cars. The furnishings: some the same, but not; some completely different. A computer: NYPSD was the screen saver; time in one corner, date in the other. April, it read. And then all she saw was *2060!*

"Oops!" She pulled Hugh close and spoke in Nester's ear. "If you can manage it, without hurting yourself, don't even stop here. We're too far into the future and we have no cover. We'll be discovered." From the corners of her eyes she thought she saw the woman reaching for something, a weapon, maybe. "Go back, Nester. Go back. Go somewhere else. Anywhere else."

Once again, Nester's signature cyan blue light began to mist and swirl to conceal them, protect them. Closing her eyes again, she thought she heard an odd beeping sound, but it was faint and gone the next second.

"Marie?" They stood together in a small, narrow alley with their backs to one another assessing their circumstances . . . no signs of a demonic dictator or flying cars. So far, so good.

Must have been a tough jump for the stone, she noticed, as they were all back in medieval linen and over-tunics.

"Are you all right, Nester? I'm sorry. I didn't know what else to do. That woman was right there looking at us. That was . . . that was more than fifty years before our time, beyond — after actually."

"And they have flying cars, Mom," her son whispered urgently, cutting off the wizard's reply. "You'll be what? Ninety something? Too old to drive. But I'll only be in my sixties and by then sixty will be the new forty with all the cool drugs and machines and stuff."

"Honey, you may not live to see thirteen." She felt Nester turn sharply and pull them into a crouching position.

Looking around he asked, "Why? What do you see, Marie?"

Hugh's eyes twinkled with delight in the moonlight and he pressed his lips together.

Marie covered her mouth with both her fists and shook her head. "Nester." She took his hand in the dark. "I was teasing Hugh. He was teasing me, about my age. We're okay. I feel like we're mostly safe here. Not where we want to be exactly, but safe enough."

He glanced down at their tangled fingers, then nodded. He offered no smile and that's when she noticed the exhaustion in his eyes. Clearly two jumps in a day was no less draining than three.

"Dang. Help me, sweetie. We need to find somewhere for Nester to rest."

The small stablelike structures nearby were ratty looking, literally. There was a moist, stale odor under the sweet smell of spring that made her think their new point in time was older than Nazi Germany but not nearly as old as the times in which the myths of Camelot were planted.

Still, she had the notion their trip across the ocean to a future New York had, at the very least, boomeranged and thrown them back over the Atlantic because there was an impression of age here that nothing man-made in the States could aspire to.

They stood at the rear of a simple house with a small, empty yard between them and the rear entrance. It was in a row of identical houses — the darkest and safest looking of the lot.

"Ready for a recon mission?" Her son turned squarely to be sure she was speaking to him. He nodded. "A very *careful* recon mission?"

"I am guessing at the word 'recon' and already I fear it is not wise. I will spy on the people in the house and come back for you."

"And when you get caught because you're so tired you can barely stand up should we just wait here for you? Open up a Kool-Aid stand in the morning? Take bets on the next lunar eclipse?"

"You study the stars, too?"

She really hated to keep popping his bubbles. "Hugh, honey, you can do this. Do not get seen. No noise. Look in windows. Do not go inside before coming back here to us first. If it looks good, we go in together. Okay?"

He nodded and she was glad to see that he looked a little nervous — he'd be more careful. She gave his arm a reassuring squeeze and he turned to go, but Nester stopped him with his own pat-'n–grab on the shoulder for luck.

Not sixty seconds passed before a stumbling, clanking noise from somewhere near the back door had them both cringing and cranking up their tired muscles to take flight again once the boy reappeared. Seconds crawled by like so many snails in a gastropod parade, one after another, and they began to sense he'd move on undetected.

There was nothing forward or romantic or . . . anything but purely weary in the act of Nester resting his head briefly on her shoulder while they waited. Nor in the action of her running her fingers into his thick, golden fall of hair, her cool fingers and palm sliding over his rough, over-heated cheek.

"From now on we take one jump a day and I don't care where it lands us, or how long it takes us to get home. Bill can just damn well sit there with his motor running, for all I care."

"If the boy is in danger, we must journey again, and again if necessary. Safety —"

"Then maybe one thing at a time. Maybe all of it is too much for Petroleon . . . I mean, beyond its share with Sellithos. Maybe it's too much to move through both space and time unless they're together. Maybe if we try just space next time and then time after that?"

"We can try." His head came up. "Is that Hugh? Do you hear that?"

Straining her ears, she picked up dogs barking blocks away and wheels on street cobbles from all directions. She shook her head.

The wizard frowned, grew tense . . . even after they spotted Hugh leaping across the yard toward them.

"Come on," he whispered almost out loud. "There's this really old lady asleep in the kitchen with one of those wicked horn things for deaf people on her lap. I don't think there's anyone else home. I looked in all the windows. Looks like one of those places you see on Christmas cards sometimes, you know? No cops or anything around that I could see."

"Was the old woman speaking to herself? In her sleep perhaps?" The wizard seemed to know how strange the questions sounded so Hugh felt compelled to answer seriously.

"No."

The golden man stood in his cyan cloak looking up at the house, actually up at a window of the house. "I feel we should choose another place to hide and rest. This dwelling is loud and it never rests." He looked down at his friends gaping up at him in concerned amusement. "A spirit dwells within."

They smiled at him. He'd jumped the Atlantic twice in one day and was, of course, allowed to believe in anything he wanted . . .

including ghosts. He was tired.

"Yeah, well, I'll take a wizard over a ghost any day," she said, lifting her skirts high because she was used to walking in jeans that didn't tangle in her . . . limbs, and started for the back door. "For one thing, they're still alive and you can hear them better."

"And they sleep and get hungry like you do," Hugh said, following her, pointing out *his* most specific needs. "And they enjoy a good water closet when you can find one."

They laughed and Nester slowly took up the rear. "He calls for Summer and he knows no true remorse."

"Tell you what," she said in a whisper from the porch. She tapped and then knocked on the old wooden door. The old woman barely moved to breathe. "Hugh can run up and open a window for him. I don't know that it's summer yet, but it's a lovely night."

# Seven

Like the practiced thieves that they weren't, the three of them slipped around the immaculate little kitchen like eels at the bottom of the sea, skirting the old woman as if she were a rock, snagging bread and little cakes and a jar of plum preserves that threatened to send Nester into a visual orgasm on the spot. They took cheese and milk for Hugh, who turned up his nose at it and, amazingly, hit upon a small pitcher of lemonade instead.

Nester was agog once more at the marvels of an early 19th-century kitchen: the baking oven beside the big fireplace, forks, and the old lady's rocking chair were his favorites . . . and the fabulous glass windows, of course, like those in Nazi Germany. But it wasn't long before he was using hand signals and covering his ears with both hands to indicate that whatever noise he was hearing in his head, it was getting louder. She shook her head, no such thing as ghosts. He pointed upward in the house. Motioned for them to come with him.

After a quick scan of the kitchen, wanting to leave it as much the same as when they arrived, minus only a few things that might not be missed right away, she spotted an expensive bottle of brandy on the counter, set to one side, unmistakably for special occasions . . . or special people — like a very tired wizard.

"How can you hear this ghost when we can't?" The stairs were dark, the hall, too, but she didn't need light to know Hugh was excited. His faith in Nester had already turned the impossible to a very likely possibility and his voice foretold that he believed he was about to meet his first real ghost. "What's it saying now? Does it know we're coming?"

"Possibly it is a simple matter of believing. Many do not believe in what they can not see or feel . . . or imagine to be possible, like traveling in time." He stopped at the top of the stairs and listened for his ghost, caught the direction, and advanced. "This is the ghost of a man and the Summer he calls to is not a season but a woman." He reached out to a door at the end of the hall and turned to them. "Beware. This one is not to be trusted. He does not know the difference between a lie and the truth."

He opened the door and they followed him into the room, first Marie, then Hugh.

The man inside sprang from his chair and looked startled to see them, but quickly composed himself and took a stance — all in something like slow motion. He wasn't real, but like a person walking through the dark reflection that actually surrounded him that he couldn't step away from or escape. He flashed them a charming smile.

"Ah. I see I have guests. Right-o. Pray come in and be comfortable."

He wasn't very tall, certainly nowhere near the size of Nester, but he was handsome in a boyish way, with short, sandy brown hair and dark, twinkling eyes under bushy brows in one of those longish faces that never seemed to age.

"Come, come. It appears I cannot bite anything, much less you . . . or drink it either so your brandy is safe." He motioned to the bottle in Marie's hand and his eyes took on a warm, envious quality. "Please, come in and enjoy your little picnic with me. I can't tell you how boring it is with so few callers."

Nester was right: Apparently the only rule

to seeing ghosts was believing in them, and believing they exist wasn't even a puddle jump from accepting a thirteenth-century wizard into your life and traveling through time with him.

"Please. My name is Reggie Cassidy and I am harmless to you."

He was trying too hard and was also kind of whiny if you asked her. "Do the people who live here know this room is haunted? Are we likely to be discovered? We need to rest awhile."

"No. I am alone here. No one is home tonight. Please stay."

"I'm Hugh," the boy said, stepping out from behind his mother's skirts. It was clearly an experiment as he shuffled forward with his hand out to the ghost.

Reggie's smile was sly and beguiling as he stepped forward as well and passed his hand straight through the boy's, who uttered, "Wow."

"Yes. And this beautiful woman is your mother." An obvious observation, but then, too, were the observations he was making of the peasant strings that held the top of her linen gown together beneath the emerald green over-tunic, and the pale cleavage they left exposed.

"Marie." She didn't bother holding her

hand out; she'd already seen his trick.

"And I am Nester Baraka of Viator. I am their protector."

"Viator? Never heard of it. Up in Scotland I'd bet." He couldn't hold Nester's unwavering scowl. His eyes fell to Marie's and then to her breasts, then made a smooth swing to Hugh. "Speaking of betting, you look like a gaming man to me. There are a few coins in the top drawer over there that you may have if you can best me in a stare-down."

"We can't take anything from where we go if we can help it, but I'll do it just for bragging rights if I can eat something first."

"Of course. You must. Young boys are always hungry, are they not, Marie?"

"Seems like it." She was pushing Nester toward the bed and he was letting her, too tired to put up much of a fight. Pillows were plumped at the head of the bed so he could eat and rest and watch over them from one position.

They divided their plunder as all good thieves do, and frankly, no food had ever tasted better. Marie went to stand at the window when her son and the ghost sat for their challenge. She hoped Nester would sleep better if she wasn't too close, but even with his eyes shut she could tell by his breathing that he wasn't asleep, that he was listening, that he was safeguarding them, as he had from the very beginning.

Reggie, it seemed, was merciless. He liked to win and blatantly did so three out of three times with a boy — a human boy, a third his age.

"You come from the future, you say. There must be gambling in your time, pray tell me about it."

Marie walked slowly across the room to the bed, smiled when the slits between Nester's eyelids closed like they had zippers.

Hugh shrugged. "Grown-ups probably bet on the same stuff you do. Horses, dogs, pretty much anything. They have million-dollar poker games in Atlantic City and Las Vegas, all over probably. They even have it on TV."

"Poker, a game, you say?"

"Yeah, a card game."

Reggie lit up like a halogen lightbulb. "Teach me. You must."

"But how . . . you can't . . ." Hugh motioned to Reggie's hands that were incapable of holding or touching or feeling anything.

Much like the rest of him, Marie suspected, after marveling several times on his all-about-me attitude.

"Drat!" Reggie held up his useless hands. "Yes, of course, but I have been pondering this gross inconvenience. Please," he said, with his most charming smile and a you-can't–resist-me light in his eyes as he floated out of his chair. "Marie, come be my hands in this new game."

It was clear that no one would rest with the lonely ghost in the room and teaching him poker would give Nester more time to relax before they traveled again. Hugh gave him a quick rundown of the rules, explained the hierarchy of the cards, and started him out with five-card draw.

Quick learner. A natural gambler. Hugh won once before Reggie started to dominate the game. He made it look so easy, whispering in Marie's ear which cards to hold and discard while he ogled her chest — a truly flexible mind — game after game as night passed and dawn threatened.

Nester rose, finally, stretching stiff muscles he'd gotten from watching them, not from sleeping too hard, and wandered over to the table to stand behind the boy — tall and solid.

Reggie distressed for a moment, but came about quickly. "I say, old man, no helping the boy now. 'Tis all I can do with my considerable skills to just keep up with him."

"My young friend needs no help." He stepped away from Hugh's chair and tried to pretend he was casually ambling around the room when Marie knew there wasn't a single, casual, ambling bone in his body. "Men of nobility and bravery and truthfulness never need help, and he is all those things." He was at the window now, looking out, and then he turned. In two strides he was behind her chair. The ghost vibrated slightly with the movement of the air. "You, on the other hand, are not, sir," he said, looking back at the ghost and Marie and himself in the mirror behind Hugh. "You are a liar and a cheat. From this position you can see every card in the boy's hand, and while you turn the lady's head with your adulation she doesn't suspect a thing."

"I had no idea . . . no . . . I hadn't noticed that the mirror was quite so —"

Nester cut him off with an angry growl, sweeping the cards to the floor in the same movement he used to haul her out of the chair.

"We must go now. Someone is coming." The arm he wrapped around her was displeased and possessive — it made her heart trill. Son and mother wrapped their arms around the wizard.

"Just the ocean this time, okay? One thing

at a time. Space this time and time the next time."

The blue light appeared at their feet and began to spiral upward as always. The bedroom door flew open and a woman entered. She was wearing a very black dress — mourning came to Marie's mind — and was followed by an amazingly good-looking man.

From a distance she heard the woman ask, "Were you gambling with some new ghost friends?"

They began to cough even before the Petroleon's light began to dissipate. Hacking, violent coughing that ripped at their lungs and made their eyes water. The stench of smoke and soot singed the insides of their noses: charcoal and tar and chemicals she didn't even want to guess at. It was killer cold and the wind was furious. It was night, but far from dark.

The earth rumbled beneath their feet as someone bumped into them and shouted in a thick Irish accent, "Head farther uptown, folks. They're blasting buildings to the ground between the fire and Canal Street, leavin' it nothin' to burn, ya see. But a fallin' thing on your head will still hurtcha."

He bonked Hugh twice on his head with a big gentle hand, gave a small grimy smile,

493

and disappeared in the black of the fire and night.

"Great. We could be anywhere." She flapped her arms at her sides as she circled, looking for cues. She stopped, facing Nester again. "Are you okay?"

He coughed into a wad of his light blue cloak. "Yes. I am fine. Let us walk as we talk, madam. The air here is unwelcoming."

"Madam?" She found herself following his broad-shouldered lead, like he knew where he was going any better than she did. But it didn't matter, really, as long as the fire was at their backs.

Walking, coughing, her head still trying to catch up with her body from the leap, it was a few minutes before she became aware of the familiar drag on her left shoulder, the easy freedom of her legs as she stumbled and bumped her way up the street through the smoke and darkness.

There were very few people on the streets, firefighters mostly, shouting out that the water was frozen and to turn back.

She heard Hugh vomiting, leaning against a building, the wizard's big hand a gentle support. It was a great idea. She would have thrown up, too, had she not automatically started to make those sympathetic mother noises, reaching for her son at the exact same moment she reached for the Sani-Wipe packet in her pocket . . . and felt it.

"Hugh! Hugh, look! My jeans. Your Pirates hoodie. My bag. We're back. We're home. Oh God!" She turned. "Philadelphia's burning?"

No. Even if it was Philadelphia, the buildings were too old, too old-fashioned, too nineteenth century to matter beyond the moment to her. They were still in the past.

"Maybe not. Too big to be any Philadelphia fire I've ever heard of, but we made it over the ocean again. How are you doing, Nester?" She handed the wipe to Hugh and went fishing in her hobo bag for clean tissues to cover their mouths and noses with.

She hugged her bag and exalted in the denim encasing her legs as they trudged along uneven sidewalks — some cobbled, some cement — passing building after building, no houses, no homes. Storefronts were boarded up, or in the process of it, and wagon- after wagonload of merchandise was being transported to safety in churches as they crossed streets called Delancey and Houston, 1st, 2nd, and 12th streets.

The farther north they traveled, the less dense the smoke became, but the stench had permeated everything. Marie watched for papers and postings for a place and a date.

"New York," she said finally. "I think we're in New York." They were stopped in front of a small neighborhood grocery, protected against looters with planks of wood across the windows and a man with a rifle seated just inside the door for all to see. "They had a huge fire here twenty-five or so years before the war."

"Which one?" Hugh asked as Nester, their normally mild wizard, scanned their surroundings and vehemently muttered, "Hell and damnation, another war? Do they never stop?"

"The Civil War, honey." She slipped an arm around his shoulders because she couldn't get enough of the feel of him next to her. He seemed to have forgotten how much he hated her during their travels. "Maybe we could try to buy some food here, huh? We'll find a hotel. I doubt they take credit cards yet, but I might be able to pass off my paper bills and coins."

Her wallet was flush for a change, having wanted to have plenty of money on hand to buy Hugh anything he wanted on their outing to the museum that was so many, many years ago it felt like — but only yesterday, or the day before, or the one before that . . .

Indicating his lovely robe, smudged and stained with dark grunge, Nester suggested, "I should remain here, unobserved. The two of you will be safer without me."

"We aren't safe anywhere without you." She wasn't surprised that the sudden panic exploding in her chest burst out in her voice as well. "We stick together. What if we have to leave suddenly? What if we get separated?"

She made a confusing and slightly deceptive bundle of the notes and flashed the coins at the guard to get them inside. It was a no-go. He slowly turned the rifle in their direction, aware of every trick in the looter's handbook apparently.

"Not many people down by the fire, mostly businesses, but the ones who come this way may not . . . be very nice. We should get inside."

Shivering on the sidewalk in the ear-piercing silence a few hours before dawn, they agreed.

"I'm hungry." Hugh mentioned it in a way that wasn't complaining a few blocks later. Tired, too, she could see, and so was her wizard.

"Me, too. This way, I think." Every time she came to New York she got lost. "Keep your eyes peeled for a decent hotel."

"Eyes peeled?" She could tell the idea perplexed and disgusted Nester.

She chuckled softly. "Watch for a hotel. Don't do anything to your eyes."

Leave the keen, clear, umber eyes in the face they were made for; leave them connected to his soul to see his interest and his caring, his amusement and concern. Leave them as that part of his heart that hers was fusing to.

Through the glass panels on either side of the main entrance to the Hudson Hotel they could see the lobby was lit with lovely gas lamps turned low as most of the guests were asleep and not likely to be milling about at that time of night. But where there was light there was probably also a desk clerk and he'd be far more curious about them than their host in war-torn Germany had been.

She looked at Nester, who was looking around, interested in everything he was seeing, soaking it all in. She smiled lamely. "I'm sorry this is the first you're seeing of my country. Normally it's very beautiful, busy, exciting."

He nodded, touching the smooth brick the hotel was built of in awe. "No great city is at its best when being burned to the ground by its enemies."

"Oh. No, this was an accident. Gas, I

think." He looked confused, as he did from time to time now that the expanse of mankind's knowledge had reached such great proportions that one man, even a great wizard, could not assimilate it all, all at once. "I'll explain later. Right now . . . can you . . . do you think you could do *just* your excellent party trick to distract the clerk away from the desk long enough for Hugh and I to slip through the lobby?"

"I told you. Child's play," he said, and was gone.

"Man." The awe and envy in Hugh's voice was understandable. It was a really, *really* excellent party trick.

They watched the night clerk scurry around the end of the desk and head for the rear of the hotel, then made their move. Nester met them on the second-floor landing with a small basket of food — really, *really* excellent. He performed his stunt once more on the third floor to determine if a room was empty and unlocked it from the inside as they had no key.

Still a little pre-indoor plumbing on the time line, they did the best they could with the grime, ate, and fell asleep as if they'd walked all the way from Regency England.

# EIGHT

Marie woke a few hours after dawn, though it was hard to tell from the gray light in the room. There was warmth in the air. She raised her head enough to see that Nester had started another of his fancy fires in the hearth . . . and was sitting in a wing chair before it.

She slipped out of bed and into her jeans, approaching him on tiptoe as if the wood floor was like ice. He looked up, gave her a weak smile.

"Can't you sleep?"

"I did, but then I was restless."

"Are you worried? Can I help? I . . . you know, you've been nothing but kind and . . . wonderful to Hugh and me. Thank you for that, Nester."

His lips bowed. "You are welcome, Marie." She smiled at him. "What?"

"Marie, not madam." She sat in the wing chair across from his and drew her cold feet up under her. "You're not mad anymore."

He looked away, embarrassed. "I admit it. I was jealous of that ridiculous ghost with no earthly cause and no right to be."

The sound she made was bemused. "Funny thing about jealousy: Women hate it in men they loathe, but no jealousy from a man they care about can be even more annoying."

And sometimes people could say more with the shine in their eyes than with all the words in a dictionary. Looking over at Nester she saw humor and caring and friendship, and possibly something more in the light of his eyes — hoped her own were as expressive, were as accepting, were as . . . unguarded.

Hugh was right, the wizard had few defenses and was vulnerable despite his super-powers. Off to study at a young age, his years in service to Lord William and then Lord Mark . . . had he been with many women? Had he ever fallen in love? Made a wizard baby out of wedlock or however it was done?

She had to look away.

"What is it?" he asked softly. "Tell me. I am your friend."

"I've gathered that Hugh didn't tell you why he was angry with me when you first met him. And you haven't asked."

"I believed that injury to be healing of late and it was none of my concern."

She nodded. "But to be my friend, and I want you to be, it isn't enough to know only the person you see before you. I have a past. I have made many mistakes and I have hurt Hugh in the worst possible way a mother can."

The mother thing caught his attention and he turned to her more fully. "I have seen you be a mother, Marie. I cannot imagine a better one."

She kept her voice low so Hugh would sleep and started at the beginning.

"I taught Honors and AP History at a progressive high school in northeast Philadelphia. My husband worked downtown as a mortgage broker and we'd already placed our order for a happily-ever-after life. Hugh came and he was healthy and bright, and four years later I was pregnant again. We were hoping for a little girl to make us the perfect family but, of course, we'd have taken another healthy boy. Everything was just what I'd always dreamed my life would be. I was actually thinking that very thing coming out of the day care that morning after I dropped Hugh off. It was a great day care, we were lucky to find it — and they'd agreed to take the new baby, as well. I ate lunch three days a week with a Social Studies teacher whose after-school child care was a nightmare. And that's what I was thinking about that morning . . . I think." She tapped her forehead with the eight tips of her fingers. "I've asked myself so often what was I thinking, what was I thinking, why was I so distracted that day?

"I'd stopped at that light every day, coming or going, for four years, and then suddenly one day in the middle of my perfect life, I ran a red light." She looked at Nester in complete bewilderment. "Red lights mean stop, and I didn't."

She explained the difference in sizes between a Ford Focus and a full-size SUV, pointed to where her collarbone had shattered, and where her right upper arm had broken in two. She demonstrated with her hands the compression fractures in her spine and tried not to cry when she took responsibility for the other driver losing his left eye. Did cry when her empty hands held no baby.

But there were no words to describe the pain in her body, the confusion in her mind, the fear in her soul, that all that separated life from death was one oblivious moment.

He seemed interested when she described

the vast array of tiny little miracle pills like codeine and Percocet and Vicodin that numbed all sorts of pain in her time. She said one worked pretty good, two worked even better. His eyes narrowed and became intense when she told him how quickly and powerfully the magic pills could take hold of one's body and mind . . . *her* body and mind. She felt, again, the anger she'd known when her doctors pronounced her healed and declined to prescribe medications strong enough to ease her continued pain; her nightmares and her increased desperation when handfuls of Extra Strength Tylenol simply made her stomach queasy — and the terror of her first buy on the streets of north Philly.

She didn't realize she was still crying until Nester stood, scooped her up, sat again, and wrapped his big blue cloak around both of them. She was an ugly crier, red nose, puffy eyes, but he didn't seem to care when he squeegeed the tears from her cheeks with his thumb.

"I'm not sneaky by nature. People never tell me secrets because I can't keep them . . . I want to, but they just sort of bubble out, you know? This explains, I guess, why my career as a drug addict was fairly short-lived. I was constantly getting caught. First by Bill, my husband, my ex-husband now, who couldn't figure out where all our money was going, our savings, even some of our retirement money. The college fund Hugh's grandparents started for him. Stake-out cops started to recognize my car, they stopped me a couple of times. I was just lucky."

For five years, all the risks she took — she'd always thought they were a matter of life and death, *her* life and *her* death . . . but she was *so* wrong. It had shattered Bill's life and, tragically, Hugh's young world, as well.

"When the streets got too hot for me, I cleverly decided to keep my eyes open at school. I think the statistic on that is that every fifth kid is a dealer . . . and I bought twice from an undercover cop." Her head came to rest on his shoulder because it was big and warm and strong enough to hold her. "They had a solid case, I pleaded guilty, and was sentenced to a month in a rehab . . . rehabilitation center — state-run and full to the gills with other addicts. I slipped out of there to find I had no job, of course; my husband had filed separation papers and he had a restraining order to keep me away from Hugh until I could prove I was completely well for one full year."

"This is too cruel, to keep a mother and

son apart."

"No. That was wise and safe and . . . I would have done the same to him, I think. I hope, for Hugh's sake." Her mind flashed back in time. "It was a blow, though, and one of the many things addicts don't handle well is divorce and custody issues . . . Stress of any kind, actually, so I went looking for something to . . . take my pain away."

She felt his body cringe and heard his low groan of foreboding, but his arms remained tight about her, accepting without judgment. She smiled. "I got caught again in less than a month. And I think that's why Hugh has found it so hard to forgive me all this time. The first time was a giant mistake and tied into the accident, but the second time . . . I think he saw that as me choosing my addiction over him and . . . I can see why he'd think that."

"I have seen men possessed by such demons that don't come from heaven or hell. Powders and roots, even flowers."

"They got their heads cut off, right?"

"If they didn't fall face first in the creek."

She smiled up at him. "Bill, Hugh's father, was . . . great. He was. He hated what I'd done. I hadn't trusted him to help me so he felt he could no longer trust me — plus I'd spent most of our money. Sometimes I wonder if we were ever really in love or if we were just . . . if we just worked well together making the perfect little life for ourselves and we didn't know the difference." She paused, it didn't matter. "But he was good to me. He vouched for me in court and promised to pay for a private rehab if I promised to stay for at least six to nine months to be determined by the doctors and after that the court. While I was there he got divorced and remarried. I left the facility eighteen months ago. The public school system won't . . . can't have anything to do with me, but I have a friend who's a principal at a private day school in Radnor. She breathes down my neck, but that's okay, too. It's a second chance and I'm grateful. I'm happy, actually." She turned her head to look over her shoulder at Hugh. "I just need him to believe I love him. I need him to forgive me."

"He knows."

"He says Laura makes better spaghetti than I do."

"To pierce your heart, no doubt."

"No doubt."

"What is this spaghetti?"

She chuckled.

"Mom?"

Marie flew off Nester's lap and stood to

face her son — T–shirt over long, naked legs, anger behind the tears in his eyes.

"I was mad. I'm still mad. You didn't come to get me like you promised. You said you would get better and Dad and you would share me like always but in different houses. You promised."

"I know. I'm so sorry, Hugh. I never meant to hurt you. It was all my fault."

"I know. It *was* your fault. It was always your fault and always about you. Never about me." His tears spilled out onto both cheeks. "Never me."

"Oh, Hugh." Three giant strides had him in her arms, her own tears falling into his hair when she felt his young arms come about her like clamps, hands gripping to keep her near. "I love you so much. I promise," she said, and knew he'd never believe that, so she stepped back to take his face in her hands so he could see the pledge in her eyes. "I will prove it to you. I'm well. I'm a stronger person now than I was even before the accident. I know I'm not alone. I know I can ask for help when I need it." Her voice got low and thick. "I know you still love me."

The hesitation before his nod was so brief she hardly noticed it — it was something she would work on. His arms around her waist, head just barely under her chin. She felt scabs and calluses and fragments of shells coming loose in her chest and falling away. It felt like her heart was beginning to swell back to its normal size.

She was aware of Nester walking toward the window and looking out, but it was Hugh who broke their embrace and joined him there. "What's happening?"

Holding back the curtain and pointing, Nester said, "I believe that the people who live up that way have just come upon the news of the fire down that way. Some appear dazed, others quite angry. The situation will soon become erratic . . . I bet."

She smiled at the phrase he'd chosen to take from Reggie.

"Then we should leave if you're up to it."

"I am." He consulted Petroleon, his expression concerned, but gave her a short nod and a brief smile when he caught her watching. "We are."

Hugh tugged on his jeans and she grabbed her best fall suit jacket that she'd worn with her jeans that day at the museum, to look solid and put together. It reeked of fire, and soot settled in the weave of the wool, but when she and Hugh locked forearms around their wizard and smiled at one another, well, there were lots of ways to feel solid and put together.

"We face the future."

"That's right. Just time this time," she said, resting her head on Nester's chest. It felt easy and natural. When had it become part of their preflight routine? "Fall. November if you can swing it . . . that would save us another jump. Less than two hundred years. That's . . . 163 years. That's nothing for you. Stay in New York, I guess, and we can drive to —"

Still holding her tight in his left arm, the wizard's hand came up to cover her mouth as the cyan light appeared to spiral out of the floor toward the ceiling around them. He closed his eyes and smiled with satisfaction. Hugh giggled.

As the blue illumination slipped away, Marie's eyes grew larger. If they weren't on the set of any police/crime drama on television then — Well, actually the sets on television were probably better funded. This squad room had paint peeling off the walls, hideous metal desks, phones ringing constantly, and one of Marie's pet peeves . . . nonbiodegradable foam cups everywhere.

Cops. They'd landed in a nest of cops and Petroleon's light was gone a full two milliseconds before anyone noticed them.

A heavy balding man in a drab brown suit

and the man standing next to him — tall, dark, and handsome in a coarse, earthy way — looked up from their conversation.

The taller of the two had a piercing gaze that he rolled at his companion saying, "Just one more reason to get away from all the crazies in New York."

New York. They'd made it. A quick glance through the window — no flying cars. The computers looked familiar. Nester was the only person in the room not in some sort of pants or slacks or jeans and even his lovely cyan cloak trimmed in white fur received no more than a second glance and a long-suffering scowl. The wall calendar.

She released Hugh's arm. "This is good, but we've got to get out of here."

Mr. Dull Brown Suit responded to his friend with something under his breath and was grinning when he turned and started toward them. "Something I can do for you folks?"

"I am afraid we made a wrong turn. Come along, Marie. Hugh." She let Nester herd Hugh out the door but turned almost immediately to take their hands and pull them into the stairwell just outside the large squad room.

"Did you see it? The calendar on the wall in there?" She laughed and looked between them. "We not only landed in the right year, it's November!"

They stood triangled on the second-floor landing smiling their pleasure to one another, laughing with their eyes, refusing to step even a microsecond out of the moment, knowing their separation was now imminent.

# NINE

"What day is it?" Hugh asked reluctantly after a few minutes, taking the step because he was young and impatient and unaware that moments once lost are gone forever. "How soon before we journey home?"

"I couldn't tell." She could feel Nester watching her, trying to guess at her reaction to adjust his appropriately. She was nauseated. "We probably shouldn't try it with Nester again; we're close now and there's no telling where we'd end up. No offense."

"None taken."

"If we're late" — she started down the stairs — "it might be safer just to tell your dad that I kidnapped you for a few days. He won't let me see you again until you're eighteen, but if we tell him the truth he'll have us both locked away."

"And I guess my essay for English titled 'My Trip to the Museum' is out, too."

She was looking back and laughing at her

son when she ran into a woman coming through the door on the ground floor. "Oh. Sorry. Do . . . you happen to know today's date?"

Righting herself the woman took one look at Nester and announced, "Halloween's over, folks."

"How over?" Marie called after her as she stomped up the steps.

"Coupla weeks." The door on the second floor slammed closed.

Nester was looking through the small pane of safety glass in the door. His soak-it-all-up and store-it-away expression is what she'd miss most about him, she decided. And the sound of his voice . . . and the safety she felt in his arms, too. And the warm, male scent of him that filled her head whenever he was near, and probably the dizzy, drunk feeling she got when he looked straight into her eyes . . .

"I need new clothes, Marie." His hand rested over Petroleon. "Do you have enough money?"

"I have better than money. I have credit cards." She wiggled her brows at him and he instinctively looked worried. She laughed and led them through a hive of busy people who looked as ordinary as she and Hugh and *at least as* odd as Nester.

Pushing through the front door onto the windy sidewalk she joyously filled her lungs with carbon monoxide and started to cough. Nester, too. She was embarrassed by how happy she was. "This is a very big city with lots of cars and lots of buildings." He'd already noticed them, his face straight up to see the tops, to see the sky above them. "Lots of tall buildings." He looked down at her and Hugh and didn't have to ask out loud what had happened to his planet. She pulled her gaze from the question in his and when she spotted a clothing store she led the way, saying, "We . . . we've made some mistakes, Nester, and we've taken everything for granted, like it would last forever, but . . . well, you know how slow and stupid and greedy mankind can be . . . we're trying to fix it. Every day someone invents something new to try to fix the problems we've caused."

"Except for the irreparable damage," Hugh said, always his teacher from the very beginning. "Almost a quarter of the Amazon rainforest is gone and the polar ice caps are melting. You can't fix those things. You can try to stop them, but you can't fix them."

Nester said nothing — hadn't since he'd informed her of his need for appropriate clothing. He listened and scanned storefront windows crammed with electronic equipment or sporting goods or fine paper products. Truthfully, she'd expected more than mild interest while picking out his first set of non-WWII-wool pants. He went with Hugh's recommendation on a T-shirt and she, amazingly, blushed red hot when the boy hurried out of the dressing room, found what he wanted, and rushed back in with a pack of boxer briefs.

She couldn't afford real leather, but the faux jacket she found was soft and lined well to keep the November chill out. It took her the whole forty-five minutes they were there to work up the nerve to ask for today's date — then she picked out a couple more T–shirts.

She was smiling when Hugh handed her the sales tickets for socks and a pair of dark-colored Nikes, Nester practicing a heel-to-toe walking rhythm behind him.

"We're a day early." Her joy wasn't all about having their journey go undetected by her husband; more of it had to do with not having to say good-bye to Nester yet, while another part wondered if he had to leave at all. "I say we send me into some serious debt and make a great day of this. We'll see what we can, eat everywhere . . . oh! . . . book a room at the Palace, I've *always* wanted to do that. What do you say?"

"What about tomorrow? What about Dad?" She could see his concern was more for her than for himself and her heart went wild with love and contentment and absolution and . . . and the most amazing freedom, deep in her soul, like a prisoner must feel leaving solitary confinement. Just knowing she wasn't alone in her life anymore.

"No worries. We'll have the concierge at the hotel find us a car to rent. It only takes a few hours to drive to Philly. Nester can see that New York is finite, see a little countryside, and we'll be right back where we started . . . and go from there. How's that?"

"Can we eat first?"

They ate in a step-down restaurant with a fifties theme — hamburgers and milkshakes that Hugh and his buddy ate with great relish, literally and figuratively. Enjoying the show, Marie mentally planned their itinerary, choosing all the places she thought would give Nester his best taste of the future, of her world, her life.

The list in her mind filled and grew long, but in the dark corners she was beginning to realize that even as smart and sharp and curious as he was he wasn't . . . hardwired for this century. Mankind is built on the knowledge acquired and accrued by each generation before; history is made and the lessons are learned in retrospection.

Nester needed to take his life one step at a time, just as she had, just as Hugh was. Anything else would not only be unfair, but she knew it was also potentially dangerous for him.

She decided that a Big Apple bus tour was the best way to see the most using the least effort. They hit the inspirational sites like the Statue of Liberty and Ellis Island from afar; then the *Intrepid* Museum, the United Nations, and Ground Zero. They were dazzled by the wonders of the Empire State Building, the Brooklyn Bridge, the Met, and FAO Schwarz. They rode through Central Park, Times Square, and got off at Rockefeller Center.

"In a few weeks, all that will be ice and people will skate on it and they'll put a huge Christmas tree over there, with a crane . . . a big machine that picks up other big things," Hugh explained, Nester accepting and filing without much question. They were a team with an interesting system: The boy seemed to automatically know what the wizard would want explained and the wizard recognized the boy's explanation as the simplest he'd ever get. "And a Christmas tree is . . ."

He looked to his mother. "One of the symbols we use to celebrate the birth of Christ. A decorated evergreen tree can be traced back to —" She looked up at the expression on Nester's face and laughed.

"I am familiar with many of the traditions surrounding the birthday of Our Lord Christ, Marie. As a boy, I recall dressing as the Wise Men with my friends and carrying a star from house to house, singing carols. And the magnificent feasts" — this for Hugh's benefit — "goose and plum porridge at my father's table and later with Lord William a great boar's head and wassail." He shook his head remembering. "I remember once, in the village square, players came to put on a show about the miracle. I enjoyed it very much."

As they walked to Fifth Avenue, then past Saint Patrick's Cathedral toward Madison Avenue, Marie talked about Broadway and California movie stars. Nester was fascinated with the scores of yellow cabs weaving in and out of traffic, and just the thought of traveling in a tube underground had his imagination reeling.

"Would you like to ride the subway?" She looked at her watch. "We have time, I think. We could —"

"No." He was eyeing his younger tour guide, who had been exceptionally tolerant and good-natured all day. He looked a little peaked. "My head is crammed with the great wonders and many delights you have shown me today, but I must admit I am weary."

Hugh nodded. "And he's hungry, too, probably."

The opulence of the New York Palace was obvious from the *outside* of the building and the inside confirmed it a thousand times over. She took pleasure in the amazement on her companions' faces and was not above owning up to being a little wide-eyed herself.

While she waited for the desk clerk to find a double room with a connecting single, she was calculating how much she had left on her credit card and if it would stretch to cover a rental car, too — barely aware of the arrival and entrance of several people through the main lobby until she heard Hugh's reverent, "Wow."

A small troupe of individuals of various sizes and shapes and tastes in clothing walked in front of, beside, and behind a very tall man with saffron-colored hair, multiple piercings in each ear, his lip, and eyebrows, a sapphire sequined jacket, and diamond-studded sunglasses.

"Dennis Rodman, Mom. See him?"

Could she miss him? "I do."

To Nester, who was comparing his very ordinary clothes to Rodman's, he said, "That guy played basketball. Great rebounder. You either like him or you don't." He didn't.

"Another game with balls?"

She and Hugh looked at one another and smiled playfully.

Unabashed, they watched until a responsible-looking man broke away from the knot and walked over to the desk where all was in readiness.

"Welcome back, sir, it's good to see you again. We've put Mr. Rodman back in Suite 606 per your request, plus the five single rooms on the same floor. Is there anything else I can do for you?"

The man politely said no and the clerk left the offer open, indefinitely, Marie suspected.

Their rooms were very fine and high enough up for a great view of the city and no street noise. While Hugh and Nester bathed, she ordered room service. When she emerged from the bathroom in her cozy white robe she found them both in the single room, Hugh showing Nester all the tricks to the video games on the television.

The wizard looked up, his intoxicating eyes going sharp and warm as he took in her hair, still damp and curly; her face, clean and flushed; the robe, concealing secrets untold.

"Hey," Hugh elbowed his pal. "Pay attention. Once you move up from the first level it gets faster." He looked askance at his mother.

"Room service should be here soon. They can set it up over here."

"Okay. Go, Nester. Quick. If they kill you, you'll have to start over."

She heard the death buzzer as she stepped from the room and smiled. Poor Nester.

Their meal was perfect. Not the food, though it was fabulous, but the camaraderie and the laughing and the joy they found in one another, the three of them. This was only the fourth night they'd spent together, but they'd been together for centuries. They knew one another's strengths and weaknesses, they'd shared fear and happiness, they'd taken care of one another. Mother, son, and wizard. The bond they shared was as real and true as they were.

And tomorrow they would break it.

That's what she was thinking about a couple of hours later — room service debris out in the hall, the blasts of Final Fantasy V fading away to the cacophony of *American Idol* — standing in the near dark of the bathroom light in a double room looking out at the lights of the city. She'd never broken a strong bond with someone before, not voluntarily, and certainly not sober. The two serious relationships she'd had in high school had been mutual breakups, and when Bill left her she simply took a few extra pills and faxed him her lawyer's phone number.

But Nester . . . well, Nester was special . . . as wizards tend to be, she suspected. If she cared to be truthful, and she wasn't sure she should be, she was probably half in love with him the moment she first saw him, tall and golden and so handsome he made her mouth go dry. The other half snuck up on her while she watched his quick mind soak up and learn, question and file; as she observed his kindness and tolerance toward Hugh . . . and toward her; his protection and his great efforts to get them home.

"Are you sad, Marie?"

She turned toward him, leaning on the window ledge. "No. Yes. Yes, a little. This has been quite an adventure. I am a little sad to see it end, glad to be home, but sad, too."

He nodded. "Tomorrow I will have Sellithos back. It will be time to fulfill my destiny . . . though I have come to realize that I could have accomplished it long ago had I the courage to simply try." He sat on the end of the bed and looked up at her. "I was a coward. I was afraid to move on in my life with only the Petroleon to enhance my powers . . . and yet who is to say that was not God's plan all along, eh? Not I. But what I do know is that I have much to see and do before my journey ends. Petroleon has served me well . . . awkward, but well and with two passengers, no less. I tampered with time when there was no need, and now I do not know what will happen. I gave up on my life, waiting for something I was not sure even existed any longer." He stood again, so close she could feel his body heat. "Until you came to me. Until Sellithos sent you to me. You are the strongest woman I have ever known, Marie. You journey with me as if you have always done so and before that you traveled to hell and back alone."

His gaze lowered to her mouth. He lifted his hand to trace the lower edge of her bottom lip with his thumb before his eyes shifted up to meet hers again. "I have great feelings for you, Marie, and I do not wish to leave you behind."

Would a kiss make it worse?

She stretched up on tiptoe to find out, his head bowing to set his mouth to hers, soft and searching at first, then gentle and giving as his arms slipped around her and the pounding of their hearts joined in one thunderous punch after another. Their embrace tightened, he raised her up, and she deepened the kiss, her senses filling with him and careening out of control, her mind screaming to stop. Stop. STOP!

Her heart refused to listen. Nester would be gone tomorrow. Tonight was all they had and she wanted it.

She pulled away, breathless and shivering despite the fire in her blood. "Nester. Nester." He looked at her and she smoothed his blond hair from his face. "I can't go with you. No matter how badly I want to, I can't." She kissed him softly. "You know that, don't you?"

He gave a vague nod. "Even if the boy did not still need you, this is the time in which you belong. I am the one who is out of place here and I am the one who must go, but not now." He sipped kisses from her earlobe to the base of her throat and she smiled at the streams of tingles jetting through her body. She could feel the frustration in his body when he finally found the difference in their heights annoying enough to lift her up onto the bed and then it was her turn to bend to kiss him, but not nearly so far. Had they more time, say a year or several hundred, they would have found a better compromise, she was sure.

He slipped the robe from her left shoulder, kissed it as his fingers curled around the ties.

"Nester," she whispered. "Hugh."

Just the name was enough to clear his brain to caution. Leaning to look beyond her to the connecting door, he stepped around the end of the bed to close their side of the door.

"How does one sleep through the *American Idol?*"

She laughed softly, watching lust light up and linger in his eyes. He put his back to the window, again reaching for her hips. She cradled his face in her hands.

Sometimes words were a waste of breath that was better used gasping in the throes of lovemaking . . . Marie was going to stitch that in a sampler someday. Someday when she was old and gray and remembering an endless night of frantic, passionate, and all-inclusive sex with the only wizard she'd probably ever know, and most certainly the only one she'd ever love.

They barely slept, telling stories and secrets between bouts of pleasure. Mostly little things . . . a hundred-thousand little things to make one night seem more like a lifetime.

He was showering, quite possibly the best miracle of all the miracles he'd seen so far, when Hugh rapped on the door. She opened it and he strode in, hearing the shower, looking first at one made-up bed, then the other, and then at her. She could hear the tumblers shifting inside his head, but all he said was, "I think we should feed him French toast this morning."

"An excellent idea." She ruffled his messy dark hair. "There's extra stuff in the bag there. Go shower. The car we're renting won't be here until ten, plus a generous six hours gives us plenty of time to get back by four, then meet your dad out front at five sharp. Sound about right to you?" He nodded, but all the excitement of the French toast was gone and he looked troubled. "What?"

"Do you think he'll forget us?"

"Never. Not for one day."

He looked deep into her eyes for assurance and truth and appeared satisfied when he walked away.

Despite all the sugar in the maple syrup at breakfast, spirits were not high during the 69-mile ride on the Jersey Turnpike. They tried, for one another, but they all felt the stress. Nester would rouse himself to ask a question here or there, and mother and son took turns pointing out what few fascinations there were to see between New York City and Philadelphia.

"I should have taken a more scenic route."

"I am glad you did not. It is hard enough for you to keep your eyes on the road when there is nothing to see."

She glanced at him — briefly. "You're complaining about my driving?"

"I believe I am, yes."

And several times she'd seen him slam his foot on the imaginary brake on his side of the car. Men.

"You, who took us back to the dawn of time?"

"I was forgiven that and it is forgotten. Unlike your accusation of being a spit and wind navigator."

"I said I was sorry." She peeked at him again. "You didn't forgive me?"

"I do not believe I did." He crossed his arms over his chest and slid down in the seat a bit to pay more attention to her and less to the road. She caught the sexy twinkle in his eye when he said, "In fact, I do not believe you are truly sorry you said it."

Her eyes met Hugh's in the rearview mirror. She winked and he grinned and they all kept trying, for one another, but they still felt the stress.

They were in Camden heading for the Ben Franklin Bridge when Nester straightened in his seat and became vigilant. Tense and pale, he calmly explained, "It is coming, Marie. I feel it catching up with us. The time we disturbed in the past is rushing forward, bringing with it the changes we have caused. Hopefully the alterations will be few and small, but the hastening of time is always irregular and can be dangerous."

She glanced at her watch. "How long? Can you tell?"

He shook his head. "The feeling is faint, but I don't think we should be on this highway when it catches up."

"Will it just change us or . . . everything?"

"Everything. The time I held in the past was small, but it spreads as it moves forward like ripples in a pond. The changes we made will have far-reaching consequences."

"Okay. Just a little farther."

Over the bridge they took 5th Street and in her head she screamed at every red light they encountered.

"Marie. Please. Pull over. We should not be hindered by being inside this machine . . . or moving slower or faster than time itself. It's coming more quickly."

They were still two blocks from the museum, but it would have to do. She parked as soon as she could and sighed when she turned the car off. She had accomplished half her goal — Hugh was within sight of where he was supposed to be when his father came to get him in . . . forty-seven minutes.

She watched for oncoming traffic before she opened her door to get out and join her boy and the wizard on the sidewalk. "What do we do now?"

He shook his head. "I don't know. Most of my life I have spent studying time, not living in it."

He turned his head then and something in his expression caused her to do the same. Like the heat waves that roll and flutter and lift up from the sand in the desert . . . horizontally . . . time came at them in much the same fashion, but vertically. Cars and buses from three blocks away came suddenly abreast of them on the street. People sauntering on Market Street near 5th were now abruptly on Market and 8th or they'd turned the corner and were heading for

Filbert. Calm, unaware of what was happening to them.

A flock of sparrows appeared overhead from nowhere and dark clouds blew in swiftly bringing lightning like a static ball. She could see her own movements and hand gestures like someone had turned up the speed on the movie projector. Her arm would flip out and grab Hugh who would jerk his head in a flash to look at her — and Nester was going with the flow but staying close, observing all, sensing more than anyone else could imagine.

This was his element: time. Fish had water, man had air, Nester had time and the space it occupied. Cars jerked to a stop at the curb, then jerked away milliseconds later; people waddled up and down the museum steps like Charlie Chaplin dolls. They had wobbled halfway up to the doors when the people around them began to slow down — though the three of them continued at full speed.

They entered the museum and stopped short before the arid display for the Dead Sea Exhibit.

"This is it. This is where it all happened." She started to lead the way but he caught her hand and held her back. "Sellithos. It's inside."

"I am aware. But the recovery must be done with the least amount of disruption to, again, avoid disturbances in the future. We were lucky this time. Please. Trust me with this."

She nodded and stepped back beside Hugh . . . who was also coming down the hallway toward them.

"Nester!" Her voice was hardly a whisper. "Look."

Immediately, he positioned his body to conceal them from sight, walking slowly to a large support column so they could spread out and watch.

The nasty scowl on Hugh's face was not something she missed though it seemed like something from long, long ago. He cast her an apologetic frown now and she let her smile say, "I love you anyway."

"Hey. Wait a second. What do you think?" Marie watched herself point to the Dead Sea Exhibit. "Mummies maybe."

After a moment he shrugged and said, "Whatever," and scuffed off.

They both looked up when they heard Nester tsking his disapproval. He was only half teasing them. "Come. We must finish this."

# TEN

Marie followed herself around the displays at a discreet distance. The waves of hair on the back of her head were lovely and she so seldom got to see them, but she needed her ends clipped and her jacket made her butt look big. She'd never wear it again.

Nester and Hugh walked parallel to her along the wall. The rain and wind battered the old windows and lightning and thunder struck closer and closer, her other self seemingly oblivious. Again she was struck, as she had been so often, by how quickly life changes.

Then it happened: The lightning struck, the lights flickered, and Marie heard herself shout, "Hugh. No! Don't touch anything."

She made her way toward Nester and Hugh; the wizard staying low, the boy watching himself withdraw the clasp with the beautiful Sellithos — plump and circular, about the size of a juicy plum; colorless and clear but for the wispy cloud of blue that hovered *above* it when the light changed — attached.

And still, she'd never seen anything like it.

They watched Hugh gently push at the haze, test the weight and the coolness of the stone in the palm of his hand. And once again she felt a prickle of dread across her shoulders when he experimented with the two prongs below the stone. Looking at the son standing beside her — who looked appalled, aghast at his own behavior — she slipped her arm around his shoulder. "Sometimes the hard way is the only way we learn."

"Don't break it, Hugh," she heard herself say from across the room. "Put it back in the case."

He looked up at her, smiled at her, and raised the ornament for her to see. But what happened next was not as they remembered . . . or as it had seemed at the time.

"Uh-oh," he said, and the first Hugh bent the tongs and closed the two blades beyond their original position, causing the two ends to touch . . . and nothing happened.

But two seconds later the stone lit up like a nova, causing them to squint against the smarting in their eyes because Nester stood tall now. He and Petroleon had captured

Sellithos's attention: They were together again and the three of them were a force that lit up the sky.

While the original set of Marie and Hugh did what they did before, she turned to Nester. "Stop it! What are you doing? It . . . it wasn't Sellithos who sent us back . . . it was all three of you."

"Mom." The Hugh at her side nudged her and she turned her head in time to see the other Hugh disappear.

"No! Stop him!"

"Look at the people."

The elderly couple and the young father with the toddler and the first-grader were posed like mannequins. She watched herself cover her face with both hands, then push them through her hair in one desperate motion. She remembered that moment, that feeling, and her stomach turned.

"You were here. You helped. You *knew?* All along you *knew?*"

"No." He said the one word with enough force to silence her and to open her mind. "I did not know until you spoke of the motionless people. I did not know Hugh when I met him or you two days later . . . but I told you, Sellithos cannot make magic, only magnify it. It cannot slow time to make it look as if it has stopped for these people

535

— that is magic."

"So . . . you knew you'd have to try to bring us back . . . but did you know all that would happen to us?"

He smiled, knowing exactly what she was getting at. "I knew only that someday we three would be in this time and in this place, repeating this act."

"Repeating?"

He nodded. "It is a time loop, where the line of time folds over and crosses itself." He reached up then and touched her cheek. "We will meet again and again." But he said the word "meet" like "love."

He turned to Hugh abruptly. "You are a fine young man and I am proud to be your friend, Hugh. I must go now." He extended a hand in friendship and the boy hid his inside. "Take better care of your mother."

"I will."

He came back to Marie with laughter in his eyes. "I hope I have saved you from becoming toast." She glanced at her watch — ten minutes to spare. The smile she gave him felt a little limp. She felt tears pushing behind her eyes and lowered her gaze to the floor. "Have you nothing to say to me?"

"I'll miss you."

"I know. I will miss you as well."

She got the impression that he tipped his

head at Hugh and the boy wandered off toward the lobby. He snaked his arms around her waist asking, "And will you think of me sometimes?"

A tear cruised down her cheek and hung on the end of her nose until she batted it off. "Yes, but I'm not coming to this museum ever again."

She smiled up into his so-familiar face and again found herself in one of those moments with him where words simply weren't necessary, they weren't enough. She lifted her arms to his neck and he bent to lift her up so she could wrap them around him tight. They held one another for a long minute and then she pulled away and palmed his cheeks.

"I love you, Nester Baraka of Viator. Be safe in your travels. Stop and ask for directions once in a while and . . . come back if you can."

They kissed, a couple of times, then finally had to push one another away. Hugh returned and stood with Marie while Nester collected Sellithos and made the pedestal showcase disappear as if it had never existed.

He held both stones in his right hand and passed his left hand over them twice to retrieve his long, pale, mossy green tunic and his thick cyan robe trimmed in white. The smirk he gave them was the same as saying out loud that he preferred being less confined. He smiled again at Hugh, but then he looked straight into her eyes, took her soul it felt like, and disappeared.

Mother and son sighed as the young father with the toddler and the first-grader passed by them and turned toward the main entrance.

"He wanted you to go with him," Hugh said.

"I know."

"I thought . . . it looked like you love him."

"I do love him."

"Then why didn't you go?"

She hung her arm around his shoulders. "Because I love you more. Because I would never, ever leave you if I had a choice . . . and because we belong here."

It was starting to get dark when they stepped out into the cool drizzle of rain. The lightning and thunder had moved on. Bill and Laura were parked at the bottom of the steps in the family SUV. Bill gave her a closed-lip smile and a nod. She'd passed another unsupervised visit with their son; he was keeping track.

She took Hugh in her arms, kissed his cheek, and hugged him again. "I don't need to tell you to keep this our secret, do I?"

He chuckled. "Who'd believe me?" He took two steps down and turned back. "I lied, you know. Laura's spaghetti sucks."

They grinned at one another and he finished bouncing down the steps to the car. They drove off.

"I told you, when a son is lucky enough to know his mother, he knows her well."

She turned, almost falling off the step. "Nester?"

Dark umbrella overhead, he stepped from the shadows of the building wearing dress slacks, a cable-knit sweater, and a different leather jacket that looked very nonfaux-ish . . . and a sly smile.

"What's happened? Did something go wrong? Why are you still here?"

"I'm not here *still.*"

"What?"

He advanced on her slowly as if she were skittish, taking one step at a time.

"I've been to visit Hugh's Amazon rain-forest, it's breathtaking . . . and it's heart-breaking. I helped build the Great Wall of China. I stood among the Romans and watched gladiator against gladiator in the Colosseum. I studied the stars from Chichén Itzá. I was good before and now

I'm better."

"You're using contractions, too."

"I can speak a hundred different languages and get by in a hundred more. I'm a slow learner, I'm afraid. I carried sandstone from the cliff buildings of Petra and when we unearthed the Terra Cotta Warriors, I journeyed to their burial."

"Oh." Could he see how green she was with envy? Could he tell that her heart was struggling in her chest, her palms were moist, and her muscles were poised to leap at him?

"I've been to the top of Mount Everest . . . didn't scale it, too cold and the challenge didn't attract me. I have been to Yosemite National Park, and the Grand Canyon and the Hermitage Museum, where I plan to take you one day to feed your love of history."

He came to the step below hers, they were almost eye to eye. His gaze roamed over her face as if he were home at last and grateful so little had changed.

"I have prayed in the Basilicas of Saints Peter and Mark, at Meenakshi, at the Golden Temple of Amritsar, St. Basil's Cathedral, Stonehenge, and Mecca . . . I even consulted the seventh and eighth Dalai Lamas and they both told me to follow my heart . . . so I have. I followed it here to you."

That was exactly what she wanted and dreaded to hear, yet it triggered her muscles and she launched herself at him, arms around his neck, a hundred kisses scattered across his face before her lips found his.

"Nester. Nester," she muttered and kissed him twice more. Twenty minutes ago they'd kissed good-bye and she'd thought no kiss could be sweeter, more poignant or more . . . momentous. And once again she was wrong.

Breathless, clinging to her last remnants of rational thought, she pulled away saying, "I love you and . . . but . . . I love Hugh, too. I —"

"Ack. He's going to *love* having me as a stepfather. Wait till he has to write a paper on the Civil War or the Continental Congress or World War II or . . . *Sputnik.*"

She laughed. "Nothing off planet, please." She slipped under his arm as she had when they journeyed, felt safe and more content than she ever knew she could. "I have to draw a line somewhere."

They started down the steps together. "What will you do here? Won't you get bored?"

He shook his head. "Study and observe, blend in as my brothers have . . . Galileo and my friend Kepler. Thomas Jefferson . . . a fine inventor." He held out his right hand. "Your beloved Ben Franklin."

*Really? Wizards?* It wasn't hard to see.

"You know," she said, just thinking out loud. "If we leave as soon as Hugh's off to school and get back before the bus drops him off, there's no telling where we —"

"I want to honeymoon in the Kashmir Valley. They say there's nothing like it in the world and I've been saving it for us."